D1789504

Psychological, Archetypal and Phenomenological Perspectives on Soccer

Soccer, or football, attracts vast numbers of passionate fans from all over the world; but clinical psychology is yet to study it in depth. In this book, David Huw Burston, a consultant football psychology and performance coach, uses a phenomenological research method inspired by Amedeo Giorgi to consider what we can learn from the spirit of the game, and how this can be used positively in the consulting room and on the field of play.

By examining detailed qualitative research with professional soccer players of both sexes, Burston identifies and considers nine particular themes, including the family, god, heroes and dreams, and discusses how what we can learn from the game of football and team culture can be applied to Jungian analysis today.

This book bridges the gap between clinical psychology and sport, outlining potential shortfalls in current youth development in sport, as well as discussing how traditional Jungian archetypes can be identified in everyday settings. It will be of key interest to researchers from both the fields of analytical psychology and sports studies.

David Huw Burston (MFT) is a Clinical Psychotherapist in private practice in the USA, and a Consultant Football Psychology and Performance Coach for 11–21 year olds at Tottenham Hotspur Football Club, London, UK.

Research in Analytical Psychology and Jungian Studies Series

Series Advisor: Andrew Samuels, Professor of Analytical Psychology, Essex University, UK.

The *Research in Analytical Psychology and Jungian Studies* series features scholarly works that are, broadly speaking, of an empirical nature. The series comprises research-focused volumes involving qualitative and quantitative research, historical/archival research, theoretical developments, heuristic research, grounded theory, narrative approaches, collaborative research, practitioner-led research, and self-study. The series also includes focused works by clinical practitioners, and provides new research informed explorations of the work of C. G. Jung that will appeal to researchers, academics, and scholars alike.

Books in this series:

Time and Timelessness
Temporality in the theory of Carl Jung
Angeliki Yiassemides

Apophatic Elements in the Theory and Practice of Psychoanalysis
Pseudo-Dionysius and C.G. Jung
David Henderson

C.G. Jung and Hans Urs von Balthasar
God and evil – A critical comparison
Les Oglesby

Bridges to Consciousness
Complexes and complexity
Nancy M. Krieger

The Alchemical Mercurius
Esoteric symbol of Jung's life and works
Mathew Mather

Archetypal Psychotherapy
The clinical legacy of James Hillman
Jason A. Butler

Jung's Theory of Personality
A modern reappraisal
Clare Crellin

Psychological, Archetypal and Phenomenological Perspectives on Soccer
David Huw Burston

Psychological, Archetypal and Phenomenological Perspectives on Soccer

David Huw Burston

Routledge
Taylor & Francis Group

LONDON AND NEW YORK

First published 2015
by Routledge
2 Park Square, Milton Park, Abingdon, Oxon, OX14 4RN

and by Routledge
711 Third Avenue, New York, NY 10017

Routledge is an imprint of the Taylor & Francis Group, an informa business

© 2015 D. H. Burston

The right of D. H. Burston to be identified as author of this work
has been asserted by him in accordance with sections 77 and 78
of the Copyright, Designs and Patents Act 1988.

All rights reserved. No part of this book may be reprinted or
reproduced or utilised in any form or by any electronic,
mechanical, or other means, now known or hereafter invented,
including photocopying and recording, or in any information
storage or retrieval system, without permission in writing from
the publishers.

Trademark notice: Product or corporate names may be trademarks
or registered trademarks, and are used only for identification and
explanation without intent to infringe.

British Library Cataloguing in Publication Data
A catalogue record for this book is available from the British
Library

Library of Congress Cataloging in Publication Data
Burston, David Huw.
Psychological, archetypal and phenomenological perspectives on
soccer / David Huw Burston.
pages cm
1. Soccer--Psychological aspects. 2. Psychology--Research. 3.
Phenomenological psychology. I. Title.
GV943.9.P7B87 2014
796.334019--dc23
2014011742

ISBN: 978-1-138-78746-9 (hbk)
ISBN: 978-1-315-76649-2 (ebk)

Typeset in Bembo
by Saxon Graphics Ltd, Derby

Contents

Acknowledgments

I would like to dedicate this book to my mother Noelle and my father John Burston for giving me the blend of strengths needed to stay the course and win a match from time to time. I thank my wife Alice for her love, stamina and patience, and my dogs Ludo and Oscarlindo for teaching me about the wisdom and spirit of animals. Henry and Libby also deserve a mention for teaching me the wisdom of children. I also want to thank Murray Jones, Demian Brown and especially Bob Ammann for his generous expertise and strength. I would like to thank all the excellent coaching staff at Tottenham Hotspur FC, especially Trevor Webb who is a great spirit in the game and whose foresight and expertise made much of my work possible. I would also like to thank the bright and gifted students who provided the material for the book as well as my illuminating teachers and mentors at Pacifica University including Richard Kelliher and Karey Pohn for their invaluable assistance in creating this document.

Figures and tables

Figures

Table

Chapter 1

Introduction

Soccer, or football, as it is known outside of America, attracts vast numbers of passionate fans from all over the world, but clinical psychology has yet to study it in depth. Thus, for this book, a phenomenological research method inspired by Amedeo Giorgi was used to interview players from an American Division One University about what it is like to be an aspiring professional soccer player. This Introduction provides a foundation for this book by presenting some background details of how this research arose and what transpired. The book will record the process of a phenomenological design and methodology and examine the insights it revealed using a depth tradition for examining the psyche.

Eight players were recruited to become coresearchers (four from each gender) on the study. Interviews were conducted using standardized open-ended questions, relating to their initial inspiration to play; dreams, achievements, heroes; playing well and poorly; and the team as family. Nine themes emerged from the responses: (1) Family as the reason they play soccer; (2) God as a source of their gifts; (3) the "first" as an achievement; (4) dreams of growth and finishing; (5) parents as heroes; (6) the unstoppable body, elevation and descent; (7) dreams of giving back; (8) the team as a *supra family* and assistors; (9) winning and losing, inner doubt, solutions, and using *shadow* language. Themes were then amplified using alchemical methodology revealing inner elemental archetypes present in soccer that would have been familiar to the Greeks and before.

Results suggest that the game of soccer strikes deep archetypal chords, stretching back to our early hunter/gatherer roots, with major achievements described as initiatory experiences. When playing well, coresearchers reported heightened states of mind, embodying mythic figures and gods, unlike playing poorly, where "thinking too much" degraded performance. Coresearchers described a *supra family* system, emphasizing values of unity and support at the heart of their experience. Coresearchers also indicated diverse gender and age family members as their inspiration to play soccer. As a result of the findings, the idea of the game being a masculine tradition was questioned. Participants described being on a team as benefitting character, confirming recent research that a team may be an emotionally healthy environment for young people. Results suggested that clinical research could perhaps discover creative ways of assisting individuals who may benefit from being involved in such an environment.

Also discussed (in the Conclusion) is how the research revealed soccer as a kind of ancient universal trinity that is being played through the game and through other sports. The study also illuminated issues relating to left and right brain functions and their importance to the individuals playing the game, which in turn correlates to Jungian ideas of the four functions of thinking, sensing, feeling and intuition. From this, implications arose regarding the wider educational syllabus, and how soccer may be a healthier occupation for the young than first imagined. The study also revealed deeper reasons as to why many important social, religious and literary figures were deeply attached to the sport, including Albert Camus, Niels Bohr and Pope John Paul II.

Soccer, the world's most popular sport (Tharoor, 2008), is a global phenomenon; its professional players are raised up into modern-day cultural heroes. Using a phenomenological approach, the study asked the players themselves to speak about the experience of playing soccer and being on a team. The specific research question explored from an archetypal perspective was this: "What is the lived experience of being an aspiring professional soccer player on a team?" Beyond soccer, this study seeks to explore the useful purpose that clinical psychology can serve sporting cultures as well as other cultures that perhaps have similar themes, difficulties, and challenges. The coincidental timing of the London 2012 Olympic Games provided a useful backdrop to the study and presented us with the opportunity to review ancient archetypal forces that still appear to be with us today, observed by an ever-growing world population of viewers.

This Introduction will first provide an overview of soccer as a global phenomenon, and of possible anthropological antecedents of the sport. There will then be a brief section on the Jungian *shadow*, with an accompanying rationale as to why this archetype may be of relevance to the study. Then, my background and interest in the topic will be outlined. Some information about the typical soccer culture will be given, in order to provide a context for the world our coresearchers inhabit. Possible relevance of the topic for clinicians working in psychology will be examined, indicating the key concerns that may be relevant to all young people in the West.

Chapter 2 will then reflect some of the previous literature related to soccer and the psyche of the performer. As the chapter concludes there will be space to state the research question. In Chapter 3, the choice of phenomenological methodology will be introduced with some background on the subject, as well as some of the contributions made by the founding practitioners of phenomenological methodology. The data collected as a result of the interviews will be outlined in Chapter 4, with coresearcher responses outlined in depth. Chapter 5 will return again to the data, in the Discussion section, exploring in more depth the repetitive themes, alchemical transference and reactions that took place, and the implications they had for the study. By means of a redactive process, the study will then culminate in the Conclusion by examining the insights that emerge from the study and the implications for further research and current trends in education.

The soccer phenomenon: A brief overview

For many individuals, identification with a team is a passion that stretches back many generations. In England, the Football League, the organization that runs the league tables, was founded in 1888 and the modern game dates to 1863, although it has ancient roots (Goldblatt, 2008). A recent observation from Yale Center for the Study of Globalization reported:

> Thousands of years ago, the Chinese, Greeks and Vikings all played games kicking balls about. But the modern game of soccer was born in England and the popularity of that particular sport has taken over the world. Thanks to satellite television, British soccer teams have hundreds of millions of fans all over the world and sport executives look to expand their audiences to more lucrative markets.
>
> (Tharoor, 2008, para. 1)

The game of soccer has a global following, now further bolstered by the communications media revolution. This has increased the size of the audience and enhanced further the profile of the sport in the global community. One team alone, Manchester United, has an estimated 659 million fans (*Daily Telegraph*, 2012), and almost half of those supporters are in Asia-Pacific. In England alone, over ten years earlier, J. Johnson (2001) remarked:

> Only 816,500 people now attend church weekly (995,700 if you count the kids they drag along). The over-64's make up the largest proportion of this population, so as in Spain, church attendance is set to dwindle in the future. Let's compare this with attendance at England's soccer grounds: over 700,000 people attended matches in the Premiership and the Nationwide league this weekend. That's nearly as many as attend church, which is especially significant when you consider that all these people actually had to pay to watch and couldn't just turn up for free.
>
> (para. 1)

Tharoor (2008), in an article discussing fans reactions to the globalization of their sport, wrote:

> Soccer is quite aptly called the "world's game." The sport's superstars are household names around the globe. Its landmark competition—the World

Cup—is watched by hundreds of millions. Even gun-toting insurgents in Iraq can be spotted wearing replica shirts of Europe's most fashionable clubs. ...The EPL [English Premier League] is already a global phenomenon—beamed to nearly 200 countries and into more than 600 million homes. Even Middlesborough, a decidedly mediocre team, has organized support groups in Indonesia and Singapore. South African football officials considered shifting kick-off times of their domestic league to avoid coinciding with those of the EPL; many fans in South Africa prefer huddling around TV sets to watch their heroes in England than follow their own club teams. Uganda is notoriously divided between London clubs Chelsea and Arsenal, with the latter's Kampala supporters making a hit music video celebrating their love for the team. Here and elsewhere, the EPL has left an indelible mark.

(paras. 2-6)

Tharoor's description of insurgents demonstrating a loyalty that transcends borders suggests something universal and significant is happening, and this study aspires to find out more.

How is it that these performers and clubs mean so much to so many people? In 2010, soccer's world governing body, FIFA reported that they expected over 700 million people throughout the world watched a World Cup™ match. According to Nicolas Ericson, director of FIFA's TV division, "the United States had reported a 50 per cent increase in overall figures compared to 2006." And he continued, "I think the audience for the final will be bigger than 2006, when it was watched by 700 million people" (Homewood, 2010). The 2010 FIFA World Cup South Africa™ website's banner headline summed it all up: "Almost half the world tuned in at home to watch."

In 2010, FIFA described how soccer was:

shown in every single country and territory on Earth, including Antarctica and the Arctic Circle, generating record-breaking viewing figures in many TV markets around the world. The in-home television coverage of the competition reached over 3.2 billion people around the world, or 46.4 per cent of the global population, based on viewers watching a minimum of over one minute of coverage. This represents an eight per cent rise on the number of viewers recorded during the 2006 FIFA World Cup Germany™.

Based on viewers watching a minimum of 20 consecutive minutes of coverage, the 2010 tournament reached nearly a third of the world population with 2.2 billion viewers, or three per cent higher than in 2006, according to data compiled by KantarSport on behalf of FIFA. The average in-home global audience for each match was 188.4 million, up six per cent on 2006, while the highest average audience measured was for the final at 530.9 million, up five per cent on 2006.

To what extent do the viewers and the players tap into or embody archetypes that resonate within the deeper nature of humankind? Most fervent supporters of soccer clubs watch matches hoping to see their teams win. For some teams, legions of fans the world over simultaneously react joyfully when they savor victory. However, opponents wish to do the same, and the supporters have to rely on their heroes to win the day. In terms of an archetypal story, the hero's journey appears to be constellated here. Favorite players must demonstrate the capacity to transcend opponents and any obstacles placed in their way:

> The hero's main feat is to overcome the monster of darkness: it is the long-hoped-for and expected triumph of consciousness over the unconscious. The coming of consciousness was probably the most tremendous experience of primeval times, for with it a world came into being whose existence no one had suspected before. "And God said, Let there be light" is the projection of that immemorial experience of the separation of consciousness from the unconscious.
>
> (Jung, 1951/1990, p. 167)

The popularity of the game suggests that its heroes and teams relate and connect to the human psyche on a significant level. This study will aim to identify at least some of the universal archetypal stories and identities that are so compelling for so many people today. Modern players are often men from comparatively humble origins now made into wealthy, national heroes. Every movement of these players is scrutinized by a hungry press and media, fuelled by the public thirst for information. Jung (1950/1990) discussed the role of the cult hero in the essay "Concerning Rebirth" in *The archetypes and the collective unconscious*. In speaking of identification with the hero, Jung used the sacred Greek ritual, the Metamorphosis of Apuleius, as an illustration. This ritual also has an element of public performance: "The initiate, an ordinary human being, is elected to be Helios; he is crowned with a crown of palms and clad in the mystic mantle, whereupon the assembled crowd pays homage to him" (Jung, 1950/1990, p. 128). Modern players are indeed paid homage, normal men "raised up," who achieve widespread adoration and fame.

Anthropological antecedents of soccer

Is soccer a purely modern phenomenon? Or has there always been a space for young men and women to work together in teams? In his book, *Your brain at work*, author David Rock (2009) uses modern analogies and case studies, complementing them with the latest advances in neuroscience, to connect the implications of research on improving quality of life. In one such case study, Rock notes that a young man had "recently been watching horror movies with friends, a modern version of an ancient communal ritual where young adult males practice emotional regulation to prepare for a hunt" (p. 221). On reflection, I had never considered that there was a ritual for preparing young people for hunting. However, this was something that became apparent to me when observing young soccer players preparing for a match. Rock's implication is that our ancestors attached importance to the idea of helping young hunters and warriors with emotional regulation. We will never know exactly what our early ancestors did, but my experience suggests that there is currently a kind of behavioral blueprint being reenacted in the playing and supporting of soccer.

Edward Tylor, one of the foremost evolutionary psychologists, was a man who influenced and informed Jung (Shamdasani, 2003, p. 274). Tylor was professor of anthropology at Oxford University (1832-1917) and asserted that from generation to generation within society we carry over traits and patterns of behavior that he called *survivals*. "These were processes, customs, and opinions that had been carried over by habit into a new state of society from that in which they originated. They were remnants of an older condition of culture" (p. 275). Is the soccer world a representation of a *survival?* To some extent, soccer is a process and custom in the literal sense, an enactment which is meaningful in some way to many people throughout the world.

Many children and adults play the game in a casual, spontaneous way on any patch of ground. However, the organized playing of soccer is mostly conducted in a league form. Teams vie with each other for a ranked place near the top. Each week the teams, comprised of eleven individuals, face a new opponent and compete for the points. In England and the US teams in professional leagues will all visit each other, and be visited by their opponents. Going "out on the road" may be an ancient situation being enacted for young men who must go and win, draw or at worst be defeated and come home with not even a point. In 1995, Harold Bloom wrote *The Lucifer principle: A scientific expedition into the forces of history*, which explored the origins of human instincts and actions from our earliest times. Bloom suggests that "Nature's amusements are cruel" (p. 25), describing how our ancestors would have by necessity encountered very precarious situations and dangers. He suggested that nature's way is to regard young men in many ways as expendable, perhaps the price to be paid for progress. Of course, historically, young men are the ones likely to fight "the enemy" or the elements. Joseph Campbell (1972), in a chapter entitled "Mythologies of War and Peace," discussed the ancient mythological lineage of warriors and war within society. Campbell identified a theme here, which could in itself be a definition of soccer as a sport:

> In India the governing law of international relations has for centuries been known as the *matsya nyaya*, "law of the fish," which is, to wit, that the big ones eat the little ones and the little ones have to be smart. War is the natural duty of princes, and periods of peace are merely interludes, like the periods of rest between boxing rounds.
>
> (p. 200)

Human history is replete with cruel conquests and battles, and Campbell (1972) then identified our own Western tradition is not exempt: "From the period of the victories of Constantine, fourth century AD, the church founded on the rock of that same good Peter's name, was advanced largely by swordsmanship" (p. 189). Is soccer vicariously playing out our attachment to this way of being? Is soccer, in fact, a kind of organized, safety first, form of warfare? This may appear an attractive proposition on the surface, however, soccer is not warfare; after all, it is a game. Warfare ultimately has few "rules of the game," but in soccer, the omnipotent referee is there to keep order, and players generally shake hands at the end of the contest.

Penalties can be harsh in soccer for foul play. Kicking or barging an opponent will result in a foul being called by the referee and play must stop. Although physical contact is inevitable in the playing of the game, violence or endangering an opponent is not tolerated, and can likely result in players being removed from the game for the duration of the contest. When this type of aggression occurs, the referee displays a red card, and the player is "sent off." In this case, players are to leave the contest, and are then automatically barred for a minimum of three games with financial penalties often issued as a further punishment.

The primary tenets of the game involve skill, stamina, and discipline with a ball. Focus on the game, rather than the opponent is encouraged, as is dexterity with the ball. While there are rules and boundaries, this also remains a deeply emotional, compelling experience for the players. This study aims to get a closer sense of what is happening in soccer to these individuals on an archetypal level. The Jungian idea of the *shadow* archetype seemed a natural place to begin looking for some answers; particularly as such pronounced, creative forces are at play.

The *shadow* archetype

What is this elusive force that seems to stalk the human condition so completely? Soccer is a creative sport, in that individuals work together to find ways of getting the ball in the opponents net. The link with the *shadow* archetype and creativity has been explored by Diamond (1999), in his book *Anger, madness, and the daimonic: The psychological genesis of violence, evil and creativity*. Diamond suggests that the *shadow* forces operating within us "are acting upon us all of the time—and we, in turn, are interacting with them—whether we are aware of this fact or not" (p. 105). What unconscious process is being played out in soccer?

In her book, *Shadow and evil in fairy tales*, Marie-Louise von Franz (1974) explored the subject of the *shadow* in depth, illuminating how the archetype is represented in common mythology and folk tales. She opened the book by attempting to define the subject:

In Jungian psychology, we generally define the shadow as the personification of certain aspects of the unconscious personality, which could be added to the ego complex, but which, for various reasons, are not. We may therefore say that the shadow is the dark, unlived, and repressed side of the ego complex, but this is only partly true.

(p. 3)

Von Franz then echoed Jung's response to overly delineating such forces within the psyche:

Jung, who hated it when his pupils were too literal minded and clung to his concepts and made a system out of them and quoted him without exactly knowing what he was saying, once in a discussion threw all this over and said, "This is all nonsense! The shadow is simply the whole unconscious."

(p. 3)

As with the unconscious mind itself, von Franz (1974) suggested that the *shadow* is a force within us that defies a systemized approach in order to comprehend. As Andrew Samuels (1986a) wrote in his book, *A critical dictionary of Jungian analysis*:

In 1945 Jung gave a most direct and clear-cut definition of the shadow "the thing a person has no wish to be." In this simple statement is subsumed the many-sided and repeated references to the shadow as the negative side of the personality, the sum of all unpleasant qualities one wants to hide, the inferior, the worthless and primitive side of man's nature, the other person in one, one's own dark side.

(p. 139)

If the *shadow* is the sum of all our unpleasant qualities, then what do we do with them? Odajnyk (1976) suggested, "Such blindness to the evil present within man is both foolish and harmful: foolish because only the fool can disregard the conditions of his own nature; and harmful because it deprives us of the capacity to deal with evil" (p. 70). Is the *shadow* archetype that is played out within the container of sport something many of us can enjoy? Or do other archetypes exist that have become subsumed and forgotten? Are they all better off forgotten because they are bad? This study also aims to step out of the shadows and also explore the brighter side of soccer. Is the *shadow* negative or as Jung suggests merely the whole unconscious?

Robert Johnson (2008), in *Inner gold*, speaks of the positive *shadow* that is also projected out onto another, the unacknowledged more positive parts of ourselves that we do not recognize. In this type of projection, light is shed upon the recipient. "The first inkling of this is when the others person appears to be luminous, that he (or she) glows in the dark" for us (p. 4). The Jules Rimet World Cup Trophy is golden and depicts Nike, the Greek goddess of victory. Soccer players such as the Brazilian Pelé remain national icons of pride, certainly worth their weight in gold to some. Now more than ever, when famous players retire they become ambassadors for soccer and social concerns. Is soccer a way of alleviating some part of us that needs to be housed somewhere, both the undesirable and the "golden" parts of ourselves? Does this explain our deification of sports heroes? This research sought to ask about heroes and where they can be found within this sport.

In 1946, shortly after his definition of the *shadow*, Jung narrowed his identification of archetypes that are somehow correlated to our instincts. He worked on this using active imagination, his primary route of connecting to the unconscious. He described how such experiences led him to conclude, "There are certain *collectively present unconscious conditions* which act as regulators and stimulators of creative fantasy-activity. These regulators, or archetypes, acted so much like instincts that he could find no argument against regarding them as identical (para. 403 trans. mod.)" (Shamdasani, 2003, p. 259).

If the *shadow* is a permanent fixture and instinct in the human psyche, then presumably we all will have to live with it. This dilemma illustrates a problem and inherent contradiction for humanity, which, appearances suggest, we are still struggling to overcome. If the *shadow* is on one hand as, Samuels suggested, "worthless and primitive" or as von Franz describes "dark, unlived, and repressed," how can we at the same time be expected to embrace and integrate it? Von Franz has suggested that "in some aspects, the *shadow* can also consist of collective factors that stem from a source outside the individual's personal life" (1964, p. 174). Our ancestors had to encounter the original jungle in all its forms as we do, in our twenty-first century, concrete version. How different are they and how far have we really separated ourselves? "To admit to the shadow is to break its compulsive hold" (Samuels, 1986a, p. 139). Why are we in this compulsive hold? This study shall seek to explore if there is a connection with the *shadow* and our past.

Researcher's background and description of interest in topic

In the spirit of phenomenological research, it is appropriate to fully bracket out, acknowledge and examine my own relationship with this phenomenon. As with many young English boys, soccer was a part of my psyche since I could kick a ball at the age of three. As described above, the game has a vast significance in England and is culturally a ubiquitous form of recreation for children. I do have an intimate relationship with the game that can help fuel the research and application demanded of this kind of research. "The first challenge of the researcher, in preparing to conduct a phenomenological investigation, is to arrive at a topic and question that has both social meaning and personal significance" (Moustakas, 1994, p. 104).

My father often appeared at the dining table dressed in black. His day job was funeral embalming, and he spent a large part of his day with the dead. Like Hermes, he would accompany the bereaved as they visited the deceased. He was also a deeply creative man, a successful inventor, and a builder. An embalming machine he invented made the family a good income at the time, and he held lectures at our home on this subject. Unfortunately though, my father was angry about how his life had turned out. It is conceivable that his experience at sea during the Second World War scarred him in some ways, and perhaps his anger stemmed from that experience. Soccer clubs also have their share of anger in them, and perhaps my work reflects an attempt to calm down my father, who died just before my sixteenth birthday.

My mother had died when I was 14, and my position in life was precarious. The situation was ameliorated by a grant to attend a local college for three years. After gaining some academic qualifications, it was my good fortune to be hired as a member of the stage crew at a prestigious local theatre called the Chichester Festival Theatre. All stage crewmembers were regarded as potential actors, and thanks to Nicholas Hytner, the current Director of the National Theatre of England, the role developed into a professional acting career that lasted for 14 years. Though my family never went to the theatre, it was a world that was familiar to me somehow. Also, Nicholas Hytner is a master at building teams of actors and crew that were cohesive. By creating cultures that were together he believed that better quality would ensue, and I was fortunate to be afforded such a role model.

Theatre is a world of play and archetype with access to a serious, disciplined professional environment that inspired me. The theatre in England has a rich tradition, and it afforded me a creative outlet that helped offset the preceding difficult and painful years. The theatre world gave my bereavement a chance to heal somewhat and allowed me to become part of a vibrant creative culture where I could express myself. The work of great playwrights became my diet, and acting in their plays was a chance to explore archetypes and learn to be able to embody them. The experience also gave me a chance to develop a capacity to focus, a crucial skill in almost all professional performance environments.

Currently, my career is split. I spend ten months of the year working in America as a psychotherapist, and the other two months working in England with professional soccer players and coaches. These players are performers as well, and my work has aimed at helping them deal with self-conscious feelings and adjust to working on the public stage. The clinical and educational culture of psychology is very different than the earthier masculine culture of professional soccer.

Until recently, my experience of working with soccer players has been solely in England. Due to my coursework and clinical commitments, there was never an opportunity to work in America. In 2008, by chance, the head coach and manager of an American university soccer program sat next to me at White Hart Lane soccer stadium in London. (I was working at the club delivering sessions on sport psychology and was expected to attend all matches.) Our sitting together was pure chance. When the head coach returned to America, he called Tottenham Hotspur, found my contact details and asked me to help his team out with "ego problems." We worked together with the team on ten occasions during the season in a manner that replicated my work in England.

Researcher's background experience in England

Tottenham Hotspur FC (Football Club) is a club in London, England. They currently employ me twice a year for a month at a time to deliver psychology sessions and to work with individuals as part of the team. My work has spanned 14 years at nine different English clubs, the smallest of which is bigger than the largest club in America. My work is full time with a requirement to be at the training ground delivering sessions on psychology and individual meetings with players. As with psychotherapy, building relationships is important in order to best assist the players. Here, we map out strategies to help them develop better mental strengths, as well as the emotional pressures and projections they face. In 2012, Tottenham Hotspur created a psychology framework for coaches relating to age-appropriate learning for children at the club aged 9 and above based on the emotional developmental stages model pioneered by Eric Erickson in 1950. Coaches were introduced to the specific stages and the implications for ways of working with children sensitively and according to their developmental stage. My recent work has included sessions for the Football Association of England, helping coaches to work with young people effectively, again based on clinically accepted models.

My work with soccer players is now quintessentially Jungian, often using myths to relate Eastern and Western philosophies. Archetypes such as animal spirits are explored as a vehicle to help scholars embody the particular traits the game demands. This study is to be phenomenological, but my work in England could be better described as hermeneutic, perhaps best outlined in Richard Palmer's (1969) book *Hermeneutics*. Palmer defined three functions of modern hermeneutics as "to say" (p. 14), "to explain" (p. 20), and "to translate" (p. 26). "Significantly, Hermes is associated with the function of transmuting what is beyond human understanding into a form that human intelligence can grasp" (p. 13). Commonly valued traits or virtues such as spirit (as in team spirit), discipline, respect, commitment, confidence, and tenacity can be explored uncovering the "spirit of the word." The hermeneutic "what is beyond human understanding" mentioned in this case refers to ideas and topics not often covered in the English curriculum. Schools currently have their own competitive league tables to contend with. It appears that this results in subjects involving unquantifiable learning such as mine are taught less frequently. In fact, when asked, scholars have reported no experience of learning about these topics at school. For example, in my experience confidence is a Holy Grail for many young people, although no one has ever directly addressed the topic with them at school. I believe that these subjects can be usefully explored and young people can be helped to achieve emotional as well as practical goals.

Since 2000, the focus of my work in soccer has been related to what may be termed the "eternal truths." This is intended to mean values that are not recent ideas, but have existed as a principle throughout generations—for example, the values of group unity, responsibility, and knowing limits. This way of working has been very successful and in my experience, it is often an unusual exercise for young men who might be expected to prefer the field to the classroom. Karen Armstrong, in her 2005 compact disc, *A short history of myth*, suggested a plausible reason why this may be. The CD concentrated on the cultural and anthropological basis of our myths and archetypes. She explained, "the shaman after all, worked with the hunters." Perhaps the shaman's role was related to the ritualized mental preparation that David Rock suggested earlier when discussing preparations for hunting. According to Rock, the young men were repeating and recreating an ancient experience without knowing it. This study shall seek to connect to these players with interviews that hope to explore their inner life and the things that matter to them.

Gender and role disparities and typical soccer culture

The culture of professional soccer is typically male and what may be considered a masculine environment. Approximately 95 per cent of the working population at the club is male at Tottenham Hotspur. In my experience of working within other professional clubs, this is typical. Young players aged 16–19 in the academy aspire to make it to the *Developmental squad*, the step below the first team. Some of them are players from abroad, and many of them have cost the club millions of dollars. However, in the main the academy takes local players with promise and tries to build them into an increasingly higher professional standard.

In England, the public attention on the game creates a lot of pressure on the younger players to succeed, as well as the crushing ignomiy of failure if you do not obtain a contract. These are acute social and emotional pressures that are relevant to us as clinical psychologists. Soccer is invariably a tough, competitive culture. But even so, this culture recognizes the social realities the players face and actively looks deeper into ways of assisting players on a personal level. A Football Association-sponsored publication about sport psychology stated that "it is primarily in the home that a child's beliefs, values, perceptions, attitudes and goals are shaped" (Cale, 2004, p. 138). What kind of priority do domestic and parental values hold for a player? In my experience, parental pressures on a young player can even potentially hinder an aspirant. Perhaps this study can reveal insights into this issue. Even simple expectations of success from family and friends can create pressure in itself, which may be greater than any imposed on players by the club they belong to.

Before emigrating to America, I had been working with professional young players for five years. My life for the last ten years has been to commute to the male-saturated world of soccer in England and then return to my other "field" of psychotherapy in America, which is comprised of more females. The cultural priorities and emphases feel different. In 2010, *The Therapist* magazine included an article on demographic profiles (in California, psychotherapists are given the official title of a 'Marriage and Family Therapist' or MFT:

> The "typical" MFT is female. This survey indicates that 78 percent of those responding are female, compared with 78 percent in 2008, 78 percent in 2006, 79.8 percent in 2004, 75 percent in 2002, 72 percent in 2000, 74 percent in 1997, 72 percent in 1995 and 1992, 68 percent in 1990, and 70 percent in 1988.
>
> (Riemersma, 2010, p. 28)

The disparity between the two worlds has always intrigued me. Soccer in England is a world full of males; psychotherapy seems the opposite, and the cultures have different mindsets. This may be one of the reasons why there have been little or any in-depth studies of sport. Cooper (1998) stated that "Jungians tend, by and large, to be pretty removed from popular culture. They're not accustomed to applying their ideas to something as much in the mainstream as sports. For the most part, we're a pretty nerdy group" (p. 59). This study can seek to counter that portrayal and explore the subject with an in-depth approach and a clinical lens.

This study sought also to explore and compare data from women who devote their ambitions towards soccer. As the study shall reveal, women's soccer is a flourishing expression in the game and some surprising results emerged from the data the coresearchers shared. This study sought to examine if women playing soccer inhabit a masculine world, or if the archetypes originate from another source. The impact of cultural barriers to women's participation in sport are also explored later, indicating that many attitudes about women and sport may indeed be "man-made."

During my acting career, high standards were expected from a professional. To be competent as an actor, the ability to focus on your performance is a skill and capacity essential for any professional live performer. If the mind of an actor wanders during a live performance, it is perhaps natural to assume that he or she is more liable to forget their lines. Fundamentally, members in a company are relying on each other to say their line, so they in turn can say theirs. The interconnectivity between participants (and audience) engaged in the activity is central to the process for companies of actors performing a play or a team playing sports. Teams indeed appear to rely on a kind of chemistry, and this study can investigate if the players themselves can speak to this dimension of the game.

The comparisons between acting and soccer are deep, perhaps deeper than first meets the eye. Professional soccer players are "guns for hire" working for one company or another for a season, as actors do. A soccer player has to focus, especially when the spotlight falls on him. The actor follows the course of play, as does the soccer player. This study explores in part how the worlds of acting and soccer are similar, where a practitioner has to concentrate and follow the course. For both parties, anxiety is often attributed to a poor performance. Does clinical psychology have something to contribute here?

Clinical relevance

Many young soccer players discover that their feelings are hurt if they are spoken to harshly or discourteously by each other or by the coaching staff. Unfortunately, for many players, if "wounded feelings" are left unattended, they can adversely affect their performance and future chances for progress in the sport. In my experience, many players develop resentments or lose their confidence after being "told off," which can set in motion an emotional, downward spiral that can jeopardize their chances of team selection. As described earlier, masculine environments are not places where, on the surface at least, personal feelings are considered to be most important. Decisions regarding selection in soccer require a manager to make decisions based on form and not on personal feelings about a player. And yet, we must also ask what is important for women on a team? This study asks questions about these issues.

In my own experience, there are professional soccer coaches who do not approve of psychology, and would not care if my work stopped immediately. This kind of attitude is a current cultural reality of that world, although at the time of writing, it is diminishing. For me, the only practical response to those who hold such views is to accept the cultural realities as the way they are, and focus on my own work to the best of my ability. As a comparatively experienced and mature man, I'm perhaps better at separating home from work issues. But in the professional sporting world, this is not as easy for the young players. Many scholars (the official title for young professional players/players in training) in my experience find themselves in emotional pain without understanding or knowing why. There appears to be a valuable role helping players make emotional adjustments under these circumstances so they recover themselves and move on as quickly as possible. Little attention is paid to the cultivation of emotional resilience or mental focus; thus, clinical psychology may be able to provide insights and knowledge useful in similar related settings such as other team environments.

My clinical experience in American therapeutic work has been with many different individuals as a licensed Marriage and Family Therapist a psychotherapist, known as a MFT. A clinic where I once worked attracted a lot of businessmen from Wall Street who flew from New York to Los Angeles to get help with addiction and emotional crises. My work with them was sometimes as their primary psychotherapist and in this role it was my responsibility to liaise with doctors and family members and to organize and implement the interventions and modes of treatment for clients. In my experience such financial brokers often have highly organized minds and very effective problem-solving abilities. Stockbrokers often rely on instinct and intuition regarding when to buy or sell. They work in teams and have deadlines, targets, and strategies.

Archetypally too, these men appear to embody the spirit of a modern hunter. Some are wonderful hunters who have made fortunes from the mastery of their skills. Their abilities in a challenging, ever shifting world are often quite apparent. What they did not appear to understand was that the rules of the hunt did not work in the same way at home. In my experience, the Wall Street "hunter" appears to apply the ideas of business relations in his domestic environment. Clients with these types of issues often arrived confused and embittered that their domestic life could not be organized as if it were a business problem. One male client told me at our first meeting, "My wife needs to be fixed; she never does what she says she will." Another once complained, "I tell her what to do and she ignores me," as if she were an employee, not an intimate relation. By taking an in-depth look at such a "typically masculine" culture, we can aim to distinguish and discern the unique challenges and difficulties as distinct to those equally demanding realities in the home environment. Businessmen and women, like our coresearchers, have to achieve targets, and perhaps this study can reveal more about the "bottom line" for individuals under pressure.

The comparative nature of this study between the genders may be able to shed light on different attitudes that exist between the sexes under pressure. High-level performance environments are intense and extreme compared to those generally encountered by the public at large, but they are not unique conditions. Evidence explored later will show how important teams may be in the emotional development of young people. Perhaps we are hardwired to work in teams. An informal poll I conducted amongst younger clients in group settings indicated that 80 per cent had no memory of ever working in a team. From the data collected, we might be able to discern characteristics that are familiar to the world of teams that many of us must inhabit outside of soccer.

Chapter 2

Soccer and the psyche of the performer

Having introduced the subject and some of the context, this chapter will outline other significant research and writing on soccer, and the psyche that speaks to soccer. As this study testifies, the subject matter is not new and there is much written about the sport. This section can help to identify and amplify the subject by including only a small portion of the work of others in the field. The main topics explored in this chapter will include sections on sports psychology and soccer, play and performance studies, the hunter archetype, the bush soul, the Olympic movement and Greek antecedents, spirit and the split *between mind and body*, stage fright and life or death experiences, and finally, Carol Dweck and mindset.

Sports psychology and soccer

In 1990, the psychologist Mihaly Csikszentmihalyi published a seminal work on his theory of flow called *Flow: The psychology of optimal experience.* He suggested that humans on a broader level are at their happiest when they are in a state of flow, or what he refers to as "focused attention." The work had a huge impact in the world of sports psychology creating a new dimension and area of investigation into the personal states that athletes must achieve in order to maximize their chances for success. Csikszentmihalyi described eight states or conditions that were consistent with the idea of optimum performance in sports. He recognized that optimum states did not involve having no stress at all, but in fact needed a certain amount of stress in order to attain a better sense of acuity. This study will seek to ask questions about the experience of playing well and what we can discern from the coresearchers about performance states.

In 2002, Graham Jones of the University of Wales, with Sheldon Hanton and Declan Connaughton, wrote a paper entitled "What is this Thing called Mental Toughness? An Investigation into Elite Sport Performers." Their study sought to investigate mental rankings and popular notions of what it is to be an elite sportsman. The introduction of the paper discussed how *mental toughness* is still a little understood phenomenon. The paper describes a study by Gould et al. (1987) that demonstrated that 82 per cent of (wrestling) coaches rated mental toughness as the most important psychological attribute in determining success (p. 206). Jones et al. then went on to say; "Interestingly only 9 per cent of these coaches stated they were successful in developing or changing mental toughness in the performers they worked with" (ibid.). This low statistic seems to indicate that the coaches are perhaps missing something significant. Presumably 91 per cent of those coaches would like to know what they are missing. Or perhaps they are fooling themselves, but it does seem the coach has a vital part to play in the development of any player.

The Jones et al. (2002) study selected ten athletes with international experience representing their country. Interviews were conducted using three methods: the first stage was a focus group; in the next stage the individual interviews were conducted, and finally participants responded to a questionnaire giving their own rankings of mental toughness. The authors then analyzed the data and placed their findings into separate categories and attributes of what mental toughness actually was. The study identified the following terms: "Self-belief, desire and motivation, focus (performance related), focus (lifestyle related), dealing with competition related pressure (external) and anxiety (internal), and dealing with physical and emotional pain" (p. 215). The authors emphasized the importance of distinguishing the above terms and then being able to help athletes achieve these characteristics. "Previous literature is characterized by definitions and characteristics of mental toughness that are too far ranging to be of help to practitioners and athletes alike" (p. 215). If we consider only one of the topics above, such as "physical and emotional pain," it is my understanding that clinical depth perspectives can provide an informed alternative that can assist with the research difficulties identified by the authors above.

Richard Thelwell and Neil Weston (2005) from the University of Portsmouth, England, wrote a paper called "Defining and Understanding Mental Toughness within Soccer." The article was based on a series of group interviews with players from different teams, and described how they interviewed elite players and identified key areas consistent with mental strength. Beyond that, however, as with Jones et al. (2002), the work had difficulty providing anything beyond a descriptive observation of the terminology to attach to a mental strength. A quantitative, empirical approach to studying sport may also have a limited resonance in trying to define and quantify the comparatively unquantifiable emotional and archetypal elements apparent within the sport. A depth lens can approach the subject in a new way; it was very hard to find any evidence of clinical psychological perspectives in any literature on soccer. So far, by attempting to quantify the unquantifiable and ineffable, studies have more often become reduced to descriptive definitions and statistics.

In an attempt to bridge the gap, the Football Association of England put together a book called *The official guide to psychology for football* (Cale, 2004). Culturally, such a holistic approach to soccer is new, and the book named many of the issues that are crucial understandings for working in this kind of environment. Aimed at helping coaches and players alike, Cale used terms such as "ego orientation" to describe ineffective mental attitudes some players have:

> Ego orientated players may be likely to demonstrate poor behavior in sessions and matches such as blaming others, moaning and sometimes even cheating. They are less likely to accept coach criticism (particularly in front of their peers), and tend to give up more easily when compared to a task-orientated player.
>
> (p. 24)

Other topics explored in the book included sections on imagery, the coach–parent working alliance, family relationships, parent relationships, empathy, anxiety, and their term "emotional temperature" (p. 147). Many of these terms are familiar to clinical psychology. Sports psychology often refers to these issues as "psycho social." Cale also suggested ideas about imagination and visualization, subjects that infer a more intuitive approach with the psyche. It is time perhaps that depth psychology had a voice as the sport investigates this kind of territory.

Sports psychology is now exploring issues that may reach into areas where clinical psychology can provide perspectives, which may benefit and support the science rather than challenge it. More recently, sports psychologists have been researching the interconnection of teams and how cultures can improve, and what kinds of cultures tend to produce successful results. In the world of soccer psychology, Pain and Harwood (2007; 2009) have recently begun to study more qualitative kinds of research into the pressures and strains that soccer players face. Things are undoubtedly changing, and in March 2014, the England soccer team announced that Dr Steve Peters would be travelling with them to the World Cup™ competition in Brazil that year. Dr Peters is referred to as a Sports Psychiatrist; although he is unlikely to dispense pharmacological medications he is a widely regarded expert on sports psychology. In 2011, he published a book called *The chimp paradox*, which looked at the levels of the mind in operation for a performer. As with this study, his book suggests that primitive, ancient forces are in motion in sport and must be acknowledged. By using a depth, clinical lens, this study complements the insights that early qualitative research by sports psychologists are reaching.

Play and performance studies

Richard Schechner (2002), in *Performance studies*, provided a rich and varied overview, insight, and introduction to major works in the field of performance studies, as well as related fields of play and ritual studies. Schechner covered a wide variety of subjects, from Bateson's discussion of the "play frame," a special ordering of time and space which allows animals and humans alike to signal that behavior taking place within it is "just play," to Geertz's work with the "deep play" of Balinese cockfighting, to Turner's classic work on play and liminality.

There is a large and varied literature on play. Other important theorists include Brian Sutton-Smith (1997), who in *The ambiguity of play* discussed different types of play, as well as "rhetorics" of play. Sports correspond to a variety of different types of play, including vicarious audience play, risky or deep play, and contests. This is consistent with Caillois' (1958/2001) four-category scheme of play, where sports such as soccer are situated under the category of *agon*. The Greeks used the term to refer to a contest or conflict. Sutton-Smith used a rhetoric that describes play as power: "play is seen as a representation of conflict, and as a way to fortify the status for those who control the play or are its heroes. This rhetoric is as ancient as warfare and the patriarchy" (p. 10). This study may be able to help illuminate another purpose beyond warfare and patriarchy.

In Huizinga's (1955) *Homo ludens*, many aspects of play and sport were explored. Huizinga argued that play is primary to the generation of culture, and even precedes culture, noting that animals played long before culture existed. This serves as a reminder of play's deep archetypal roots. It also appears from the literature on play that there are several different aspects to consider regarding the archetypes encountered during research with these elite players.

In *The future of ritual*, Schechner (1993), a discussion of social dramas in a chapter entitled "The Street is the Stage," mentioned the celebrations leading up to the fall of the Berlin Wall as an example of festivals whose outcome is unknown. He likened this to soccer:

> The excitement of such social dramas—not unlike what grips whole populations during some sports matches, especially those like the soccer World Cup where team and nations are closely identified—is rooted in the tension between known patterns of action, stunning instantaneous surprises, and a passionately desired yet uncertain outcome.
>
> (p. 97)

Schechner (1988), when discussing various aspects of performance, linked play, sports, ritual, and other types of performance to hunting. He posited that these various forms of play and ritual had their origins in hunting, and practicing skills that would be useful in hunting. Hunting requires long periods of stealth, sudden outbursts of energy and lots of practice. Species who play the most also engage in activities that expend kinetic energy in sudden quick bursts, such as fighting, fleeing, mating, hunting, maintaining dominance, and protecting turf. According to Schechner, "crisis—the sudden and unstinting spending of kinetic energy—is the link among performance, hunting, ritual, and play" (p. 97).

Play, Schechner (1988) related, keeps kinetic energy in practice, "to be spent in behavior that is not only harmless but fun. *Decisively, play allows kinetic potential to be maintained not by being stored but by being spent*" (p. 97, original emphasis). Schechner asserted that

> play is a form of hunting and that hunting is kind of playing. This kind of playing is strategic, future-and-crisis-oriented, violent and/or combative; it has winners and losers, leaders and followers; it employs costumes and/or disguises; it has a beginning, middle, and end; and its underlying themes are fertility, prowess, and animism/totemism. This kind of playing at killing emphasizes individual or small-group action and teamwork.
>
> (pp. 99-100)

Schechner noted that play may also be the result of displacement behavior.

As described earlier, Csikszentmihalyi's, (1990) work, *Flow*, identified a state he called "flow." He describes a feeling often referred to as being "in the zone," which occurs when people are fully immersed in an activity. This is a state of complete absorption, where things just seem to happen naturally and temporal concerns are absent. There do appear to be relationships between spiritual practitioners' optimal states and those reported by sports players when in the "zone."

The hunter archetype

It may be noteworthy that it is very hard to find any reference to the terms "hunting" or "hunter" when looking in the index sections of books on psychology. These words are curiously absent given the importance and social significance of hunting to early peoples, which was surely fundamental before the advent of agriculture, hunting and foraging (or gathering) were predominant ways of securing food. To assert that hunting was an important cultural element for our early ancestors may appear to be conjecture. But, thanks to recent advances in science we can now analyze hunting and cleaning tools and find evidence of the high level of meat in their diets; so it appears that hunting played a crucial role in the priorities of early cultures.

In 2009, Richards & Trinkaus discovered that high nitrogen and carbon isotopes indicated that Neanderthal diets were concentrated on meat. Their research called "Isotopic Evidence for the Diets of European Neanderthals and Early Modern Humans" included samples of over a dozen bone fragments gathered from all over Europe. By measuring the levels of collagen in the bone, the study concluded that Neanderthals were "top level" carnivores. This study will investigate the correlations that may exist between team sports and the hunting dynamic of our ancestors. A noteworthy exception to the exclusion of psychological discussion regarding hunters is Erich Neumann who actually did refer to the role of the hunter in his book *Origin and history of consciousness:*

Hunting and war are conducive to the development of an individual ego capable of acting responsibly in a dangerous situation, and equally conducive to the leadership principle. Whether the leader is chosen to deal with a specific situation, say for the specific purpose of canoe-building or for a hunting expedition, or to act as the permanent leader, the situation of leader is bound to arrive sooner or later in the male group, even when this is co-coordinated within the matriarchal nucleus.

(1954, p. 147)

Laurens van der Post was an iconic figure in the world of nature and hunting. A friend of Jung's, van der Post studied the Bushmen of Africa and spoke widely about the inner essence of such indigenous peoples and tribes. Van der Post (1961) traveled with the Kalahari tribesmen and wrote an account extrapolating their myths and folklore in his book *The heart of the hunter: Customs and myths of the African Bushman* as he traveled with them. This book, dedicated to Jung, helped to inform this study, exploring the archetypal stories and legends that appealed to the hunters. Van der Post was a commando for the Allies in the Second World War and was a supreme soldier himself. Jung's appreciation of archetypes appear reflected by van der Post's own writings:

But at least we can know there is a pattern in us, communicated through images that came like starlight into our spirit, and that by serving them with all our heart and mind, life on Earth can become richer, freer and greater than it has ever been.

(p. 266)

This may be one potential origin of the hero archetype. The Bushmen of the Kalahari are renowned ancient hunters, and van der Post (1961) asserted that they have a gift, which we have lost. He remarked that twentieth-century rationalism had robbed humankind of an inner spiritual awareness crucial to the soul "the primitive spirit stands in rags and tatters, rejected by the contemporary mind" (p. 145). He went on to say that this might be caused by "the unawareness of man whose vision is so tied to the world without, that he is incapable of seeing the spiritual content of his own inner world" (p. 145). Van der Post is not the only author or psychologist to have this perspective, so what has been lost or left behind?

The bush soul and identification with animals

But what can we illuminate of this inner world? Many books have been written about soccer legends. Players who reach the heights obviously demonstrate remarkable physical strengths and abilities. Some part of their psyche must also have great strengths: what are these and where do they come from? Jung noted that certain "primitive" cultures have a soul that lives outside the normal bounds of domestic life: "Many primitives assume that a man has a 'bush soul' as well as his own, and that this bush soul is incarnate in a wild animal" (1964, p. 6).

Is there such a thing as a Western "bush soul"? Malcolm Gladwell (2005) has recently explored the idea of a separate soul or entity with its own intelligence operating within our lives. In his book, *Blink*, Gladwell suggested that humans possess what he calls a "locked door." He described events and experiments that explore the efficacy of intuition and instinct when using perception. He illustrated this concept by describing an experiment designed by the psychologist Norman R.F. Maier. For his experiment, two ropes where hung from a ceiling, surrounded by various domestic objects. Candidates were asked to think of as many ways they could of joining the two ropes together. Maier discovered that most candidates could think of three ways, but a fourth idea, to swing the rope like a pendulum while holding the other, was beyond most. Maier gave this group an extra ten minutes to think, entered the room and then deliberately brushed a rope as he passed it in view of the candidate. The moving rope inspired many to guess the fourth solution, but only one person was able to realize that Maier's actions provided the clue. Others made no connection, claiming instead other reasons.

Gladwell (2005) concluded, "Maier's hint was so subtle that it was only picked up on an unconscious level. It was processed behind the locked door, so, when pressed for an explanation, all Maier's subjects could do was to make up what seemed to be the most plausible explanation" (p. 70). Echoing the idea of the "bush soul," Gladwell suggested that "everyone in that room had not one mind but two, and all the while the conscious mind was blocked, their unconscious was scanning the room, sifting through possibilities, processing every conceivable clue. And the instant it found the answer, it guided them silently and surely to the solution" (p. 71).

Can we locate this "other soul" in the sports world? Is this represented by the archetypal symbols common in modern sports? Steve Claridge was a famous soccer player and is now a commentator in England. In the Introduction to a biography about Claridge, co-author Ian Ridley employed a commonly used metaphor to help us identify the nature of a player: "He turned cleverly and took on defenders bravely. Above all, he had the heart of a lion" (Claridge & Ridley, 1997, p. 7). Earlier, I cited Jung who suggested that the "bush soul" is "incarnate in a wild being." What is it these footballers display, in common with other sporting legends, that embodies and captures so many psyches across the world?

Early Egyptian cultures also indicate that the animal was of supreme relevance to the soul of humans, as demonstrated in the mummified remains of animals, the significance of which is only beginning to be understood. Many animals, such as the "Apis Bull," were ceremonially selected, raised, and worshipped by Egyptians because their individual qualities related directly to the gods (Owen, 2004, p. 2). Similar to the Kalahari Bushmen, the Egyptians created Bastet, a feline god, as a protector of the Pharos. What is the human link with the animal spirit and why does it remain so embedded within sports culture? We cannot fail to notices that animals frequently serve as mascots for teams, and that many teams are named after animals. For example, the 'three lions' is the symbol for the Football Association (FA) and the England team, a lion wearing a crown is the symbol for the Premier League and, in 2014, of the clubs involved in the Premier League, eight had crests with birds, three with lions, one with a dragon, one with an eagle, one with a tiger and one with a red devil (which closely resembles a lion).

Jung declared that his inner guide Philemon, told him "thoughts are like animals in the forest" (1961, p. 183). The identification with animals is an ancient human trait, at least because of our relationship to animals for food. Stanislav Grof (1988) wrote about this identification in his book *The adventure of self-discovery* suggesting that this identification related to early hunting tribes and their ability to stalk prey by identifying with the animals they hunted:

> They were able to tune into them and identify with them so fully that they got to know intimately their instincts and habits. Following this experience, their success in hunting increased considerably, since they were able to switch from the consciousness of the hunted animal and outwit their prey.
>
> (p. 55)

This state of altered consciousness enabled the hunter to fully embody the archetypes that they were hunting, to enter into their spirit by becoming their spirit. The coresearchers in the study might offer insight into the states they have to enter and if this is of benefit to them also.

In the US, Phil Jackson, the one time coach for the Los Angeles Lakers, has written many books on the psychological/spiritual connection between players and their work. *Sacred hoops: spiritual lessons as a Hardwood Warrior* (1995) became a bestseller and introduced the world to his shamanistic style of team management. Jackson has moved away from empirical approaches to sports psychology towards a more spiritual connection with the game. He is known for having dressing rooms that contain totems and other ritual and tribal symbols. In *Sacred hoops*, Jackson spoke about many spiritual and ancestral issues connected to sport. He described the American Indian Lakota warriors and how they "had a deep reverence for the mysteries of life. That's where there sense of power, and sense of freedom came from. It was no coincidence that Crazy Horse, the greatest Sioux warrior, was a holy man" (p. 109).

Van der Post also suggested that there was a direct benefit to the hunters of the Kalahari for taking their ancient myths seriously. For hunters and warriors, achieving their potential may have meant more chances of better food and safety. "Through this increasing awareness, particularly in the story of Mantis, he discovered in himself the power to achieve a greater and more authoritative, a finer and more accurate statement of life and personality on Earth" (van der Post,

1961, p. 178). In 2009, Marvin Close and Chuck Korr wrote *More than just a game*, a book about the notorious Robben Island prisoners in South Africa who were able to stay alive and develop a resistance to oppression within a prison by organizing a football league. The game provided a structure for learning that gave many individuals careers after the end of apartheid in the government of a free South Africa. This seems a noble aspiration for any individual: Can we help young soccer players in this way or can they help us? Has an archetypal and ancient kind of learning been lost to us, and if so, can we rediscover it?

The Olympic movement and Greek antecedents

The only apparent rival to the soccer World Cup™ competition for television viewers is the Olympic Games. Figures are not precise, and some independent companies like to exaggerate their figures for their own purposes and marketing. Ceremonies or matches are also subject to variables that obscure accurate declarations of figures or statistics. Some figures cannot be quantified, for example, public screenings of live events, others in a household watching, radio listeners, and online viewing. Variations in world time zones also produce inevitable variations for the populated zones, with China being a notable example. One claim refers to the Beijing Olympics in 2008. Ben Wyatt, staff writer for CNN News, suggested that the 2008 Olympics in Beijing attracted the largest recorded viewing figures in history. He quoted Kevin Alavy, a director of Futures Sport and Entertainment, a global sport research and evaluation consultancy: "Our research found that there was a global audience of 593 million people who watched the opening ceremony live, while 320 million watched the World Cup final in Germany in 2006" (Wyatt, 2010). In 2011, the American Super Bowl football game recorded a "record" number of viewers—111 million (Levy, 2011). Whatever the real numbers are, these figures seem to suggest that the spectacle and sporting traditions of the Olympic movement also holds a great significance to the world's psyche. Jungian analyst Ronald Schenk suggests: "In providing an alternative understanding of television, I would suggest that television, when seen as an entity with a life or essence that has an intention of its own, is a response to the soul's need to transcend subjectivity and unify the material "reality" of the modern world with spirit." (2010, p. 96) The world is connected and becoming exponentially more connected by the internet, and sport appears to have a major role to play in this spiritual modern reality.

In 2003, Phil Cousineau wrote *Olympic odyssey*, a treatise on the deeper meanings and history behind sport, in particular the Greek tradition of the Olympic Games. "The Olympic movement began in the city of Olympia in the eighth-century BCE and lasted, with sporadic cessations, up until the fourth century, when it was outlawed by the Roman tyrant Theodosius" (p. 3). The games were given a modern incarnation in 1896 thanks to the vision of Baron de Pierre Coubertin (p. 110). Cousineau's account detailed the mythological origins of the movement by exploring the cultural origins and purposes of the games. He argued that the founding of the Olympics was designed to satisfy a higher purpose to the State than just competition or entertainment. Cousineau suggested that the origins of the Olympic movement were born from a need to maintain peace and not allow city-state rivalries to weaken the overall strength of a united Greece. Interstate violence was endemic for much of Greece's early history, and internal wars could ultimately be self-defeating. In times of wider world conflict, a robust army would be needed, an army that knew how to live and work together. "For the hope of the ancient Games was that the inspiring spectacle of young warrior athletes competing peacefully might break down walls of suspicion and enmity between rival city-states, who were rarely on peaceful terms with each other" (p. 48). Spectators or athletes travelling to the Olympics were safeguarded by law; such was the importance to the Greeks of this sacred spectacle dedicated to Zeus. Competitors were awarded laurels, and as today, some achieved notoriety and fame for their achievements. Certainly, history shows that the celebration and appreciation of skill for skills sake was a significant passion for the Greeks.

The global shared experience of witnessing these events still appears to transcend the religious or political divide. Can this be a helpful influence on the world community? Issues such as conflict and poverty remain in the world, but perhaps the coming together of sport can be a vehicle of unity as the Greeks intended? Baron de Coubertin hoped this would be the case when he revived the movement in 1896. "Coubertin believed fairly contested games might bring an age of global harmony" (Cousineau, 2003, p. 110). However, it would be erroneous to suggest that the Olympics replaced or contested with the idea of battle for the Greeks. Greek culture was still attached to warfare and military power, none more so than the Spartans. Cousineau cited the historian Will Durant, who wrote in his book *The life of Greece:* "Religion failed to unify Greece, athletics—periodically—succeeded. ...Under the rubric of athletics we find the real religion of the Greeks—the worship of health, beauty and strength" (p. 33).

The mythological union of Aphrodite, symbolizing beauty, and Ares, the god of battle and warfare, is perhaps a fitting emblem for the ideals of sports at least. This marriage of combat and beauty produced an offspring called Harmony. Echoing Coubertin's desire for world union, Cousineau (2003) stated, "as their mythic marriage shows, the fusion of the two—love and combat—can bring Harmony (the name of their love child) into the world" (p. 33). Perhaps harmony is the attractive side of sports for the viewer as well as the essential state of union for the athlete as he or she endeavors to immerse themselves in the challenge at hand. This study sought to discover what harmony might mean for our coresearchers, and if it is in the same spirit as the Greeks once knew.

Conceivably, the popularity of modern sports and the global union created by the internet and media are adding impetus to an ancient phenomenon without us knowing it. As described earlier, one protocol of soccer that appears universal is the shaking of hands at the end of the contest. As a gesture, it is perhaps symbolic of the spirit behind sport and fair competition, in that there is always a re-connection at the end. Cousineau suggested that for the Greeks, "the recognition of teammates and opponents alike as brothers or sisters remains one of the goals of modern sports" (p. 28). The study asked questions about relationships seeking to discover if they are familial or competitive in nature.

Spirit and the split

Rather than primarily seeking an understanding of the global phenomenon, this study aimed to look deeper into the inherent emotional realities for an individual athlete. Cousineau (2003) detailed a discussion about athletics he had with Joseph Campbell. Campbell told him emphatically:

> You have to channel all the energy or they'll burn your cities down. I don't know what I would have done without athletics when I was a young man. It gave me discipline for a lifetime. I still swim forty-four laps a day, meditating on a different tarot card during each lap.
>
> (p. 61)

Campbell made reference to the inner values and qualities behind sporting expression that can be of use to any individual. "Life's tough. Running taught me how to pace myself in everything I've done in my life. It takes real guts to make your way through this world. The discipline you can learn in sports can give you that" (p. 61). The study will seek to explore the ways involvement might contribute to personal development by interviewing players of the game. Sports at a high level are to a greater or lesser degree dependent on psychological strengths and abilities beyond technical ability. Campbell suggested deeper virtues are accessible in sport and this study sought to identify what they might be.

Spirit is a term often used in sport, for example the notion of team spirit. What does this term actually mean? What about the spirit of the individual, and how does this relate to team spirit? The author Michael Novak was also interested in the deeper essences behind sporting performance. In his book *The joy of sports*, Novak (1993) suggested that "sports are creations of the human spirit, arenas of the human spirit, witnesses to the human spirit, instructors of the human spirit" (p. 158). Perhaps this is an idea that was more naturally understood by our ancestors. Can there be a connection between the sporting sense of spirit and spirituality? In his book *Buddha's brain,* author Rick Hanson (Hanson & Mendius, 2009) made such a comparison; "For thousands of years, contemplatives—the Olympic athletes of mental training—have studied the mind" (p. 1). Cousineau (2003) suggested that twenty-first century cultural ideals have separated traditions that were once naturally more unified:

Rather than living in a culture that encourages athletes to meet with philosophers, artists with politicians, and soldiers with poet—as the ancient Greeks did for nearly twelve hundred years during the festival of Zeus at ancient Olympic—we live in one where priests disdain the body, athletes dismiss thinkers, and everybody is suspicious of poets.

(p. 5)

He suggests these splits are a modern phenomenon and were not the case in the past. He referred to the aikido master and journalist George Leonard, who wrote extensively on the relationship of mind and sport. In 2001, Leonard published a book called *The ultimate athlete* where he outlined his theories in more detail and defined a modern "mind-body-spirit" split which he regards as "a major error in Western thought" (p. 290). Goodchild (2001) also suggests a split in the wider public psyche; "it reflects our cultural bias spanning the past four hundred or so years: of control over an inanimate world by all powerful ego and a rational consciousness separated and distanced by both the larger cosmic fabric, and the deeper levels of the psyche, of which we are in fact an intimate thread" (p. 205).

If a modern lacuna exists within the psyche of Westerners at least, then what precisely have we lost? Robert Johnson (1987), in his book *Ecstasy: Understanding the psychology of joy,* investigated the mythological figure of Dionysus, who was once widely celebrated in ancient Greece as a source of creativity and fertile expression. However, Johnson charted the rise of a more removed, Apollonian tradition in the Roman culture compared to Greece. The Romans replaced ancient Dionysus with Bacchus, more associated by them to drunkenness.

When Western society chose to follow the erratic footsteps of the degraded Bacchus instead of the joyful dance of Dionysus, it began to confuse materialism with sensation. As a result we citizens in the late twentieth century can truly be said to have lost our senses, or at least to have lost contact with them.

(p. 22)

Along with many of the authors cited such as Campbell (1972), Novak (1993) and Leonard (2001), Robert Johnson suggested that a separation of some kind within the human spirit has occurred and we may not be as whole as we once were. This study investigates whether coresearchers express identifications that would be familiar to the Greeks, embodied by the gods such as Dionysus and Apollo.

If deeper ideas about life and the mind are useful, they why aren't they naturally a part of our modern sports culture? Perhaps it is that modern sports cultures naturally reflect the cultural values of our times. Alan Wallace (2006) wrote *The attention revolution,* a book summarizing his research into meditation and the relationship it has with the power of attention. He expressed his belief that "especially in the modern West, where so many people are in a hurry, intent on finding quick fixes and short-term gains, it is easy to take a shortsighted view on meditation" (p. 88). The power of attention is an issue very relevant to a live performer of any kind. This study aims to shed light on the priorities and attachments that athletes express concerning attention and the pressures they might experience in order to perform.

The original ethics of sport in early Greek culture incorporated philosophy as a routine requirement for athletes (Cousineau, 2003, p. 5) and philosophers were known to have attended sports centers to give lectures. One such place was called the Academy, outside Athens. In ancient Greece, training environments were also social places where lectures were publicly delivered. "Aristocratic and educated men also visited them daily for physical and intellectual exercise" (p. 80). Sports enthusiasts such as Socrates were known to visit the Academy, and after Plato established his philosophical school there, those who studied with him were called "Academics." Have then, the thinkers also dismissed the athletes? As this study will demonstrate later, there are numerous contemporary examples of modern great thinkers drawn to the philosophy of sports and who have an intimate connection to the playing of the game. Academy is still the title for all centers of soccer (and most other team sports) learning and apprenticeships in England. Perhaps there are other similarities beyond just a name?

Landon Donovan is a major US soccer player who sometimes plays in England, in one of the elite soccer leagues in the world. At a press conference before the FIFA World Cup Germany™ on June 9, 2010, Donovan endorsed the role of psychotherapy in his life, as well as his deep relationship to meditation. One reporter described how "Donovan turned a news conference last month at Princeton into a 30-minute psychoanalytic session" (Bondy, 2010). Donovan suggested that inner disciplines were essential for him, and were as relevant as external training requirements. He went on to become the star player for the United States in the soccer 2010 World Cup™ in Germany, twice scoring last-minute crucial goals and keeping the hopes of his team alive. Although Donovan's views may be regarded by some as eccentric, research suggests his approach to inner spiritual discipline does have historical antecedents.

The relationship of a coach working with an athlete is not a modern incarnation. The role of trainer was natural in ancient Greece; athletes were not expected to learn alone. Of course, many coaches may have once been competitors themselves and may have experiences to share with a student of sports. The struggles an Olympic athlete could expect were described by Epictetus, who suggested to the aspirant:

> You say, I want to win at Olympia. …If you do, you will have to obey instructions, eat according to regulations, keep away from desserts, exercise on a fixed schedule, in both heat and cold; you must not drink cold water nor can you have a drink of wine whenever you want. You must hand

yourself over to a coach as you would a Doctor. Then in the contest itself you must gouge and be gouged, there will be times when you will sprain a wrist, turn your ankle, swallow mouthfuls of sand, and be flogged. And after all of that, there will be times when you lose.

(Cousineau, 2003, p. 87)

For an athlete, to lose in ancient Greece might have been just as painful as it is now. Coaches have had to help their charges through times of defeat and struggle, more often perhaps than victory. Epictetus' suggestion to the athlete is to work with a coach as if he were a "Doctor." The contemporary sports psychologist Willi Railo said of performers "we can be unduly self-critical, and, in the end be our own worst enemy" (Eriksson & Railo, 2000, p. 47). How can a performer be his or her own "worst enemy," and what does this mean? Perhaps there is also a modern split between clinical psychology and sports that can come together.

Stage fright, anxiety, and life or death experiences

For the purposes of this study, I would like to draw a distinction, as Aaron Beck (1976) did, between anxiety and fear. "Anxiety is generally considered not only a universal emotion but a mark of man's humanness" (p. 132). But does it serve a purpose? In his book *Cognitive therapy and the emotional disorders*, Beck suggested that "when anxiety encroaches on coping behavior, it is likely to have a disruptive effect" (p. 134). This would be expected for many public performers, perhaps shown by distracted thinking or physical tightness. But what is happening? Hanson and Mendius (2009) believed that "anxiety also makes it harder to bring attention inward for self awareness...since the brain keeps scanning to make sure there is no problem" (p. 42). Beck (1976) ascribed no particular useful function to anxiety, as opposed to "the essence of fear: the appraisal of potential harm" (p. 137). He cited Freud's distinction of "realistic fears" and "unrealistic fears" with the latter being Freud's definition of anxiety. Beck suggested that "fear is a particular kind of ideation; anxiety is an emotion" (p. 136). Did Freud suggest that there could be such a thing as an unrealistic emotion? This study asks questions about the tensions that exist for public performers and also the universality of the experiences that they face. Soccer players may fear physical injury that could prevent them from playing, but what about internal injury?

"Stage fright" is a familiar term and many people may understand it to be anxiety or social phobia for performers or actors on a stage. Actors, athletes, and soccer players may share similar fears; as I alluded to earlier, my experience suggests that the worlds of theatre and sport are very similar. My initial connection to sports was based on my professional experience as an actor coping with stage fright, comparable to an athlete's performance anxiety, and dealing with these feelings. Cousineau (2003) explained:

The Greeks were acutely aware of these connections. Their word for "actor" was *agonistes,* which was also the word for "competitor." To them, athlete and actor were kindred spirits. Each played in a drama in which occurred an unfolding of fate or destiny, a symbolic life and death.

(p. 64)

Due to the physical nature of athletic performance, most of our competitors in the public arena are young. What significance is there to this fact? This study concerns young people and the pressures they face when taking this path in life. Young professionals in soccer academies are in the 16-19-year-old age range, which, according to Erik Erikson (1950), places them at the "identity vs. role confusion" stage of their development. Erikson stated that children at this stage "are now primarily concerned with what they appear to be in the eyes of others as compared to what they feel they are, and with the question of how to connect the roles and skills cultivated earlier" (p. 261). Perhaps they face an uphill struggle, having to overcome the pressures of public performance combined with the vicissitudes of adolescence. In 2010, Sagar, Busch, and Jowett conducted a study that seemed to corroborate this idea. The research was aimed at investigating the emotional needs and priorities of young males in British soccer academies. In the study, the researchers discovered that "shame and embarrassment" was the greatest fear that the young men expressed. Shame and embarrassment appear to be universal issues for young people navigating developmental milestones.

On February 2 2014, the Oscar-winning actor Phillip Hoffman was tragically found dead in his home in New York, apparently from a heroin overdose. During his life, he made connections between acting and sport, saying that

I don't understand people who are actors who don't love sports. I think it's the same thing. What it takes to be a great athlete is the same thing that it takes to be great actor, I think—that kind of concentration, that kind of privacy in public and that kind of unselfconscious kind of experience are very similar, and that kind of pressure of the people watching, and finding privacy.

(Hoffman, 2014, online)

Much of an athlete's life is spent in comparative solitude, training on their own, with a coach and perhaps a few colleagues. Some of these individuals then also have to be able to perform in front of an audience, sometimes vast in numbers. These performers require a flexibility of approach and psyche. Can this be learned?

Sports performers are not the only people who have to appear in public. Many people have to speak to a group or are put under the spotlight at some stage. Interviews, weddings, family events, managerial presentations, all can be anxiety-provoking situations. The fear of public speaking, glossophobia, is a common experience. According to a recent study at the University of Nebraska at Omaha by Karen Kanger Dwyer and Marlina Davidson (2012), it is the most common fear that people experience. Dwyer said: "In answer to the question of whether or not public speaking is the number one fear, the answer is yes, it is the most common fear." She then adds: "However, it is not the top-rated fear—that belongs to death."

What kind of death is being described here that is almost as powerful as the actual fear of dying? The neuroscientist Louis Cozolino suggested, "Psychotherapists deal with a wide variety of anxiety disorders based in the fear of what can be called social death" (2007, p. 237). Do performers vicariously live out this ongoing struggle for us, having to endure the risk of loss and social death? In his book *The divided self,* R.D. Laing (1960) explored the psyche from a clinical perspective. He sought to uncover the mechanisms of anxiety including issues we might normally call self-consciousness, which for Laing "implies two things; an awareness of oneself by oneself, and an awareness of oneself as an object of someone else's observation" (p. 106). To describe these feelings and states, Laing also used terms implying psychic splits, such as "embodiment" and "disembodiment." Laing noted:

> This split will be seen as an attempt to deal with the basic underlying insecurity. In some cases it may be a means of effectively living with it or even an attempt to transcend it; but it is also liable to perpetuate the anxieties it is in some measure a defense against.
>
> (p. 65)

This perhaps resonates with Cousineau's earlier objections to modern splits and cultural disconnections. Cozolino (2007) suggested that we may be wired this way, in that "compounding the problem, the left hemisphere interpreter provides a rationale supporting and reinforcing avoidance" (p. 237). In *Models of the mind,* Edgar Levenson (1985) identified heavily with the contribution of H. Sullivan (1953), calling his own Interpersonal Model "Sullivanian." He developed the system for specifically working with anxious patients, describing their experience as "more akin to dread, terror and so disruptive to both the patient and the necessary people in his life, to avoid its contagion, they do not see what there is to be seen" (Levenson, p. 50). This seems to resonate with the spiritual ideas of Hanson (Hanson & Mendius, 2009) when he wrote that "delusion is holding onto ignorance about the way things really are—for example, not seeing how they're connected and changing" (p. 43). Again the idea of a split permeates the experience, implying that the psyche can get lost in some kind of fog. But what is the nature of the experience for those who become separated from themselves as the authors suggested?

Laing (1960) stated that disembodied individuals usually "feel most closely associated with the 'mind'" (p. 65). How can this be? He suggested that the healthier "embodied" psyche is not so much associated with thinking as it is with a state of simple being. Instead of negative fantasies, he described embodied individuals as having "a sense of being flesh and bones, of being biologically alive and real: he knows himself to be substantial. To the extent that he is 'in' his body, he is likely to have a personal continuity with time" (p. 67). Experiencing a sense of being within the body is a concept that often resonates with spirituality, yoga, and meditation. Our coresearchers may describe experiences that resonate with ideas and sensations more normally described in writings on spirituality or their own sense of religion.

Yoga, for example, has achieved increasing popularity in the West as a form of exercise and has now to some extent become part of popular culture as an exercise:

> But yoga is more than exercise—it's a complete system for living harmoniously in the world and for attaining peace. In Sanskrit, yoga can be understood at different levels. For instance, yoga, meaning yoke or union, can be interpreted to mean the unifying of body, breath, and mind.
> (Treschel, 2002, p. 61)

Depth psychologist Lionel Corbett, MD, in his book *Psyche and the sacred* (2007), also suggested that transformations will not happen by exercise alone:

> No amount of yoga or other attempts at relaxation will release these bodily constrictions until our attitude surrenders. Without a surrender of attitude, the body is always sensing danger. Properly understood as a gesture of surrender to what is, to breathe deeply and relax the body fully is a powerful statement of trust in the ground.
> (p. 230)

Corbett suggested that attitude has a fundamental role to play in the orientation of the psyche, and that a surrender needs to take place and a "letting go." Is attitude the missing link that needs to be changed or reunified? This study explores how important the role of attitude is in the fortunes of our coresearchers. Recent research in American clinical psychology has suggested that attitudes can be crucial for the development of a team culture or an individual, so much so that the soccer world in England has begun to investigate this.

Carol Dweck and mindset

Stanford Magazine (Krakovsky, 2007) reported that a performance director from the soccer club Blackburn Rovers in England had visited America to meet clinical psychologist Carol Dweck. In her 2006 book, *Mindset: The new psychology of success,* Dweck had attracted wide acclaim for the results of her ten-year study (1999), conducted on young children and college students. The performance director's interest in Dweck's work had been sparked by this study, which provided new insights into the optimum way that young people learn. Dweck's study was a step forward because she started to look more deeply at the way we interact with young people, and how we may be hindering rather than helping them due to our own preconceived culturally formed ideas about talent and success.

Dweck's (2006) results suggested that in order to transform and realize their potential, children need support and encouragement for their efforts, not for their talent. Dweck's study divided a group of children and gave them a task to complete. Half of the group was praised for their talent, being told, "You must be smart at this." The other half was praised for their effort, being told, "You must have worked really hard." Those praised for their effort became much higher achievers. They were prepared to tackle challenges and not so quick to view lack of success as failure. Significantly, they were then offered a second test where they could choose an easier or more difficult set of challenges. Of those praised for their effort, 90 per cent chose to try the harder test.

These students exhibited what Dweck (2006) called "mastery orientated" approaches. Less than half of the talent group chose the difficult test, suggesting that those who rely on their talent will avoid most challenges when they cannot be sure of succeeding. It appears that the shift of emphasis to "what" you do, rather than "how" you do a task somehow hinders self expression. In my own experience I conducted an informal poll of three psychotherapy groups and 75 per cent considered themselves "perfectionists." Perhaps they are frightened of the "social death" that Cozolino (2007) described above. Dweck called this type the "fixed mindset" individual, being someone who will play it safe and refuse a challenge so they can best hope to do it right. Those prepared to get something wrong accordingly possess a "growth mindset." Dweck emphasized the value of a positive approach by leaders and individuals towards learning friendly cultures: "In one world, effort is a bad thing. It, like failure, means you're not smart or talented. If you were, you wouldn't need effort. In the other world, effort is what makes you smart or talented" (2006, p. 16). Dweck identified problematic cultures that often endorse ideas such as rank according to talent and favoritism for the few. In these groups talented individuals carry status and struggling individuals often become demoralized, disconnected, and even end up ridiculed or humiliated.

The study implied that in negative sporting cultures, survival of the fittest becomes survival of the favored. This, in turn, creates cliques and corrosive atmospheres that can be harmful for the favored as well as the excluded. Evidence suggests that especially within schools, this type of sports culture may even become a potent source of malignancy and alienation rather than inspiration. Perhaps it is no coincidence that the Columbine High School sports culture was identified as extreme, with many of the faults described above. The sports team appeared to symbolize for the perpetrators much of what was wrong in their world. The young killers reportedly began their rampage in the cafeteria with the words "jocks stand up first" (Adams & Russakoff, 1999).

Dweck (2006) suggested that people with a work ethic that can incorporate and interpret failure as a part of growing will learn more and faster. Her book described an account of how a group of untrained artists, in the short span of five days, were able to transform rudimentary self-portraits into competent art. "This is so important, because many, many people with the fixed mindset think that someone's early performance tells you all they need to know about their talent and their future" (p. 70). She included a chapter dedicated solely to sports, "Mindset of a Champion," where she integrated her ideas into the world of a performer—giving examples of great athletes, performers, and coaches who shared mindsets that accompany success. Her research suggested that an inclusive, ethically-minded team culture would be more secure and integrated.

Are these ideas a modern equivalent of the contribution that philosophy made to sports before the split? Like Dweck, Cousineau (2003) believed that talent and spirit are different: "talent is admired, but spirit is embraced" (p. 69). What is this spirit that joins and connects us? "Psychiatry defines mental disturbances according to symptoms but does not elucidate the processes that generate them. This means there is no understanding of the processes themselves" (Symington, 2002, p. 51). The phenomenological design of this study allowed room for the study to ask our coresearchers about the processes they experience for themselves.

Research question

Soccer culture has rarely been studied with a clinical, depth lens, despite being regarded by many as "the world's game" (Tharoor, 2008). What can be discovered about this world by taking a look from the inside, recruiting players as coresearchers? What archetypes can be discerned and recognized that have so far remained hidden or obscured by the public glare? This study aims to illuminate the lived experience of being a soccer player in a team by interviewing coresearchers on both sides of the gender divide. The specific research question explored was: "What is the lived experience of being an aspiring professional soccer player on a team?"

For the purposes of this study, *archetypal* is defined as the universal, innately existing patterns of the psyche that typify patterns in collective human memory. *Experience* is defined as the lived-experience of the subjects as they discuss concrete situations, thoughts, and feelings around the phenomenon of being a member of a competitive soccer team. *Professional soccer team member or players* will be defined generally as students from both sexes playing competitively at the Division 1 level of collegiate soccer in the US, who are working towards playing in the major leagues of professional soccer.

Chapter 3

A phenomenological and alchemical approach to investigating soccer

Having introduced the subject and some of the background, this chapter will concentrate on the phenomenological basis of the study and its choice as a suitable methodology. The following section will seek to explicate the relevant concepts related to phenomenological design such as *bracketing*, *epoche*, *noema*, and *noesis*. Language and meaning will be discussed; returning to the work of Giorgi, Hillman, and Romanyshyn as references to the direction of the study. Then there will be a section on the reason for including the unconscious in the design, a description of alchemical hermeneutics as well as the use of word clouds. The role of participants will then be described as well as the materials used. As part of the *epoche*, the rationale behind the selection of questions will be explored. After that, the procedures of the research will be described, as will induction interviews, the selection of the candidates, along with potential drawbacks, and ethical considerations. The final section of this chapter describes the procedures for gathering and analyzing data, study limitations, and ethical concerns and issues.

Choosing qualitative design for studying the psyche of soccer

My own research suggests that this topic lends itself to a qualitative or human science approach. Whereas natural sciences seek to explain the world, human sciences seek to understand a person in the context of their life (van Manen, 1990, p. 4). Qualitative inquiry asks "how" or "what" questions, instead of quantitative questions that focus on asking "why," and seeks to establish some kind of relationship between two variables or cause and effect. Research that explores social or human problems "analyzes words, reports and detailed views of informants, building a complex, holistic picture" (Creswell, 1998, p. 17). Creswell emphasized the role of the researcher as an active learner who tells a story from the participants' point of view rather than as an expert passing judgment on the participant (p. 18).

This study endeavors to take to heart the idea that we can move clinical psychology beyond the consulting room into less familiar territory. "And it is this experience, which is part of our everyday lives, that must be the source of material for human sciences" (Polkinghorne, 1983, p. 26). As suggested earlier, soccer is a relatively unexplored culture for clinical psychology, so the spirit of the inquiry will be in keeping with Pacifica's motto to "tend the Soul in the world" (Pacifica Graduate Institute, 2012, mission statement). British Jungian analyst and author Andrew Samuels (1986b) spoke of this idea in his book, *Jung and the post Jungians*: "What I would like us to do is create multidisciplinary partnerships with people from other disciplines, so that we can contribute our psychological 'bit'" (p. 29). A qualitative depth approach may provide some fresh insight and new knowledge into a culturally familiar subject like soccer.

As described earlier, the sport of soccer has an unrivaled global following, which stimulates much interest. The private lives of players and managers are always under scrutiny, apart from the building interest outlined earlier as the match day approaches. For such a public game, very little is known about the inner life of players from their own perspective as coresearchers. Therefore this study uses open-ended questions, seeking to elicit insight into the *erlebis*—the inner life of the player. And how does that inner reality relate to the team, and being part of this group?

Investigating individuals in team settings can reveal new insights, and it appears to me that a phenomenological approach is indicated as the best way to do this. "The purpose of this type of interviewing is to describe the meaning of a concept or phenomenon that several individuals share" (Marshall & Rossman, 1999, p. 112). The authors go on to describe a particular form of research called "elite interviewing," a title that is suitable for this project. These coresearchers are involved in a distinct environment and face different personal challenges when compared with other students who may study academic subjects only. "Elite" individuals are those considered to be influential, prominent, and/or well informed people in an organization or community; they are selected for interviews on the basis of their expertise in areas relevant to the research" (p. 113). The coresearchers involved in this study represent the highest level possible that a young amateur sportsperson can reach in America. In this case, they are selected as representatives of a university team because they are well informed about soccer and already possess a level of skill deemed to have the potential for a professional career. But it can be considered to be an exclusive world. Few enter inside the changing room, but thanks to the coaching staff of this team, this study can try to gain access. The research will aim to aspire to the psychologist Michael Patton's idea of qualitative research: "The basic criterion to apply to a recorded observation is the extent to which the observation permits the reader to enter the situation under study" (2002, p. 23).

This work incorporates phenomenological ideas from different researchers, but in particular those recently outlined by Amedeo Giorgi (1985), who has been fundamental in reasserting phenomenological design as a robust method of investigation. Giorgi himself referred to the work of Edmund Husserl as an inspiration. It was Husserl who developed modern phenomenology as a method that tries to take a more interior view, aiming to go "back to the things themselves" (Husserl, 1954/1970, p. 252). Giorgi (1985) suggested that this means "to go to the everyday world where people are living through various phenomena in actual situations" (p. 8).

Although there are potential drawbacks that will be outlined later, evidence suggests that this is an unexplored approach for investigating soccer. Many have studied soccer as a subject, from the outside looking in, but what about from the inside? What can we learn by listening to what they say about this path they have adopted? Did they choose it or did it choose them? "We believe that many important aspects of these phenomena *as lived experience* were either overlooked or severely distorted because the methods of the natural sciences were invented to deal primarily with phenomena of nature and not experienced phenomena" (Giorgi, 1985, p. 1). This study aims to follow in the traditions of Husserl, Giorgi, Moustakas, and others by listening closely to what players from both sexes have to say. What exactly is it that rests on their shoulders? The phenomenologist Gadamer (1980), in *Dialogue and dialectic,* wrote: "no one could seriously contend that the ability to think correctly is acquired only through a detour through logical theory (p. 5).

The research approaches employed are a blend of hermeneutic and phenomenological methods. The word "method" comes from two Greek words, *meta* meaning "after" and *hodus* meaning "journey" (Ayto, 2008, p. 332). Naturally, therefore, a blended hermeneutic and phenomenological method would involve a journey of understanding taken after the data is collected in which new, veiled meanings are discovered. Hermeneutics is the study of understanding, and the word *hermeneutic* comes from the Greek word *hermeneuin*, "to interpret." Palmer (1969) suggested that this word has three functions: to say, interpret, and translate. All three of these functions spring from the oral tradition and remind us that hermeneutics seeks to open a dialog between the interpreter and the work. As will be described in more detail below, the phenomenological element of the study involves a stage of reflection, where Giorgi suggested the researcher can "integrate the insights" (p. 19) of the data collected. This stage suggests openness to meaning through intuition and reflection.

Research suggests that this study shall also have another claim to be a distinct approach. According to Roger Brooke in his book, *Jung and phenomenology* (1991), phenomenologists have mysteriously "largely bypassed Jung's work" (p. 55). He suggests that this may be based on reasons other than practical merit or application; citing Lauri Rauhala to support his case: "Even a superficial knowledge of Jung's thought gives grounds for supposing that a phenomenological–existential analysis would apply even more fruitfully to his views than to Freudian psychoanalysis, bound as it is in a natural scientific tradition of research" (from Rauhala, 1984, p. 229-30). Brooke explores the methodology of Jung and how his work is implicitly bound up in a hermeneutic approach, as well as utilizing a phenomenological approach to the understanding of others. He speaks to the spirit of this particular study when he points out that: "As Giorgi proceeds to illustrate, there is a conditional dialectic between the approach, the method and the object of the study. Approach and method mutually imply each other. The approach structures the method, and the method brings the approach into being" (p. 56). This concept will be explicated in more detail later as the methodology is described in greater depth. Considering the above, there are grounds for optimism—by using a Jungian lens, combined with Giorgi's methodological ideas, a worthwhile synthesis can be created.

Creswell (2003) suggested that phenomenological research distinguishes itself from other designs in that "understanding the 'lived experience' marks phenomenology as a philosophy as well as a method, and the procedure involves studying a small number of subjects through extensive and prolonged engagement to develop patterns and relationships of meaning" (p. 15). Moustakas (1990) noted that: "dialogue is the preferred approach in that it aims toward encouraging expression, elucidation, and disclosure of the experience being investigated" (p. 47).

By adopting a phenomenological method, this study endeavored to discover experiences from the players, illustrating what sets them apart from each other, and even from us all. Reason and Rowan (1981) also suggested that this kind of inquiry has to be situated in the very experience the inquiry is exploring. The interactions with coresearchers are conceived as cyclical, a "personal, circular process of knowing, of inquiry, harkening back to research's etymological origins." Marshall and Rossman (1999) assert that phenomenological design is not abstract or ethereal but must, however, be grounded with important, distinct approaches (p. 136). They believed the very beginnings of a study are as important as the other stages;

> Initial insights and the recycling of concepts begin the process of bounding and framing the research by defining the larger theoretical, policy, or social problem or issue or practice that the study will address. This complex thinking also begins to establish the studies parameters (what it is and what it is not) and to develop the conceptual framework that will ground the study in ongoing research traditions.
>
> (p. 32)

My professional relationship with the game had already stimulated within me many questions that one could propose to ask a player, but did that mean they would be useful here? Hillman (1982) suggests that before any questions are asked of coresearchers, the phenomenological method dictates that the first dialogue researchers must have is with themselves, to discover preconceptions and ideas about what might lie ahead:

Breaking the vessels is the return, the turn again to the world, giving back what we have taken from it by storing inside ourselves its soul. By this return we regard the world anew, having regard for it as it shows its regard for us and to us in its face.

(p. 129)

To study this subject in this way, research suggests, is going to be an intimate exchange of information, digestion and revisiting material through dreams and intuitive responses.

In phenomenological enquiry, this process is known as *bracketing*. In a more quantitative style of research this would be represented by a *control* sample, the constant factor. This occurs when the sample is constant or one where external influences are removed. The implication of this for this study, implies that my questions and interpretations need to avoid any bias my experience has provided, for example, making assumptions about culture. This study aimed to maintain an objective stance wherever possible, one reason why standardized open questions were used. The means for doing this important early work in phenomenological research will be considered in more detail in the following section. Later in the study, my projections and reactions to the material are detailed in the discussion chapter in a section entitled "Alchemical Reflections," where there was a chance to explore my deeper reactions to the data and the project.

Epoche, noema, and noesis

Interviews were conducted with eight scholars, four from the men's team and four from the women's team. As described, a phenomenological approach suggests that careful consideration is required in the formulation of the questions to ask coresearchers before beginning the study. For example, even the idea of "aspiring professional soccer players" could be misleading and presumptuous. Do we know absolutely that all the coresearchers want to be professional players? It was my expectation that all of the coresearchers would want to be professional players like the individuals that I work with in England. Why do they have to want to do this for a living? This example is perhaps an illustration of why care had to be taken when creating questions. There would not be a second chance to get this right so this had to be a deliberate phase of the enquiry.

Clark Moustakas emphasizes the importance of the pioneer Edmund Husserl in developing the importance of restraint for the researcher. The goal is to achieve "the freedom from suppositions, the *epoche*, a Greek word meaning to stay away from or abstain" (1994, p. 85). The world of soccer is very familiar to me, which may be a blessing and a curse for this study; hence the need for a conscious period of reflection and inner searching. Husserl (1954/1970) suggested that "the *epoche* creates a unique sort of philosophical solitude, which is the fundamental methodological requirement for a truly radical philosophy" (p. 184). A sustained effort was required here to be able to fully grasp the opportunity of research this project presented by creating a space resisting all of my previous experiences and intuitions in soccer to the best of my ability.

This stage of the research necessitated my discovering ways of stepping back from the subject, in order to fully appreciate the phenomenon we were observing. "One learns to see naively and freshly again, to value conscious experience, to respect the evidence of one's own senses, and to move toward an intersubjective knowing of things, people, and everyday experiences" (Moustakas, 1994, p. 101).

Moustakas (1994) described Husserl's impressions on the subject and a method called *transcendental phenomenology*. Husserl wanted to understand the act of consciousness of a subject. Moustakas stated, "Husserl's transcendental phenomenology is intimately bound up in the concept of intentionality. In Aristotelian philosophy the term *intention* indicates the orientation of the mind to its object; the object exists in the mind in an intentional way" (p. 32). This observation requires the study to proceed in a way that acknowledges the separateness of our perception and the object being perceived.

Moustakas stated that "every intentionality is comprised of a noema and noesis" (1994, p. 29). This divides the perceived object of thought (*noema*) and the separate meaning and subjectivity inspired by the object or way in which it is experienced (*noesis*). This is a philosophical perspective about how we view things rather than how they are in reality. There is always a potential for a single thing to have two meanings. For example, a visit to the dentist is logically about the maintenance of dental hygiene, an act of self care. But someone with a phobia of dentists may experience accompanying fantasies of dread and discomfort, not care and hygiene.

An alternative anecdote may also help to illustrate the point. I was present at a local café when a young lady barista told every customer, "this is my first day at this store," which may be considered the *noema*. It was the literal truth, of course, but was she also saying another message? Perhaps she meant something else, for example, "I don't know what I'm doing so please be nice"? Moustakas suggested: "The 'perceived as such' is the noema; the 'perfect self evidence' is the noesis. Their relationship constitutes the intentionality of consciousness. For every noema there is a noesis, and for every noesis there is a noema." (p. 30). This study aspired to look closely at what coresearchers contributed and what layers of meaning might exist in the language our coresearchers used to describe themselves.

Alchemical hermeneutics

Alchemical hermeneutics is a method that appears to complement the presence of the transcription text with an alternative view relating to my experience of the subject. This work mostly took place after the initial comparisons and units of meaning were discerned, although of course my relationship to this work began before I began to write. Hillman (1983) suggested that active imagination as research method seeks to remove or reduce any intentional focus on the subject at hand (p. 78). This study provided an opportunity to analyze a substantial amount of dialogue from eight coresearchers, in an attempt to discern some kind of deeper insight and understanding of the material. Hillman (1983) referred to the "care of interior images" (p. 93) when discussing the imagination and memory, citing Albert the Great, who suggested that "it should not distend the soul" (p. 93). This means that for all of the data collected was only worth as much as the quality of the analysis afforded to it. Phenomenological inquiry here needs to go beneath the obvious and be open to seeking deeper truths. Hillman warned against a distention of the soul where there are a "myriad of images, the soul a supermarket with a little of everything" (p. 94). Instead, he suggested, this is less likely to happen when we remember that "the psychological space is one of depth and not extension" (p. 94). Highs and lows feature significantly in the data coresearchers related, which will be addressed later. But before that, how do we go deeper?

One reason this approach was attractive to me was based on the necessary suspension of presuppositions by the researcher towards the subject itself. It is understood how my past experience could be an impediment to the empirical nature of the results. By contrasting and comparing unadulterated data, the hope is that some deeper themes can emerge, the form of soccer and what is happening. The quest for an insight into the true nature, or form of things, is not a new one. One early philosopher interested in this kind of enquiry was Plotinus, a Greek who lived in Rome in about 200 AD. Much of what we know about him came from a friend and student, Porphyry. Porphyry described how Plotinus was not interested in spelling or handwriting, for him, the idea was all-important. Eventually Porphyry had to compile much of his work himself, and wrote a preface in *Enneads*, a collection of writings, which contains many of Plotinus' writings and beliefs.

Plotinus suggested that ultimately, all things reduce down to a single "one" within an inner light. He believed, along with Plato, there was a true essence to things and, like the phenomenologist Giorgi, that the true essence of something could be discovered by reduction, not addition. Plotinus also sought to disarm himself of prejudgments in order to gain insight. As for the gods, he suggested in *Enneads,* "It is for them to come to me, not for me to go to them." Hillman (1976) discussed the work of Plotinus in his book *Re-visioning psychology*: "If the style is repetitious it is because the way of the soul, according to Plotinus, is the way of the circle" (p. 213). For my part, the "way of the circle" represents a spirit of openness and receptivity to the subject being explored. The idea of circularity emerges later in the study, and was of immense significance.

Epoche and active imagination both seem to share a common approach; removing oneself from the subjective into a more whole awareness and synthesis. "After more than a century of evidence for the unconscious and its formative influence on all aspects of life, it appears naive in the extreme not to take it into account in our ways of knowing and researching" (Romanyshyn, 2007, p. 106). This research aims to leave a space for the unconscious, which is of course appropriate for a psychological depth study.

Steps for analyzing phenomenological data

Giorgi stated "the task of the researcher is to let the world of the describer reveal itself through the description" (1985, p. 74). The primary material for this study, the interviews, were digitally recorded and then transcribed into individual bodies of text. Material was then analyzed using phenomenological methods and approaches. For all of the suspension of judgment in the *epoche*, the method of rigorous, empirically-based phenomenology is not without structure. The phenomenologist Christopher Aanstoos (1985) remarked that "a phenomenological method arrives at this through a rigorously specified means of engaging the naïve descriptions and discerning their psychological sense" (p. 90). Without the structured approach it would be easy to dismiss the validity of the results as subjective. However, phenomenological method has to have the courage to suspend judgment and wait for insights to emerge relating to the subjects, themes or ideas we cannot know in advance.

So, in order to remain grounded and empirical, Giorgi (1985) explicated four steps that constitute effective analysis, beginning with a "sense of the whole" (p. 10). He explained that once interviews are completed and the data is at hand, an emphasis should be placed on digesting the material for its own sake. He advised the researcher to read the text many times over, which should produce a more informed sense of the material. In my acting career, when I was learning to write screenplays, it was suggested to me that a rough draft should be analyzed as a whole. This was achieved by conducting an uninterrupted reading of the entire screenplay. It was believed that only then could one truly understand the material and begin to see the forest for the trees. The data collected became such a text, our window inside the mind of the coresearchers, and with it came responsibility to treat that information carefully. As researcher Bruce Krajewski pointed out, "there is the question the text puts to us (we are called into question), a point that often gets overlooked when critics seek to demonstrate their superiority to the text" (1992, p. 9). By now it was quite clear that I must resist immediate interpretations of the data and just keep reading, restraining my desire to start "thinking too much."

Secondly, a process begins when the data is analyzed for *meaning units* (Giorgi, 1985, p. 11). The gathering of meaning units aims to separate the language the coresearcher uses into significant and less significant parts. These statements may or may not have an intrinsic meaning for the research, and at this stage begins the process of teasing those meanings out. Moustakas (1994) called this stage *horizonalization*: "Later, statements irrelevant to the study or topic as well as those that are overlapping or repeated are deleted, leaving only the horizons (the textual meanings and invariant constituents of the phenomenon)" (p. 97). The phenomenological reduction that begins with the process of *epoche* continues as we distill the data into evidence that can reveal something about the life of a soccer player.

In the book *Phenomenology and psychological research,* Giorgi (1985, p. 16) described a third phase he entitled "Transformation of the subjects' everyday expressions into psychological language with emphasis on the subject being investigated." Remembering *noesis* and *noema,* this stage involves a rigorous approach to the language that is being used, and the refining of the germane root meanings behind statements. The subject of this study is the world of soccer through the lens of the coresearcher, and a fresh understanding of terminologies and meanings could emerge by exploring connected meanings and themes.

Lastly, Giorgi (1985) suggested a "synthesis of transformed meaning units into a consistent statement of the structure of learning" (p. 19). At this stage of the study, the researcher attempts to piece together the evidence through deep self-reflection on the data and to some extent, a return to the subject, taking into account the transformed meaning units producing a coherent sense of the world we have attempted to investigate. "In the process of explicating the phenomenon, qualities are recognized and described; every perception is granted equal value, no repetitive constituents of the experience are linked thematically, and a full description is derived" (Moustakas, 1994, p. 96). It is here that the themes emerge: the consistent links or connections that can be discerned. It is at this point in the research that my work with active imagination was employed relating my responses to the data. As the following section will describe, active imagination is a distinct step that is not obviously associated with phenomenology but for the purposes of this study a natural step to take.

Amedeo Giorgi, Hillman, Romanyshyn, and a role for the unconscious

This study is a phenomenological study that incorporates a hermeneutic approach in accordance with the work of Amedeo Giorgi. As part of his work at Duquesne University, Giorgi, along with co-authors Knowles and Smith (1979), described an approach to the research that sought to go beyond earlier applied methods and approaches. Giorgi's work built on the philosophies of great phenomenologists before him such as the German philosophers Heidegger and Dilthey. In 1927, Heidegger published a series of papers called *Being and time* (2008), where he emphasized the importance and role of interpretation in the experience of being human. In what way does this world move our participants, and how do they endeavor to move it?

Giorgi (1985) distinguished his phenomenological approach by comparing phenomenology with the more conventional, logical empirical approach to understanding our world. He suggested that such an approach first posits the criteria for the learning, then looks for matches that accord to the criteria being sought (or perhaps not), and then draws out implications from there. He called phenomenology the practice of science that remains "within the 'context of discovery' rather than in the 'context of verification'" (p. 14). Giorgi holds a space for the unknown and uncertain, suggesting that this approach to research has a valid place in science: "Verification is important for science, but it does not exhaust the definition of scientific practice because nobody just verifies" (p. 14). Giorgi suggested an approach where two perspectives are desirable for interpretation of the data. He called these "circumscribed indeterminateness" or conversely "empty determinateness," which accompany the analysis of the data, allowing for openness to the material as well as the rigorous questioning of the possible meanings the material holds. For the researcher in phenomenology, it appears that not knowing will be as important as knowing. The accompanying alchemical hermeneutic aspect of this study aspires to be able to make some sense of my own reactions to this work.

Giorgi's approach is the model for this study, although the works of other phenomenologists have surely made this work possible. Moustakas (1990) suggested that modern phenomenology owes a great debt to Edmund Husserl, who "stood alone a determined self presence, pioneering new realms of philosophy and science" (p. 25). Moustakas recounted how Husserl withstood much criticism and even public ridicule, but nevertheless arrived at a recognized "science of pure possibilities carried out with systematic concreteness" (p. 28). Giorgi et al. (1979) sought to develop the science in other new directions, complementing the possibilities developed by the pioneers of phenomenology Husserl and Heidegger:

> Up to now, empirical phenomenological psychology proceeded by collecting protocols descriptive of the subjects' experience (e.g. learning, envy, anxiety, etc.), and then systematically and rigorously interrogating these descriptions step by step to arrive at the structure of the experience. Hermeneutical psychology suggests another data source and a different method of analysis.
>
> (p. 179)

This research intends to look at things on the smaller scale and not lose touch with the larger pictures the material suggests. After the completion of the interviews, a substantial amount of data had been collected, which was then analyzed on the small and large scale. As stated earlier, individual items or "units" were selected as the investigation of the data progressed. But before this stage, to attend to the larger scale, Giorgi et al. (1979) suggested an intentional reading of the material as one whole element. He proposed a simple two-part model of the process:

The researcher reads the entire description of the learning situation straight through to get a sense of the whole. Next, the researcher reads the same description more slowly and delineates each time that a transition in meaning is perceived with respect to the intention of discovering the meaning.

(p. 83)

Starting from the picture as a whole, the analysis continually teased out the material until individual meanings were left that could be interpreted, achieve significance, or be discarded.

Research suggests that the search for meaning is not a casual aspiration in phenomenological study, and openness to the material presenting itself has to be held. The approach to analyzing the data from coresearchers is a process of potentially uncovering meaning from what on the surface may appear insignificant. Giorgi (1985) stated:

We can let the phenomena speak for themselves, and when we do we discover that whatever appears suggests in its very appearance something more which does not appear, which is concealed . . . the given that is in the appearance of phenomena is "directionality," a direction is offered or a significance is held out which we pick up and follow, or turn away from.

(p. 151)

This kind of approach to analyzing data suggests that the further we go with the material, an inevitable process of reduction is in operation. A comparative set of responses from coresearchers emerged that can be observed individually and also as a whole. Jung spoke of the process that will need to take place in this study, when speaking of the psychotherapeutic encounter. He said that "for better or worse the therapist must be guided by the patient's own irrationalities. Here we must follow nature as a guide, and what the doctor then does is less a question of treatment than of developing the creative possibilities latent in the patient himself" (Jung, in Storr, 1983, p. 211). Phenomenological process will seek to follow the nature of the responses as well as the words themselves.

In his book *Phenomenology and psychosocial research* (1985), Giorgi cautioned the researcher to attend to the process of continually "working through" the material, which translates as the continual effort of reading and re-reading, following Jung's advice above about working creatively with what is offered not what is sought. Giorgi's concern was that the researcher may become lost in interpretations, not grounded in the situation being observed or superficial assumptions. Regarding these problems, Giorgi advised the researcher to persist: "the very 'working through' solves many of them before they become problems" (p. 20). Giorgi's emphasis seems continually to encourage the researcher to keep stepping back from the material with an informed ear, continually listening for deeper meanings to emerge. As it happened, many problems did occur during the course of this research, there were empty moments, which will be described in the Chapter 5.

The work of Robert Romanyshyn (2007) informed a significant part of this study, in particular his ideas concerning alchemical hermeneutics. He acknowledged the importance of Giorgi in his book *The wounded researcher*, where he described Giorgi's book *Psychology as a human science* as "groundbreaking" and his work as that of a "pioneer" (p. 239). Romanyshyn's work will be covered in more depth below, but of particular significance here is that he also expresses concerns about Giorgi that this study hopes to address. Romanyshyn stated that Giorgi's aforementioned book has "no mention of the depth tradition, especially Jung's work, apart from a few critical remarks about Freud" (p. 240). Giorgi himself suggested Paul Ricoeur as a model for methodology in phenomenological design; however, Romanyshyn echoes Rauhala (1984) in lamenting the absence of the truly depth perspective: "Paul Ricoeur has noted that philosophy cannot ignore a confrontation with the unconscious, and if philosophy cannot afford to do so, no psychology whether as a natural or a human science, can afford to do so either" (p. 240).

As this investigation is informed by the depth perspective, I sought to bridge this lacuna by deliberately holding a place for the unconscious in the design. It is not just Romanyshyn who described concerns over this relatively unexplored aspect of the work. Hillman (1976) stated that "when we turn to the events themselves, and let them tell us what they are, our work is phenomenological" (p. 138). Like Romanyshyn, Hillman pointed to the archetypal messages that phenomenology presents: "Phenomenological reduction becomes an archetypal reversion, a return to the mythical patterns and persons. We see through the logical by means of the imaginal; we leave the intentional for the ambiguous" (p. 139). The decision to observe the material with this lens appears germane what with the traditions of depth psychology and the concerns of both Hillman and Romanyshyn. Perhaps the unusual step of observing and recording data from this world is in keeping with Giorgi (1985), who spoke earlier of "empty determinedness," which we can perhaps consider as a route to serving the demands of the unconscious on the material and context.

Imaginal alchemical hermeneutics

A hermeneutic method seeks to understand the underlying meaning of particular lived experiences by inviting participants to describe specific events and situations in their lives. Data is then analyzed through the lens of a particular interpretive set or sets, in this case, that of archetypal psychology. As described earlier, alchemical hermeneutics was utilized in the hope of complementing the phenomenological research. Creswell (2003) stated, "Two primary characteristics of design are the constant comparison of data and the emerging categories and theoretical sampling of different groups to maximize the similarities and the differences of information" (p. 14).

Alchemical hermeneutics utilizes many of these forms of knowing, and such methods were adopted aspiring to inform the work on a deeper level. Romanyshyn's (2007) special brand of hermeneutics—imaginal alchemical hermeneutics—shares many similarities with phenomenological research. Moustakas (1994, p. 44) referred to the process of "imaginal variation," a process whereby the observer enters a kind of reverie, which is neither an empirical inquiry nor, more to the point, even seeks to be. As with Romanyshyn's alchemical hermeneutics, this process leaves a place for intuition and the process of active imagination on the results. For this study, there were good reasons to reserve a place for my unconscious and the unconscious of the topic to be observed. The spirit of active imagination seems to accompany the spirit of *active learning* (mentioned by Creswell, 1998) naturally as a component of this research method. "Alchemical hermeneutics as an imaginative method honors these ways of the soul as an alternative means of bringing new depth, presence, and shadows of the soul of the work into view" (Romanyshyn, 2007, p. 264).

Romanyshyn suggested, "Alchemical hermeneutics is a creative method. The spirit of inquiry, therefore is open-ended, giving the structure of one's research a freedom to arise out of the ongoing relationship between the researcher and the topic" (p. 265). As my relationship to soccer is a rich one, new possibilities may emerge. Using the material gained from the initial interviews with coresearchers, a process of in-dwelling on the results accompanied the more conventional methods of phenomenological analysis outlined by Giorgi. It must be acknowledged that there is, however, at this stage, a potential to drift into the poetic and therefore inevitably confine the analysis to the realm of the subjective. But there is a value and it is an ancient one.

As mentioned earlier, Socrates was known to have visited academies where athletes were trained. Socrates is depicted as discussing the subjective in Plato's *Apology*. Socrates was shocked when it became known that the oracle had declared him to be the wisest of them all. He decided to interview the wisest and most successful Greeks he could find, an investigation that was more of a bid to discount the oracle's idea. However, he concluded that of all those he met, many had belief systems that they thought were certain but could not be so. Significantly for this study, however, he did set aside one category of thinker for special attention in this regard, the poet.

He did so because for Socrates, poets enter into a state of suspension like that of the oracle. They become the interpreter of the message only. In this sense, Socrates identified a way of knowing or thinking that seemed to lack the subjectivity of the author by using a means of a kind of suspension. Socrates admired poets for being able to ask for the material to come to them, echoing Plotinus' sentiment that "the gods must come to me," mentioned earlier. The process of *epoche* likewise resonates with this idea. This research intends to embrace the spirit of these works in an attempt to make a genuine inquiry that allowed the players to speak for themselves and even for the data to interpret itself to some degree. Like poets, soccer players interpret and express themselves in the course of the play. Like Plotinus, being open to what comes to them, in their case a ball pass or a tackle or an opportunity to advance.

Word clouds

Although this is essentially a qualitative study, this research intended to be open to the latest opportunities that science can offer to compare data and identify themes, patterns, and connections. The free online service Wordle (www. wordle.net) is a word cloud generator that compares the words selected in any text document and produces exaggerated images of each word depending on the frequency with which it is used. The images produced can be illuminating and serve to complement the voices they represent. Although care needs to be taken about making any concrete conclusions in relation to this data alone, as part of a data set it may highlight useful topics that can be explored in the alchemical hermeneutic element of research. Frequently used words may well support or indicate connections and correlations. In the case of this study, the word clouds produced data allowing us to compare the answers of both sexes directly. The different frequency of words used by both sexes produced images where revealing distinctions appeared that may also be relevant in light of the other data sets.

Participants

The soccer squad at the American university from which participants were drawn has a men's team and a women's team, both comprising of 24 individuals. This was the pool from which the coresearchers were chosen for the collection of data and research. Participant age ranges varied from 20 to 25 years of age, and all were full-time students. Along with their academic major (for example, kinesiology or business management), students became part of the team for three years as they completed their other studies. The head coach gave me full permission to work with players, and official university permission was also granted. Likewise, the interviews were approved by the Pacifica Ethics Committee. The prospective ideas were discussed with the scholars, and they expressed a desire to be involved in this project.

The head coach of the women's program also expressed an interest in the study and agreed to participate and facilitate work in parallel with the men's research. This was an opportunity to include members of a women's team in the study by running an identical model and approach originally designed for the men's team. My research as yet has failed to discover a serious psychological study of women's soccer. Comparative research between the genders has the potential to reveal new insights about differences and observable distinctions in traits and approaches between the sexes involved in the same sport.

Materials

The interviews conducted with the student-player coresearchers was a standardized open-ended interview, meaning that all questions were the same, and were designed to stimulate open responses, rather than a fixed, closed response like yes or no. Careful consideration and research was given to the selection of questions that all coresearchers were asked. As described earlier, because of my background in professional soccer and my interest in the subject, an effort was made to minimize my input by using a standardized approach with consistent conditions. In particular, as the research involved both sexes, an approach that standardized data seemed in keeping with the overall desire to reduce the influence of the researcher on the data collected. Keen (1975) suggested that:

> the goal of every technique is to help the phenomenon reveal itself more completely than it does in ordinary experience. The goal may be stated as to uncover as many meanings as possible and their relations to one another as the phenomenon presents itself in experience.
>
> (p. 41)

The creation of suitable questions was not a straightforward task. There would be no second chances, so again, a patient, methodical approach was required. As it transpired, the process of designing the creation of questions became part of the *epoche*, as each one had to be considered with the minimum of contamination with presuppositions and ambiguities.

Selection of questions

Considering that my experience working with players is substantial, I took care to remember Giorgi's warning that we must remove our preconceptions and initial beliefs, requiring the use of *bracketing*. There was perhaps a danger of creating leading questions that would fit my impressions of what it is to be a soccer player. An illustration of this is the very first question that came to mind while preparing questions to ask coresearchers. "To what extent is soccer like hunting?" For many years this has been an idea that has not left me. The question seems innocent enough. However, for this study, it could easily be interpreted as a *leading question*, one designed merely to support a preconception that may be totally erroneous. I realized that questions can have the potential to be manipulative, and a conscious effort was made to avoid this as far as possible.

Giorgi suggested that only "by so deliberately avoiding concentrating attention on any predetermined aspect, the researcher is able to escape the danger of finding only what one expects to see" (1985, p. 91). The actual process of the *epoche* involved sitting with a notepad and pen and simply allowing my mind to ask questions and use an imaginative approach to pose them. Any prospective questions would then be scrutinized with regard to the discussion above, considering whether the question was leading the coresearcher into a meaning of my own making. Josselson and Lieblich (1995) spoke to this pitfall by suggesting that the researcher:

> might similarly advocate an "empathetic stance" within research, a way of approaching data that allows for discovery rather than seeks confirmation of hypotheses and that fosters more exhaustive quests for explanation rather than the illusion of finding a preexisting truth. If we listen well, we will unearth what we did not expect. This becomes the paradigm for discovery.
>
> (p. 30)

This project did indeed reveal unexpected results which will be explored later in the Discussion section and the Alchemical Reflections section in Chapter 5. In order to best eliminate my own preconceptions and ideas, the foci of my attention concerned issues relating to the day-to-day experiences in their lives. Hillman (1976) suggested, "When we turn to the events themselves and let them tell us what they are, our work is phenomenological" (p. 138). Questions had to be to some extent generic, and at the same time be able to give the coresearcher a chance to speak at some length. After a period of reflection, and trial and error, the following questions were formulated with the above considerations in mind.

Selected questions for the study and rationale

Why do you think it is you have become a soccer player? This first question was intended to be an opportunity for the coresearchers to introduce themselves and ideally settle down into the exercise, hoping to provide a platform for the rest of the questions by asking the coresearchers to share a bit of background regarding soccer and how they became interested in the game.

Where do you think your gift for playing soccer comes from? A *gift* is an idea that presumably every player on the team can relate to. A gift or a talent for something is an idea this question is designed to explore in terms of where a player believes this has come from. We return briefly to the work of Dweck (2006), as described earlier, and the idea that talent is very significant to an individual, and his or her attitude towards it is crucial in his or her development. Does the way we regard our gifts relate to where we think they came from? The question could possibly reveal responses from coresearchers that refer to the *survivals* discussed by Edward Tylor, those "processes, customs and opinions carried over" that were "remnants of an older condition or culture" (Shamdasani, 2003, p. 274). Will the gift be described as coming from an external or internal source?

Who are your heroes? The world of soccer does create heroes—those who attract wide public attention and the status of the hero. These are individuals who can, with their talents, save a team from loss or raise them to victory. What do players say when asked about a hero or heroine? This question sought to elicit more perhaps about what a hero is or what a heroine is to our coresearchers. It gave a chance for coresearchers to share on many levels, from just naming individuals to something related to the archetype and where they sensed it could be found.

How would you describe your inner experience of when you play well? Deeper reflection revealed that this question in fact relates closely to the following question inviting the coresearcher to describe the opposite experience. The question concerns the coresearchers' experience and identification with the performance of their craft. It can be assumed that the experience of playing the game is not consistent, in that sometimes a player plays well and sometimes a player will know defeat, with his or her "touch" becoming elusive. The variations of mindset are an experience that a player can relate and distinguish as an inner experience.

The work of Schechner (2002), Sutton-Smith (1997), and Huizinga (1955) were described earlier relating to the subject of play. Schechner related play to hunting, and these questions left an opening for coresearchers to mention this as a possibility. Csikszentmihalyi's (1990) concept of *flow* might play an important role as well. Huizinga noted that play has deep archetypal roots, which may be revealed in the responses to this question, whatever data is collected. Previously, the American player Landon Donovan publicly stated his affiliation with meditation and the importance of this practice for his game. Coresearchers related psychic and embodied states that related to the Greek gods, which will be explored in more depth in Chapter 5. These questions hope to probe into the experience of play, the good and the bad side. Can we relate the spirit of prayer and meditation to states present in play?

How would you describe your inner experience of when you play badly? As stated above, this question follows on from the previous question about playing well. The possibility of discussing both sides of this actual play experience enabled players the possibility of offering new insights that could be significant. Players may not have had the opportunity to explore this issue in any detail or treated it as an experience to remember.

Remembering Levenson's ideas (1985), a bad memory can be repressed. "To avoid its contagion, [people] do not see what there is to be seen." It was revealing to compare responses from coresearchers and seek a common thread in the experiences. Along these lines, it was anticipated that individuals would be more likely to try to focus on recreating those feelings of when they are playing well, leaving investigation of the negative experience relatively unrecorded. As Symington (2002) stated earlier "psychiatry defines mental disturbances according to symptoms but does not elucidate the processes that generate them. That means there is no understanding of the processes themselves" (p. 51). This question attempted to make room to identify the archetypal processes that the coresearchers experienced and shed some light on the darker side of play.

However, perhaps there is a purpose served in remembering when things go badly. This question pertains to Laing's (1960) work noted earlier regarding the "divided self." It gives an opportunity to compare coresearcher responses concerning the sensations and experiences of integration and division. The sports psychologist Willi Railo (Eriksson & Railo, 2000) was earlier described as believing that a performer can be "unduly self critical, and, in the end be our own worst enemy" (p. 47). Will we be introduced to this enemy perhaps? This question allows players to reveal answers along these lines. Data collected could possibly also indicate gender differences in relation to dealing with challenging situations.

Tell me about a time when an achievement of yours stood out for you. This question is designed to allow the coresearchers to reflect on an occasion that was significant for them. Hillman (1976) suggested that "the art of memory is relevant in another way. It also suggests something about the care of interior images. When going into the imagination it seems one should remain close to the images" (p. 93). This open-ended question was designed so that the answer may or may not relate to a soccer experience, but given the context of the interview, it is natural to assume that coresearchers would likely relate to such an experience.

And what was important about that event for you personally? The supplementary part of the question hoped to encourage the coresearcher to share more about the significance and meaning of the event. This question was also designed to encourage exploration of the symbolic, inviting the coresearcher to go deeper as to their attachment to the event and the inner meaning it might hold for them.

Can you describe a dream you have for your life? This question aimed at exploring ideas the coresearchers had for their futures, inviting the coresearchers to speak in terms of a vision and aspiration on a personal level. Within this there is the opportunity to compare data between the sexes as to what they share about their dreams. Romanyshyn (2007) stated in *The wounded researcher* that "to follow a dream is, however, no easy task" (p. 68). The question was designed to allow a deep dimension within the coresearchers to be accessed, revealing possibly more about their fears as well as their aspirations.

Is being on a team like being a kind of family? In what way does it resemble a family, or not? As described earlier, the sports psychologist Andy Cale suggested, "It is primarily in the home that a child's beliefs, values, perceptions, attitudes and goals are shaped" (2004, p. 138). This question aimed to explore how coresearchers feel about the culture they are immersed in, and what this means on a deeper level to them. The question does label an archetypal identity, that of the family. This can mean many things to many people, and in case the coresearcher feels differently, the supplementary question was offered for the contrary idea about "or not." Cousineau (2003) remarked that "the recognition of teammates and opponents alike as brothers or sisters remains one of the goals of modern sports" (p. 28). Answers from coresearchers to this question might shed light on whether this is an aspiration or a reflection of an archetypal presence in sports culture. How does it all work when individuals are at the same time pitted against each other competing for places as well as presumably needing each other for co-operation?

What does it feel like to lose? Loss is an experience that all soccer players will face eventually, and it is in losing that some players might find their hardest challenge. It is here that, to some extent, soccer replicates real life—none of us can win all of the time. Research suggests that how players respond to defeat is, again, a relatively unexplored area. Romanyshyn (2007) explained, "What we love we lose, and in that moment we begin to see the love that claims us by means of our complexes through different eyes" (p. 64).

What does it feel like to win? As with the question above about playing badly or playing well, this question poses the polar opposite, counterpart question about losing. Winning is a very important theme in America generally, and coresearchers will relate strong feelings about the subject.

Procedures for selection and interviews

During a visit to the club on a normal training day, the study was introduced to all potential candidates. After outlining the nature of the study and the responsibilities for coresearchers, a request was made for volunteers who would like to participate. Volunteer names were then written down and a random lottery system identified the candidates fairly, reducing any chances for sampling bias. Each head coach agreed to this selection procedure, selecting four candidates from each team in this manner.

The individual participants were then interviewed again, where the outline of the study was more formally introduced with full explanations of expectations, confidentiality, and the purpose of the study. This standardized introduction was included in the Informed Consent Form (see the Appendix). The candidates were informed that he or she could withdraw at any time. If the candidate agreed to participate, they signed the form to indicate his or her consent. Next, the more formal interview commenced, which was recorded and transcribed for the purpose of analyzing the data. At all stages of the research, care was taken not to interfere with the broader responsibilities each player had with regard to education or time commitments for the team.

Potential drawbacks: Limitations of the study

Phenomenological design as a method has its critics, and it is responsible to explore the limitations that this approach may have. Creswell (2003) listed four limitations that interview methods can create. Creswell pointed out (p. 186) that studies will provide indirect information filtered through the lens of the particular coresearcher, which is by no means therefore a representation of the whole. Research will be conducted at a place separate from the actual setting where soccer takes place, the field. Creswell went on to note that the presence of the researcher may influence responses, with coresearchers trying to provide the best answer for the researcher, rather than an honest answer, which may be less clear or positive. Finally, Creswell pointed out that as a method, phenomenology can be flawed, as it creates a data set from a selection where "people are not equally articulate and perceptive." Nevertheless, Creswell maintained that there is an advantage, in that "participants can provide historical information and that also the researcher can control the line of questioning and therefore we hope to make genuine comparisons from consistent questions" (p. 186).

The study aimed to ask questions that relate to relationships experienced in the game. Coresearchers might have been unwilling to make statements because the dissertation would be a public document. For that reason, the greatest care has been taken to protect the identity of the individual performers. Players cannot be expected to criticize the system or the management, which, in my experience they often do during unguarded moments. To some extent I have a "reputation" in the game, in that I already work for a prominent team known to the coresearchers. For many of these players, my current club is an organization they could only dream of being a part of, and therefore coresearchers may have tried to answer questions in a manner that might seem the "best" answer rather than the honest one. The pressure is not so much to impress me, as more a potential desire to answer in a way that might meet my approval.

Ethical considerations

This research complies with the American Psychological Association's standards for conducting research with human subjects as well as adhering to Pacifica Graduate Institute's Ethics Committee guidelines. Approval from the Pacifica Institutional Research Committee was received in August 2011, and all Ethics Committee standards were applied and observed. In December 2011, permission to conduct the study was received by the university concerned. The risks and benefits were noted on the Informed Consent Form that the coresearchers received before the project began.

At the outset, the coresearchers received a participant letter acknowledging and welcoming them into the study, included in the Informed Consent Form, which described the nature and purpose of the research. Coresearchers were given a pseudonym to protect their confidentiality and provided with the means of reaching the researcher if needed. They also granted me permission to record the interviews for the purposes of analyzing data. As well as being informed that they could withdraw from the study at any time, if distressing psychological material arose, they would be referred to a psychotherapist, but individual coresearchers would then be responsible for paying for any subsequent treatment. However, this was an unlikely scenario as this study is about the experience of playing soccer and not the reliving of any previous trauma beyond losing a game. Before commencing meetings, individuals were again informed as to the nature of the study, its limitations, and parameters. At the conclusion of the study I offered to meet with the coresearchers to go through the findings of the research.

Chapter 4

The interview transcripts and situated structures

Transcripts of each interview were created from the digital recordings made on campus, which lasted for an average of 15 minutes each. As prescribed, individual transcripts were read and then read again many times in accordance with Giorgi's (1985) methodological approach, taking care to not necessarily jump to early ideas or conclusions. This period was created to allow time for the material to sink into my conscious and unconscious processes. Then came the process of identifying meaning units from the transcripts by separating the specific essences of responses, which tended, in my experience, to reveal themselves rather than needing to be discerned or sought. On the advice of a colleague, a Microsoft Excel spreadsheet was created to enable material to be easily regarded side by side for each answer.

By the time the transcripts had been created, much work had already been done. Typing the material was laborious, but the benefit of this was that it familiarized me further with the voices of the coresearchers. My first task was to distill the data into recognizable chunks that reflected the significance of the sentence by retaining only the original words. Meaning units were not translated or interpreted at this stage, but simply collected as they were stated, to maintain as much integrity to the data as possible. Remembering *epoche*, there needed to be a confidence that the material could speak for itself.

First, I gathered together the meaning units expressed by coresearchers individually for each question. Answer sets that indicated an attitude, belief, or impression were clustered together. The task was now to begin to discern how answer sets compared with each other, and each of the sexes. The purpose was to search for comparisons, similarities, and repetitions, in order to identify themes as they revealed themselves. Each stage was, in effect, a redaction, a process of distillation from individual meaning units to themes and then onto deeper understandings, connections and alchemical responses. Exploration of the ideas and connections that arose will be included in the Discussion section in Chapter 5. This chapter will detail the responses of each individual as they were stated, leaving interpretation for later. After that, the themes that emerged will be introduced (see the General Situated Structure section) and developed further for the discussion that follows.

Individual Situated Structures

Below is a summary of each individual interview. For the purposes of this particular study, personal details about the individual participants have not been disclosed to protect anonymity. As they are currently public performers, details about the personal backgrounds of the individuals have been omitted. All of the coresearchers are aged between 20 and 25, and are students of a four-year university program. Participants came from a mixture of cultural and ethnic backgrounds.

Jane. When Jane spoke of her gifts for soccer, she spoke of "love" twice and that, for her, the game also involved "realization." When asked about where she thought her gift came from she again spoke of "the love of it" and also made a bodily reference to "my feet." Jane stated that she knew she just "wanted to play" but also named "God" as a source, and then later twice ascribed her gift to her coaches. When asked to describe an achievement Jane spoke about a time when she felt as if she had been included as a senior member in the team although she was the youngest player. She described setting the goal for herself to play at such a level and then described how she helped the team score an important goal. She repeated how the important factor was setting a goal and achieving it. She repeated the reason this event was significant for her: She "set [her] mind to do it and we did it." She then stated, "I set the goal and we did it."

Jane described a current well-known Brazilian professional soccer player called Ronaldinho as one of her heroes. She then described her "Dad" as another hero, and her "number one fan," describing his presence at every game she plays. When asked about playing the game well and how that felt, Jane spoke about feelings on four occasions rather than thoughts. She stated: "just a really good feeling I don't know how to explain," "feel a sense of accomplishment," "just a really good feeling," "you feel accomplished." When asked about the contrary experience of playing badly, Jane used the word *talk* twice, stating that she would "talk to yourself a lot mentally, not always in the negative as she would "talk to myself and say 'come on pick it up.'" However, she went on to describe how "it's not like just disappointment but 'why can't I do good just now?'" On a deeper level she stated, in talking about this "it's, hard to know that you can't control the outcome, so I think that's what it is."

Jane said that her dream for her life was to be "successful in anything I do," and "I don't want to settle for anything." She spoke about a vision for her life where she could "see myself also being successful." Unusually, for a soccer player perhaps, she described the comparatively mathematical activity of wanting to be an accountant, stoically reporting that "either way I have to work hard," but that "right now I have no doubt." Jane believed that being on a soccer team is like being in a family. She reasoned, "you're always working with one another, helping one another." She added, "you just have to learn to get along," suggesting that "on the field you automatically become a family" and that "you can't just do well for yourself." Jane cited "emotional support" as an important aspect of being in a team. She said that the lessons available do not "only relate to sport," suggesting she learned "life lessons" and that she could "always relate life to soccer." Jane remarked, "if you learn those small things in a sport you can apply it to life when situations come around."

Jane described the feeling of winning as "liberating," and that there was a sense of "accomplishment." On the other hand, losing to her is "not just being disappointed, it feels more than that." She said she was "disappointed in myself and my feelings." In terms of blame, she said, "I'm not down on my teammates; I'm down on myself."

Carly. When Carly was asked about how she became a soccer player, she suggested her family experience, mentioning her "Dad" twice and how he "put me in a soccer match." As for where her gift came from, she used the term *blood*. She used the word *nature* twice regarding her gift, it "naturally came" and was a "natural thing." Again she pointed to her "whole family" as a source.

When asked about an achievement, Carly described a time in her soccer career when "we won our league," adding she "realized I could go and play Division One" soccer. She said that this achievement helped her "realize a lot of things," and "grow as a player." She first suggested her "Dad" as her hero, then mentioned her "brother," as she did earlier when speaking about why soccer is so important in her life. Carly suggested that these familial bonds were significant and that they "helped me through everything."

When Carly described the experience of playing well, she stated that she had "butterflies in my stomach," something normally associated with nervous discomfort. Twice she used the word *excited* to describe her state. As for the experience of playing badly, she described "disappointment" and how she was "unhappy with myself." She did not report thoughts in the experience of playing well, but she did when playing badly—saying that she "can't stop thinking about it." She went on to describe how she is just "down on myself, I'm just really down on myself." She went on to refer to a bodily impact of feeling this way: "I don't really keep my head up."

Carly's dream for her life involved education first, saying that she wanted to go "off to college." She included soccer in her dreams, hoping that she could "have soccer within my career path," as well as broader life goals of "family, kids, everything like that." When asked if being on a soccer team was like being a family, she stated that "it is, definitely," going on to say that she had to "spend a lot of time with them," adding that "you win with them you lose with them" and that you are "happy together, mad together." She also described the necessity of having to "deal with confrontations."

Carly said that winning was a "rewarding feeling" and "good reward for hard work." She repeated that it was a "very good feeling," and that she had a "big smile on my face," that she "did something good." On the contrary, she described the experience of losing as being "very down on myself." Again thoughts were referred to, saying that she was left to "think there's more I could have done," again reiterating that it was "not a good feeling."

Diane. Diane first suggested "a lot of encouragement" as the initial reason why it is she came to play soccer at this level. She describes how she "got an opportunity" and that "you can do it with encouragement and praise." Diane spoke about her desire to be "making my parents proud," but, ultimately, she hoped that this could all contribute to "making myself feel good about myself." She believed that her gifts came from an "athleticism that God gifted me with" followed by "the attitude of wanting to do well for myself and be good at something" adding, "it was an extra, it wasn't something someone else could do." She ascribed more values to do with the work ethic: "If you don't have the drive to do anything with it, it's not really a talent."

When asked about an achievement that stood out for her, Diane was less certain: "It's difficult to pick something." She then reflected and spoke of a memory from a previous team and being a "big fish in a small pond wasn't a good enough achievement." In broader terms, she defined her achievement as "the last three years of playing college, everything I've learned about myself." She added, "to have the discipline to learn about it and finish up, and do this for me." She summed up her achievement as if her current life was at a kind of pinnacle: "I don't think anything will ever be as challenging as managing a college life with school, social, and academic side of it and having a job as an athlete, because it really is a job." The importance of this event for her was "five or six years work," speaking about a "sacrifice you've made with your social life and stuff," "I mean if you keep working towards something, a bigger goal, that you can get there." As if coaching herself, she added: "It's a long process but I can do it and it's doable through the ups and downs; keep going and you'll get the new season."

When asked about heroes, Diane again spoke of *sacrifice* three times and spoke certainly that it was "definitely my parents, and all the sacrifices they made in their lives, without them I could not do it, I didn't even have a driver's license." She identified a matriarchal heroine: "My mom because everything I've been able to talk to her about even more sacrifices that she's made in my life." Diane suggested that this enabled her to "not worry about things that kids shouldn't have to worry about." She used the term *role model* for her mother, "a really amazing role model," "she's taught me so much life lessons that she's learned from her own experience." Diane added with humor in speaking about her mother "she tends to be right!" She then spoke about a hero in soccer who was obviously a significant relationship, "my pro coach when I was 13 he really liked me, helped; he wasn't just the coach in the sense that he was also a friend and he helped me go through what would be considered a rough time." She added that he "helped me stay motivated."

When playing well, Diane described "a feeling of such happiness and stability." "You feel like you're on top of the world," adding "at that time nothing could go wrong." Diane expansively described a heady experience: "it's almost like a kind of a high, like adrenaline junkies will search for that, it's a high once you have it, you crave it, you get motivated to practice every day to go out and do your best, because the feeling after a game is almost indescribable." Conversely, she spoke of playing badly as a "disappointment, it can shatter your confidence with one game." She continued, "all the confidence you build in the matter of the season and a few games, one game can just turn it around." She reflected, "I think it's hard to come back from that," and "it's almost the opposite of when you play well, you get to such a low point it's hard to come back." Diane spoke of an isolating experience when things are not going well: "one of the hardest parts about playing bad is like, looking around at your teammates and realizing that you let them down," adding "it's definitely disappointing, the whole experience is disappointing for yourself." Again Diane referred to thoughts of others and her responsibilities as significant to the experience: "you could've done better, you didn't do what you needed to do, looking at your teammates knowing you didn't support them as well as you should look after your family." A bad result for the team was her responsibility.

When asked about a dream for her life, Diane said, "being happy and successful in the career that I want to go into—physical therapy." She described a bright scene: "every day being up to learn something new with it and being engaged in it." The emphasis here was on learning: "any medical field you have to keep learning; it's always advancing." She returned to happiness, "I want to be happy with my family and happy with my life and happy with who I am day to day."

In terms of the team resembling a family, Diane remarked, "yes absolutely, it resembles a family in every way I can think of." She spoke at length about this side of soccer, more than any other coresearcher. She reflected that "when you see someone down on themselves and having a hard time, there is always someone picking you up, that's what family does," which she believed involved, "telling you that it is not as bad as you think; you're doing fine, just take it one step at a time." She offered that this might be a virtue forced by necessity as well as any other factor, suggesting that "we spend so much time with each other that we have to each support each other." She emphasized the importance of mutuality in this regard saying, "you can't do it by yourself," "we depend on each other," "the way we spend so much time with a person, when you get to see the good and the bad of each person, that's what a family is," "we have to be around each other with the highs and lows of the season." She again repeated her philosophy that "it's all about building each other up, keeping each other together because we're all in it together, it's a team thing that's more of a family than anything else I've experienced before outside of my own family." Diane related an idea of family identity and sharing "that's one of our biggest strengths is acting like a family, the more you're family the better you do as a team," "to have the support of a group is like a family in knowing that your teammates take care of you; in that way it's unbelievable, it's a huge difference. I've never had both sides of it before."

Diane continued with benefits she believed impacted on her broader life experience. She said soccer had "taught so many life lessons that I can't even explain." "The fact that you had to take so much more responsibility as a student athlete, and the discipline to get out here and motivate yourself every day, not just have someone motivate you." Diane suggested consequences for those who do not take responsibility: "The coach can't be the only person to motivate you or you will die." She described that the skills she is learning are transferable in that "all these different characteristics that I'm learning here on the soccer field that's been a transfer into like, my job, and stuff in my life, I'm so glad about the opportunity to learn that and live it here, and let it take me places."

Diane described the experience of losing as a kind of limbo: "it makes you question what you're doing and if it's worth it." She recounted, "you have to dig deep and try and remember why you're here." She spoke of remembering: "you have to remember those moments when you do win." Diane also spoke of her deep investment in the game, "losing can be really tough, especially if you pour your heart and soul into something." She related to a battle on the internal level: "you are challenging you, moving forward, but being an athlete you have to learn how to do it." Winning to Diane was a feeling that inspired her to reach new heights, stating that it "feels fortunate, I gear up." She returned to many ideas that she had spoken of earlier in the interview, connecting a winning team to "being a good family." "Bringing football together and the individual." Diane returned to the belief that winning is "just like a high, unexplainable," remembering "all the sacrifice." She suggested that something is gained in an experience that lasts for five minutes that can be retrieved, "that little five you get again and again." She returns to her idea "that five minutes just makes all of it worth it, and it's just like, an essential accomplishment."

Gabrielle. Gabrielle believed she became a soccer player because her "whole family played, especially my sisters." Also "it was fun to be outside and play." She said that her gift for soccer came from her family "my parents were very athletic," but again she referred to *play* twice more in relation to her gift: "I just wanted to play." She expressed a philosophy of love "just loving the game helps you be good," "I wanted to get up every day and play." The achievement that stood out for her was her "freshman year of high school." Gabrielle spoke again of getting herself up, and her work: "I worked really hard to get up to that point and then achieve the goal." She said this gave her "a sense of accomplishment," adding that "just so much goes into soccer," then described her important virtue such as "a sense of pride," "so I just persevere towards this."

For heroes she described heroines and returned to her family for her inspirational figures, "my sisters" and one in particular she called a "good role model." Gabrielle said she has to "look up to her expectations." Gabrielle then referred to her mother "my mom," "she's worked really hard to keep us going," "she's always with me," "my mom is really supportive," followed even again by "my mom is really supportive, it's really probably my mom." When asked about the experience of playing well, she described a feeling: "I just feel so happy and I enjoy it," referring to her bodily experience and how "it's easier to breathe," "it feels like I'm light and it's fun." As to the contrary experience of playing badly Gabrielle again described the bodily sensations: "I feel heavy, I feel like a walk is testing," "I feel kind of down because it's harder to lose." She lamented, "It's hard to lose."

When she thought of a dream for her life, Gabrielle said she wanted "to graduate with my degree and become an elementary school teacher," with an intention to "still stay involved with soccer somehow" repeating a similar statement she spoke of earlier "to just have fun with life and succeed." As for the idea of teams being like family, Gabrielle affirmed the idea that "it is a family, it's a big family," "because if you mess up they are just like, all, they catch you." Gabrielle then remarked that there are benefits: "they'll always have your back, too; they are there to help you, encourage you." Gabrielle again suggested the idea of a sorority, "you have the opportunity to have more big sisters to look up to essentially." Gabrielle related the experience as inclusive: "I feel you learn more being part of that kind of family because it's kind of different cultures coming into your life."

When she loses a game she said that "it's always hard to lose," but stoically she explained, "okay, I messed up as a team but what can we do to fix it?" She answered her own question, "you can strive to be better." Gabrielle returns to the experience: "it stays with me more than winning because it's harder to get rid of the feeling." She expressed a descent, "I feel like it's easy to be pulled down than it is to be brought up, as it's harder to lose." As for winning, she returned to the themes that made her happy earlier on: "it feels great," "you get to celebrate with your family on the field and you just raise up." She continued, "it's work and yet it's just, just so happy."

Jamal. Jamal explained that he became a soccer player because "I've grown up loving the game and been playing it since I was a kid." He identified the game as "just the one I loved the most, and I was good at it." Jamal described a higher power as the source of his gift "being a Christian, I believe that it comes from God." He then added his father as another source: "but my dad was also pretty athletic," but then returned to his central theme: "I think the initial thing comes from God." Jamal regarded a soccer achievement "scoring my first goal against Santa Barbara," adding that it was "the first college goal of the school." He described the event: "it kind of got me over the hump of being able to actually put the ball in the back of the net." He went on to elaborate when asked about why it was significant to him personally: "before then I was always coming close," "I wasn't finishing them," "I feel like with the confidence that I can actually do it and the connection," "that I can put the ball in the back of the movement and finish the chances." He qualified the statement at the end by adding it was "like a mental thing for me."

For a hero, Jamal named "dad and my grandfather." Then he also added his wife: "My dad because he is so supportive of me, and my wife, the two people that I look up to most of my life." He qualified this by saying: "there are bad things and there are also good, but I try and pick the good." Jamal went back to the theme of his deeper roots, "my grandfather also supports me and loves me no matter." He emphasized the depth of the relationships when he repeated, "they just love me unconditionally," "they just guided me through life and, and that made me into the man that I am."

When playing well, Jamal said the experience "gives me an unbelievable amount of confidence, like I can just lick [defeat] him and be able to play with anyone." Jamal distinguished between feelings and thinking: "I feel like I can do everything right, not just think about it," "it feels like playing well puts me into a good mood." The experience of playing badly he explained is "kind of the opposite," "it kind of puts me in a bad mood and it kind of makes me initially worse." With an exasperated tone he added, "it just, kind of, drives me crazy."

Jamal described a dream for his life as "making a living by playing soccer," relating that back to his previous themes "having a family and being able to support them by playing soccer," "being able to give my family and the people who have supported and loved me something back what they deserve," "I could just glorify God." For Jamal, the idea of a dream involved a space where he could "give them back" something. Jamal felt that soccer teams were indeed families: "yes, I think it is exactly like being in a family, sometimes more like my own family." He gave reasons for this "we are always together," "so there are actually emotions you shared that when you lose and the emotions you share with when you win." Jamal shared that he believes "it brings you together, it's kind of an emotional attachment," "the ups and downs and it's kind of like a family." For Jamal, this is something he obviously believes in passionately, "it resembles more of a family than an actual family."

When winning, Jamal stated, it "feels good," and on three occasions he used the term *give*: "I feel like it gives the team confidence and I feel like it gives you an edge," "we know we can do it, and it gives to you," "it gives me confidence." Losing for Jamal was "actually the opposite," of winning, although not an entirely wasted experience. He suggested that losing can "also make you humble" and "I try and take losing as a positive sometimes but it does feel bad, but I feel like it's necessary sometimes to lose."

Andrew. Andrew initially stated he became a soccer player because of his family: "all of my sisters played soccer." He described a scene of "watching them going out," adding, "I've always been around it." He referred to his deeper senses: "the passion keeps me going in my daily life"; referring to a more global perspective: "it just keeps me in line, a lot of people don't get the chance to play sport." Andrew was expansive in his attributions, saying that soccer "is just a great way to keep young men and young women and young people grounded for the love of life keep going each day." In response to where his gift came from, he replied, "I am a very spiritual person." He mentioned *God* on three separate occasions. "I've been born and raised a Catholic so I have to say, Dave, my talents come from God." He remarked philosophically, "at this point in my career there is a reason for everything," "I think God did do something significant here not somewhere else." "That's where I think my gifts come from, God, and he has a plan for me each day."

Andrew stated his greatest achievement as "making LA Galaxy," the largest soccer club in Los Angeles. Again he used a religious term to describe it "I felt very blessed to be a part of it," "I felt very proud," "it can take a lot of hard work, but I come here and I've done a lot of work my whole life and I totally think I can achieve that," "so I'm very proud of my LA Galaxy," which he described as "an awesome experience." The significance of this for him was "reaching my dream as a young boy," "it was one of the benchmarks in my life," "and one of the things that I could check it off and say that I did it." Andrew reflected, "I was overjoyed."

Andrew spoke more about heroes than anyone else. For his first hero, he described a male English soccer star "Matt Le Tissier," because "he always strives for perfection," and "he never missed a penalty, which shows how much you put in the strive for perfection." However, Andrew returned to family for his source of inspiration: "my parents are my biggest heroes; they give me a lot"; "they give me the right opportunities financially funding my soccer." He related how "I got the opportunity," adding his other siblings as heroes: "also my sisters," but then returned to a more spiritual theme to describe his heroes by identifying "Gandhi," qualifying himself with "I'm a very peaceful guy and my main thing is kind of meditating each day and meditate and relax, take all the hustle and bustle of each day and kind of think about what each day has given me." "Thanking God for what opportunities I have, to try and help the others around me and try and give them enough of me to share some of their success and win." Andrew referred to a professional American cyclist who had a won a widely publicized fight against cancer: "Lance Armstrong never seems to give up." He adds, "Michael Jordan, his competitive nature." But he ended by returning to "most of all my family."

Andrew described the experience of playing well as an impervious sense: "when I'm playing well, things keep going well even if I make a mistake." He spoke of an inner dialogue as if he was parenting himself: "what's really worked for me is positive self-talk," "not trying to get too high but some sort of consistency." He expressed the omnipotence of the activity, suggesting a new clarity: "when I'm out there on the pitch I leave everything else behind." He related, "good touches keeping things up," "I think that's the main thing is positive self talk." He spoke in a more sober, stoical manner about the experience of playing badly, saying, "the past is the past," and "I have to make sure the next one I do better." He combined forgetting with knowing in his next statement on this: "So I get on with it, short memory during the game, try to do the things I know I can do right. So I know I have that full control for doing that."

In response to being asked about a dream he has for his life, Andrew shared, "I have special dreams, several of them." His first was to "play with the Southampton in England." Staying with the theme of a dream, he continued, "several times a week I would envision myself playing in some game on a cold crisp English night you know, I could just see it." His sense of a dream involved giving, too: "I will give back to this world whether that be with people around the world less fortunate than I am," "obviously everyone lives to leave some sort of significant legacy here," "I think we all in some ways will leave something behind, the footprint, whether that be in the game of soccer in any sport, in life, with group of friends or anything."

In response to the idea of a soccer team as a kind of family, Andrew shared, "I think this is totally a family," "For me it's more of a brotherhood, I've not much experience of having a brother so I love it." Andrew extolled the virtues in the team: "we support each other, giving each other a shoulder to lean on if you're not doing so great." He added, "we have to support each other, and it totally is a family," "and I think also we are in it together till the end, which is exactly like a family, never give up on your family."

When asked about the experience of losing, Andrew said that it "depends on the result, if it's a tough loss, you can feel miserable." He again returned to stoical ideas: "I think you can't really sulk in the loss, you can't get down and out about it; yes, it might feel sour at first, but you've got to push on, do creative things and go back to the practice field," "the end of the day, looking at the effort you made individually and as a team and if it's not good enough then that's why you're not getting the results," "many people always say that they hate to lose, but are you changing anything?" Retuning to a theme he described earlier, he suggested, "people think too much about losing, and that's why they continue to lose, and I try to move on." When asked about the experience of winning, Andrew enthusiastically remarked, "it feels tremendous to win and I love winning, I have the mindset of a winner and I feel tremendous, but I only feel tremendous if things I've been practicing were accomplished."

Oscar. Oscar stated that his involvement in soccer "primarily all started with my dad." He expanded on this: "and everything I think my brother and I have learned from his experience. I kind of took his guidance and everything and put it to work, even right from the start." He made an association between life and soccer "from that I learned to love the sport, I learned to live my life," curiously adding, "it's a way for me to not forget what's going on." He remembered, "there were problems in the family, but I think playing soccer you're able to forget those things, for those 90 minutes." He believed that he will "have an excellent future if hard work is put into it." Oscar returned to his father when he discussed the origins of his gift: "again I think it came from my dad's influence and coaches who saw some promise in me, early on in my career." He modestly referred to his successful experience of the past, "I scored some lucky goals but I think that helped me believe in myself." He then affirmed the statement by referring to his work ethic: "dedication and hard work is a kind of gift for me, and the motivation too."

For an achievement, Oscar cited a challenge in his life: "playing young with the club teams," also "my junior year in high school when we won." Oscar ascribed the credit to the quality of those around him, "I was able to help lead to alongside some seniors and players that were really talented." He referred twice more to the theme of working hard: "I think the hard work, aside from the talent, helped get us through the games," and "I feel like in that time I was able to accomplish something through the hard work." Again he returned to modesty and relating achievements to others: "I was able to accomplish that for not only me, but for the team and the school." As for the personal significance of his achievement, he said, "I think it has strengthened the idea, or strengthened my belief in myself that I could accomplish, I could accomplish a lot in soccer." Oscar checked himself and said with caution, "I do have doubts, even going into every game as always doubts the, 'oh my gosh, it's not going to go well.'" Oscar expressed faith that others could rescue him from those doubts, giving an example: "once I'm on the field, and everybody assured me that it was going to go well, I think it was the kind of motivation that everything will be well and that doubt went away."

For his hero, he returned to his father: "my dad is my first hero." "He talks to myself and my brother and he tells us that about his experiences, and he says that he doesn't care what's going on in life, or any problem arises that we should always just go ahead with what we are looking for in life." Perhaps echoing the sentiments of his father he said, "if it's soccer we go out, do the most with what we have, and there's no problem great enough." Oscar then referred to his mother, whom he also cited as a source of inspiration: "My mom is one of those that kind of, she's a motivation in a way because she has been back from doubts, she instills that she never doubted me." "She helps me get motivated and focus on what I need to do better, that what I can do is better and we are not supposed to worry." At this point Oscar thought for a moment before adding, "outside of the family I would say the two goalkeepers that played for my favorite club, and the one is still playing in Mexico." "I want to be like him, but I also want to learn the most from what he does, and how he plays, and make it my own."

When describing the inner experience of playing well Oscar used a spiritual reference: "I think it's humble, I think it's humble." Then he remarked, "I have a great sense of respect for the opponent." He suggested that something is gained that can be kept, "and all the rest of the game that there is, or even in life, I'm positive about things and I'm looking forward." Oscar referred again to "feeling positive about the future." For the opposite experience of playing badly, Oscar described a sense of forgetting and remembering: "forgive and forget, but learn because if you forget about that game just like that, and don't take anything from it, then that was a useless." He said optimistically, "if I played badly I just get motivated to continue to work hard." Oscar again spoke of some kind of veneration, "even if I'm playing bad I still have to remain positive and stay humble and continue."

For Oscar, the dream for his life would be "playing professional soccer," and something he accentuated, "having a family," which he referred to three times. Oscar distinguished dreams and fantasies: "being true to myself, not I mean dreaming big, but not falling into fantasies that might not just be there." He returned to the family theme and the theme of giving back: "and hopefully giving back to my family with what I can accomplish, love always," "I would love to give something to the family because they're my motivation that keeps me going."

Oscar affirmed that "being in the team is like being in a family." He spoke of unity, "you're always together your united by your beliefs and your name." Oscar continued to describe the experience in familiar terms, "being in the team you learn to love your teammates as brothers and you grow with the same ideas in the same goals for each other." Oscar reflected again about something being given that can be kept, he remembered "every time I see them, I feel as if they all part of me and that they've left something in me that I continue to use on and off the field."

Oscar was philosophical about losing: "There is always two sides of it. You could always lose by lack of effort, concentration, or hard work," adding optimistically that "with both of those you can learn something." However, as Oscar attempted to relate his experience of losing, he went to the other side of the coin: "I mean the feeling, it just kills me inside," suggesting that he has "wasted that time." He then suggested stoically, "regardless of what's going on around in life, you've got to focus on what you're doing in the present," "it just feels depressing in a way, because you've just thrown it all out there and given everything you worked hard for." He countered this with an attempt to find meaning: "you have to look towards the result in the future, and ask what I can do to make that victory in the next game? So it's optimism." The experience of winning he described as "exciting," but he qualified this: "there's a great difference between getting a win against a good team and getting a win against bad team," "getting a win against a big opponent this just more motivating."

Kevin. Kevin believed the reason he came to play soccer was a need: "when I was little it was more for the need to burst out some of my energy." But now he spoke of heartfelt feelings "that ended up growing into the passionate love I have for the game," "but soccer just stood out and that's why I continued playing." As for the source of his gifts, he shared: "first off it comes from God,

that's given me a kind of plain blueprint and the resources I need to succeed."
He then spoke of his work ethic: "the second part comes from my determination
and hard work to become better."

When asked to describe an achievement in his life, he referred to a recent
game when the team overcame a highly rated opponent: "I think last year the
Irvine game for me was a very big achievement—we were able to beat them
2-1, and I just felt awesome about that." He related the significance to him as
a realization: "it was being able to tell people whatever the number, however
hard they tried, they can always be overcome and we be out on top." He
indicated other people as a part of this "I was able to prove to them and myself
that I was able to overcome many difficulties."

For his hero, Kevin first named a professional player "Gareth Bale," "I really
look up to him and I tried to model his play" adding, "but just coming out of
nowhere really these last few years and beyond to make it as one of the top
players in the world." He then referred to his family heroes, describing the
sacrifices his father made and difficult times: "in the family wise, I think both
my parents." He added in a sense of reverie, "my dad has worked his whole
life, we've been in a lot of tough times in my life when we haven't had enough
money for lots of stuff," adding, "As well as my mom."

Playing well for Kevin had an irresistible quality, according to his experience:
"I feel like there's no one on the field that can stop me." He referred to a
"weird feeling when everything is going your way and anything you try and
do will always come off well for the team." Again he returned to the feeling of
omnipotence, in that he felt "pretty much unstoppable." He says he is unmoved
by the experience of playing badly: "It doesn't have as much a bad effect on me
as long as I know I'm giving 100 per cent." Suggesting an attitude of self-
acceptance, he says, "if I'm giving 100 per cent throughout the whole game, I
can keep my head high."

As for the dream for his life, Kevin stated he would like to be "a professional
soccer player; that is my main dream." Alternatively, he said, "I'm studying to
become educated in sports medicine on the sports field." Speaking of heartfelt
feelings, he remarked, "I just have a passion for all athletes." Asked whether a
team is like a family, he answered, "I think it is," and explained, "we have that
parent figure with our coaches that we look up to for guidance or anything you
need," "then all your team members are like your brothers and sisters." For
him, the relationship was one where "they will hold you accountable," but also
he believed "they'll be there for you, keep you, be there for whatever you
need."

When asked about losing, Kevin expressed a defiance: "I hate losing, you
know I hate to, I just wish I could play the game after the game" and "just
show them that you cannot win this next match, I'll stop you." Describing the
experience of winning, he referred to his *feelings* three times, suggesting that
winning is "a good feeling," "and it's good feeling coming out off the field."
Kevin explained, "knowing that you beat your opponent on that day and

you're triumphant over him...it kind of makes you feel like in a way, like, not that you're better than the other person, but just on that day you're better than them."

General situated structure

In this section the common themes that arose from the Individual Situated Structures along with my early observations will be outlined. There is a lot of data to consider. Moustakas (1994) explained that "the composite structural description is a way of understanding how the coresearchers as a group experience what they experience" (p. 142). In practice, interpretation of the data shifted continually from that of the individual, to the team, to comparison of the genders. After analysis, themes did emerge between and amongst the male and female coresearchers. Below, we shall begin the process of tying them together and looking for the patterns and differences. In his book *The Descriptive phenomenological method in psychology,* Giorgi (2009) remarked, "at other times there may be a repetitive theme, the psychological significance of which is critical" (p. 134). In this study, we have had the opportunity to get a sense of some of the critical issues for our coresearchers. There may be archetypes here, which are also significant because they are the same between the genders.

After careful analysis and time spent with the data, certain themes did indeed emerge, as well as other interesting statements which, although they may not have been shared by the majority, may nonetheless themselves point to other themes that deserve note. In terms of the quantity of words spoken by the coresearchers, the males spoke 5,524 words in total and the women 4,438, exactly 20 per cent less than the males. Although the words spoken by the women were fewer, this didn't appear to have any effect on the richness or significance of the data to be interpreted.

In addition to the themes that were the same for both sexes, some answer sets to questions differed between genders. For example, when coresearchers were asked about personal achievements, female coresearcher answers seemed to speak of growth, whereas male coresearchers spoke of finishing and closing. When asked about their heroes, the majority of male coresearchers identified someone other than an immediate family member such as a professional player, whereas only one female coresearcher did. When asked about the experience of playing badly, the majority of women spoke about "disappointment," whereas only one male coresearcher related this. The majority of males instead spoke about a solution to the issue, but not the experience. In a similar manner, when asked about losing, the majority of female coresearchers spoke about going into a world of inner doubt, whereas the male coresearchers again spoke about solutions to the problem rather than the experience. All coresearchers indicated that the team was like a family, describing positive experiences as a result.

These issues are explored further below, keeping in mind Giorgi's caution about taking words too literally in themselves. Giorgi (2009) cited the work of the philosopher Daniel Dennett (2003), who believed that the strict interpretation of words only was an effective form of phenomenological inquiry. In a method Giorgi called *heterophenomenology*, strict adherence to the text only is needed (2009, p. 136), without acknowledging the context or other factors, including responsibility for my own interpretation of the work and a place for that in the work. The coresearchers have played their parts, and now, using a phenomenological lens, I will explore and explicate the themes and any sense that can be made of them.

Emerging themes

The following section will explore the connections that emerged from the transcripts. A relationship to the material had arisen over time, often simply as a result of writing them down from the audio recordings. First, I shall provide an overview of the themes that emerged, outlining the subject matter and the number of coresearchers who identified the theme. Themes, correlations and individual answers will then be outlined in greater detail in the following section.

Overview of themes

Theme 1: Family as the reason they play soccer. Five out of the eight coresearchers identified parents as the reason for why they play soccer.

Theme 2: God as a source of gifts. Five out of eight coresearchers identified the role of *God* in their lives as the source for their gift.

Theme 3: Achievement and Initiation. Five out of eight coresearchers identified a *first* in soccer as their achievement in their life, for example, a debut, debut goal, or playing at a young age on an older team.

Theme 4: Dreams of growth and finishing. In terms of the above achievement, coresearchers were asked about the personal significance of that achievement. A majority of female coresearchers related the experience in terms of growth; the majority of male coresearchers spoke of finishing and closure. All male coresearchers expressed the significance of the achievement as a chance to give back.

Theme 5: Parents as heroes. All coresearchers named a member of their immediate family as a hero.

Theme 6: The unstoppable body, elevation, and descent. In response to being asked about the experience of playing well, seven out of eight coresearchers described feelings of elevation and freedom. The experience of playing badly was described by the majority of female coresearchers in terms of descending and contraction, but not by the male coresearchers.

Theme 7: Dreams of giving back. Five out of the eight coresearchers expressed a desire to somehow give back to their family or the community as a whole.

Theme 8: Team as a supra family and assistors. All eight coresearchers suggested that a soccer team is like a family, a relationship that earlier evidence suggested did not conflict with their own affiliations to family, a kind of *supra family.* All eight coresearchers qualified this idea by referring to the team as a source of assistance and support.

Theme 9: Winning and losing, inner doubt, solutions, and shadow language. Three out of four female coresearchers suggested an inner doubt in response to losing. Three out of four male coresearchers expressed solutions but did not relate the inner experience. There was a change in the language used by the male coresearchers, who used expletives, which appeared a significant deviation from the rest of the data.

Themes in depth

Theme 1: Family as the reason they play soccer

Question: Why do you think it is you have become a soccer player? Five out of the eight coresearchers identified parents and wider family members as the reason for why they now play soccer. Carly identified "my Dad," "my brother," and how "my dad put me in a soccer match." Diane spoke of a sense of "making my parents proud." Gabrielle explained that her "whole family played, especially my sisters." The family as an inspirational role model appeared from the data as not necessarily based on gender. Andrew said that "all of my sisters played soccer." Oscar continued the trend by saying that his playing "primarily all started with my dad." He added that "everything and I think my brother and I have learned from his experience, I kind of took his guidance and everything and put it to work, even right from the start." The role of the family consistently appeared as a crucial element in how the coresearchers have come to pursue this path. As later data will demonstrate, the family was a theme returned to many times in the way that coresearchers related to the playing of soccer and being on a team.

For those who did not refer to their parents, another theme emerged that distinguished this subset. Jane spoke twice of a *love* for the game, saying that she "realized" it was her path. Jamal also spoke of *love* twice: "I've grown up loving the game and been playing it since I was a kid," "that was just the one I loved the most, and I was good at it." He, too, suggested a kind of realization in that he "learned to love the game." Andrew spoke of his childhood, "when I was little, it was more for the need to burst out some of my energy." Echoing the idea of love and realization, he also said "that ended up growing into the passionate love I have for the game." Those who did not describe a parental influence described a relational experience of *love* for the game and of a process of realization within the relationship.

Theme 2: God as a source of gifts

Question: Where do you think your gift comes from? Five out of eight identified the role of *God* in their lives as the source for their gift. Jane stated, "I believe God and the coaches I've had." Diane described an "athleticism that God gifted me with." Jamal suggested that "being a Christian, I believe that it comes from God" and that "I think the initial thing comes from God." Andrew said that "I've been born and raised a Catholic, so I have to say, Dave, my talents come from God," "I think God did do something significant here not somewhere else," "that's where I think my gifts come from, God, and he has a plan for me each day." Kevin also directly attributed his gift to God: "first off, it comes from God, that's given me a kind of plain blueprint and the resources I need to succeed."

Carly did not refer to God, but described her "blood" as the source, adding "my whole family." Carly referred to her talent as being "natural," stating that her gift "naturally came," and was a "natural thing." Oscar was the only male who did not identify God as the source of his gift. Instead, he spoke of his father again, who was a successful soccer player. All coresearchers spoke about either family or God as the source of their gift. Three of the female coresearchers used the idea of *wanting* in response to this question. Jane said, "I knew I wanted to play." Diane spoke of "wanting to do well for myself," and Gabrielle said "I just wanted to play," and how she just "wanted to get up every day and play." After revisiting the entire body of answer sets for male coresearchers, none of the men used *want* in any of their statement about the source of their gift. The potential meaning of this will be explored later, but is *wanting* a kind of longing or desire?

Theme 3: Achievement and initiation

Question: Tell me about a time when an achievement of yours stood out for you. When directly asked about an achievement "for your life," it may be natural to assume that answers might tend to describe an accomplishment that has a sense of being completed. However, six out of eight coresearchers identified some kind of soccer achievement as a *first* achievement in their life—for example, a debut game, or playing at a young age on an older team. Of course, being a debutant is an achievement in itself, but the recurring issue was being a young initiate who manages to make the grade.

More specifically, Jane said that she was "the youngest but felt like I led the team." Carly described a time when "we won our league," certainly an achievement, but she then emphasized how the gift was that she "realized I could go and play Division 1." Gabrielle described her "freshman year of high school." For the male coresearchers, Jamal answered the question by saying, "scoring my first goal against Santa Barbara," which was "the first college goal of the school." Andrew described a debut in the academy at a large professional team by "making LA Galaxy." Oscar described the experience of "playing young with the club teams." He also spoke of "my junior year in high school when we won CIF," relating the significance as being "able to help lead alongside some seniors and players that were really talented."

Of the remaining coresearchers who did not indicate this kind of experience, there are echoes of these themes. Diane spoke of her dissatisfaction in terms of longing, of "being a big fish in a small pond," which "wasn't a good enough achievement," and how that was "easy" but also "not enough." Kevin also referred to his current team and a match experience in the recent past. He related a time when he and his team beat a highly favored opponent at their own ground. As we shall see below, coresearchers of both sexes indicated a change in the way they perceived themselves after a significant achievement in soccer.

Theme 4: Dreams of growth and finishing

Question: What was important about that event [an achievement] to you personally? In terms of the above achievement, female coresearchers related the experience as significant for reasons of growth, whereas male coresearchers spoke more of finishing and closure. Jane related that the significance of the achievement was that she "set a goal for myself and accomplished it," and that it was a time of things coming together "the work I put in paid off in the end." Carly described her achievement as winning Division 1, a soccer league, and that then went on to help her "realize a lot of things," and that helped her "grow as a player." Diane remembered the significance of the event "because everything came together," then reflected, "it's a long process." Gabrielle's immediate response was an exclamation: "just so much goes into soccer!" Then she described a "sense of pride" that she felt when she became a freshman. Stoically, she ended her answer with "so I just persevere towards this."

While female coresearchers spoke of things from the past coming together and were retrospective about their achievement, the male coresearchers appeared to speak with a different emphasis. Jamal spoke of a debut goal, as if it was a harbinger for his future: "I feel like with confidence that I can actually do it and the connection that I can put the ball in the back of the net and finish the chances." Jamal lamented, "before then I was always coming close," "I just wasn't finishing." Andrew said, as if something had been finalized: "I think it was reaching my dream as a young boy." He described his debut at the LA Galaxy professional soccer team academy as a "benchmark" in his life, conveying the idea that a literal mark had been carved somewhere, a transformation had been made. He endorsed this idea but referred to it as "one of the things that I could check it off and say that I did it," adding, "I was overjoyed." For Oscar, his debut for a team represented a staging post, a "belief in myself that I could accomplish, I could accomplish a lot in soccer." He described how his teammates embraced him, overcoming his doubts: "once I'm on the field and everybody assured me that it was going to go well. I think it was the kind of motivation that everything will be well, and that doubt went away." When Kevin spoke about his relationship to others outside of the team, he refers to as "them," and how as a result of the win "I was able to prove to them and myself that I was able to overcome many difficulties."

The male coresearchers appeared to speak of significance in terms of themselves and the other, whereas female coresearchers appeared to describe internally significant feelings and sentiments. Only the male coresearchers described their relationship to other people when recounting their inner thoughts on the subject.

Theme 5: Parents as heroes

Question: Who are your heroes? In an increasingly media-influenced age, any question about heroes may be expected to elicit evocations of many of the celebrities and stars on stage, screen, and in athletic fields. However, all coresearchers named a parent in their immediate family as a hero. There was no distinct difference between the sexes between the choice of parent as hero, with Jane and Carly mentioning their fathers, and Diane and Gabrielle focusing on their mothers. Jamal mentioned his "dad and my grandfather" and also his "wife," who, along with his father, are "the two people I look up to most in life." Andrew gave the longest response to this question, declaring initially that "my parents are my biggest heroes, they give me a lot." Oscar named his father: "my dad is my first hero." Oscar and Kevin also named "mom," and Andrew stated "both my parents."

All coresearchers spoke of a parent, although there was a difference in the answer sets beyond this. In addition, the majority of male coresearchers also described an external person outside the family as a hero. Andrew mentioned Matt Le Tissier, and Kevin spoke of Gareth Bale. Oscar mentioned his father, who was also a player, but then discussed "two goalkeepers that played for my favorite club and the one is still playing in Mexico." Only Jane described Ronaldinhio, a Brazilian professional soccer player, as her hero. Andrew went on to describe the spiritual leader Gandhi, the professional basketball player Michael Jordan, and the professional cyclist who overcame cancer, Lance Armstrong. The female coresearchers were distinguished in that all except one, Jane, who did not suggest a person outside of the family as a hero. Comparatively, the female coresearchers had little to say about heroes, whereas the males spoke at much greater length on the topic, especially Andrew and Oscar.

Theme 6: The unstoppable body, elevation and descent

Question: How would you describe your inner experience of when you're playing well? In response to being asked about the experience of playing well, all coresearchers described feelings associated with elevation and freedom. Evident from the responses was a focus on the expression of *feelings*, rather than any specific thought process to accompany them. Jane stated that it was "just a really good feeling," adding "you feel accomplished." She said that she couldn't adequately describe the experience when she repeated, "just a really good feeling, I don't know how to explain." Carly spoke of an actual sensation "butterflies in my stomach." She then spoke of being "excited" twice, and that the experience was a sensation "just full of joy." Diane described "a feeling of such happiness and stability," adding a sense of elevation when she then spoke of how "you feel like you're on top of the world." Diane echoed Jane's sense of an altered state, and how an invincible state arrives when "nothing could go wrong." Diane suggested that something has a power over her, "it's almost like a kind of a high, like adrenaline junkies will search for that, it's a high once you have it, you crave it, you get motivated to practice every day to go out and do your best, because the feeling after a game is almost indescribable." Gabrielle followed the theme by stating, "I just feel so happy and I enjoy it." She then described a bodily effect, "it's easier to breathe," using the same phrase as Diane: "you feel like you're on top of the world." Gabrielle again related a bodily reference to feeling and sense of elevation in that "it feels like I'm light and it's fun."

As for the men, Jamal continued the emphasis on bodily feeling and a sense of omnipotence, saying, "I feel like I can do everything right, not just think about it." He spoke of being moved by events with a new sense: "it feels like playing well puts me into a good mood." He spoke of something with a lasting quality, in that "when I'm playing well, things keep going well even if I make a mistake." Andrew mentioned "self-talk," "what's really worked for me is positive self-talk." He declared a virtue of "not trying to get too high but [to maintain] some sort of consistency," perhaps also expressing a desire to keep hold of something he received. To describe playing well, Oscar expressed an idea that may seem surprising for a sportsman, "I think it's humble, I think it's humble." As with Andrew, Oscar expressed a cautionary stance with the exuberant feelings expressed by others: "I have a great sense of respect for the opponent." He described an affirmative experience "I'm positive about things and I'm looking forward," speaking again of the future as "feeling positive about the future." Kevin was not so cautious about the experience, confidently asserting, "I feel like there's no one on the field that can stop me." He also expressed a sense of the unknown in the experience: "it's this weird feeling when everything is going your way and anything you try and do will always come off well for the team." As if nothing lies in his path, he repeated his earlier statement of omnipotence: "I just feel pretty much unstoppable."

Question: How does it feel to play badly? Previously, coresearchers had described being in contact with an experience when playing well, as a process of everything going right, being unstoppable and on a mountaintop, and their responses were filled with bodily sensations and emotions. For the opposite experience of playing badly, coresearchers offered some very different accounts. For her initial response Jane said, "you talk to yourself a lot mentally." "I talk to myself and say 'come on pick it up.'" Carly said she "can't stop thinking about it." Rather than the elevated expressions of the previous answer, Carly said she was "down on myself, I'm just really down on myself," then expressing a bodily effect: "I don't really keep my head up." Echoing the references to height earlier, now Carly spoke of diminishment: "you get to such a low point it's hard to come back." Jane and Carly used the word *disappointment* to describe their experience, as did Diane: "it's definitely disappointing, the whole experience is disappointing for yourself." Gabrielle spoke of the body again, "I feel heavy, I feel like a walk is testing," and repeated the theme of descent as opposed to elevation in the experience of playing well. "I feel kind of down because it's harder to lose." Although it can be expected that coresearchers would describe a more negative experience when asked about losing, negative internal dialog appeared to have replaced the buoyant feelings of playing well. Coresearchers also consistently described different relationships to their body in terms of heaviness, depth, and losing control.

Theme 7: Dreams of giving back

Question: What is a dream that you have for your life? As could be anticipated, all coresearchers provided a positive idea or scenario. As for the female coresearchers, Carly and Diane both mentioned *family* as a dream, Jane said she wanted to be "an accountant" and Gabrielle said she wanted to be an "elementary school teacher" with Diane wanting to go "off to college." In terms of playing soccer as a dream, Carly stated she wanted "soccer within my career path," and Gabrielle said she wanted to "stay involved with soccer somehow." This appeared to contrast with the much more definitely expressed aspirations of the male coresearchers—all four immediately expressed a desire for a professional career in the game. Jamal said, "making a living playing the game." Andrew said, "I have special dreams," wanting "to play in the English Premier League." Oscar purely stated "playing professional soccer." Kevin said "a professional soccer player that is my main dream."

There may be simple explanations or reasons why the female coresearchers were less certain about a professional career, which will be outlined later. However, the male coresearchers also expressed another set of responses, which were more subtle. All four expressed a desire to "give back" something to their origins somehow. Jamal said he saw himself "being able to give my family and the people who have supported and loved me something back, what they deserve." Andrew wanted to "give back to this world," whereas Oscar said, "and hopefully giving back to my family with what I can accomplish, love always." Kevin did not use the term but spoke about an alternative career in "sports medicine," expressing his caring and "passion for all athletes." The word *success* was indicated by three out of the four female coresearchers, whereas none of the male coresearchers used this actual word. Although we cannot fully hope to interpret why females used the word *success* and males did not, it is perhaps significant that females spoke of general ideas related to "success," whereas the men seemed more interested in expressing ideas about "giving back."

Theme 8: Team as a supra family and assistors

Question: Do you think being on a soccer team is like being in a family? And if it is, how is it so? Soccer is a naturally competitive environment at the level our coresearchers play. At one time, as many as 30 students are competing for 11 places in a starting team. During the course of a game, substitutions can be made, when players out of the game can be exchanged and get to play. Even so, selection for a team is based on ability and competence. At a game as many as 50 per cent of the group will not get to take part in play and will remain on the bench as potential substitute players. A mutually competitive culture may not be what one might associate with ideas of family, although every psychotherapist knows that families are sometimes very competitive!

However, our coresearchers invariably spoke about the team using terms associated with the family archetype. Coresearchers had previously shown a strong trend in unanimously relating their involvement in soccer to their immediate family. However, their answers indicated that coresearchers believed the team was also a family. It appeared that the team represented a *supra family*. From the answers given, this family was not an improved version of their family of origin, but more an overarching group system. This family provided an extension of family rather than a replacement. This indicated that the word *supra* was an appropriate label to use for this kind of collective.

All eight coresearchers expressed a belief that a soccer team is like a family. Jamal even suggested, "yes I think it is exactly like being in a family, sometimes more like my own family," a statement he repeated later: "it resembles more of a family than an actual family." The coresearchers all went on to express ideas about why they agreed with this particular belief. All eight coresearchers also described the team as a source of assistance and support. Jane explained, "you're always working with one another," "helping one another"; she qualified her ideas by expressing a simple thought embodying her sense of obligation: "you can't just do well for yourself." For Jane, the team was a source of "emotional support." Jane also hinted at a deeper level to the experience in terms of learning ideas that last, "life lessons," she said definitely that she can, "always relate life to soccer"; "if you learn those small things in a sport, you can apply it to life when situations come around." Carly reflected, "you win with them, you lose with them," adding they were "happy together, mad together." She suggested that as in an actual family, she inevitably has to "deal with confrontations."

Diane spoke more than anyone else about the family, suggesting it was the same "in every way I can think of." Her first concern is for others: "when you see someone down on themselves there is always someone picking you up, that's what family does." She focused more on the supportive side to the team: "either your parents or your siblings telling you that it is not as bad as you think." Diane echoed Jane's statement that "you can't do it by yourself," alluding to a sense of importance when she said, "we depend on each other." She, too, emphasized the point about family being essential: "it's all about building each other up, keeping each other together because we're all in it together." Diane suggested a practicality behind the togetherness: "the more you are like a family, the better you do as a team." Diane is the only female coresearcher to mention anyone else than her direct teammates in speaking about the team as family. For her, the matter seems almost to relate to issues of life or death: "the coach can't be the only person to motivate you or you will die." As with Jane, Diane ended her answer by relating her learning in soccer to the outside world: "learning here on the soccer field that's been a transfer into like, my job, and stuff my life, I'm so glad about the opportunity to learn that, and live it here and let it take me places." She finished with a sense of the numinous power she attached to this experience in her life: "your teammates take care of you in that way, it's unbelievable."

Gabrielle agreed, absolutely "it's a family, it's a big family." She then related a sense of always being looked out for, in that "if you mess up they will catch you." She immediately followed with a positive note: "they'll always have your back, too." She also joined in the belief, or the expectation, that "they are there to help you, encourage you" saying that she has "more big sisters to look up to." Gabrielle talked of different *kinds* of families. "I feel you learn more being part of that kind of family because it's kind of different cultures coming into your life."

As noted earlier, Jamal spoke of family using heartfelt expressions. He talked of sharing, in that there are emotions you share when you win and when you lose. He again emphasized a depth to the relationships he perceived available: "It brings you together; it's kind of an emotional attachment." Andrew referred to the "the ups and downs, and it's kind of like a family." He added a personal significance and a slightly different angle: "for me it's more of a brotherhood; I've not much experience of having a brother so I love it." However, Andrew repeated the theme of a family of assistors: "We support each other, giving each other a shoulder to lean on if you're not doing so great." For him it is a necessity: "we have to support each other," "and I think also we are in it together till the end, which is exactly like a family. Never give up on your family."

Oscar noted a subtle similarity to a family of relations in that "you're united by your beliefs and your name." He repeatedly used terms related to a sense of a family indistinct from his own. Of his colleagues he said, "being in the team you learn to love your teammates as brothers, and you grow with the same ideas and the same goals for each other." He also summed up his opinions with an allusion to the values of life skills and the broader nature of the learning available. He spoke of his interconnectedness to his team in visceral terms: "every time I see them, I feel as if they are a part of me, and that they've left something in me that I continue to use on and off the field." If the players universally believe a soccer team is like a family, then who are the parents? As with Diane, Kevin was the only one who referred to the idea that coaches were a part of that family: "we have that parent figure with our coaches that we look up to for guidance or anything you need," then "all team members are like your brothers and sisters." Just as Gabrielle did, Kevin suggested a natural responsibility to others "they will hold you accountable," he then immediately expressed an affirmation of this idea and a sense of being held, he added, "they'll be there for you, keep you, be there for whatever you need."

Theme 9: Winning and losing, inner doubt, solutions, and shadow language

Question: What does it feel like to lose? Three out of four female coresearchers described an experience of inner doubt in response to losing. Jane was even prepared to carry the weight of losing on her own: "I'm not down on my teammates, I'm down on myself." Carly's first response to the question was also being "very down on myself." She also seemed naturally to look to herself first, and admitted that "there's more I could have done." Diane, who spoke the most about family, said, "it makes you question what you're doing and if it's worth it." She then encouraged herself: "you have to dig deep and try and remember why you're here." She suggested a depth to the investment that feels lost when "you pour your heart and soul into something." Only Gabrielle went to the team and a solution first: "OK we messed up as a team, but what can we do to fix it?" She then reflected on the personal experience: "I feel like it's easy to be pulled down than it is to be brought up."

Male coresearchers did not appear to differ in the quality and emphasis of their responses to losing, and both sexes appeared to have an equal amount to say on the subject. Jamal expressed a philosophical idea on losing, that "it can also make you humble and make someone." He continued with his stoical attitude and said that "I try and take losing as a positive sometimes." He concluded in a similar vein: "it does feel bad, but I feel like it's necessary sometimes to lose." The other males spoke minimally on the internal experience. Andrew's response to how it feels to lose was "if it's a tough loss, it can feel miserable." He went on to suggest solutions: "I think you can't really sulk in the loss, you can't get down and out about it." Then after more suggestions for dealing with loss he said, "I just move on."

Oscar followed suit beginning with a consoling notion: "losing, there's always two sides of it. You could always lose by lack of effort, concentration or hard work." He continued to explain, "with both of those you can learn something." It was only at this point that Oscar related a personally-felt expression when he said, "I mean the feeling, it just kills me inside when I lose because of lack of effort, because again you have just wasted that time." Only Kevin from the start expressed the inner anguish related by Oscar, "I hate losing, you know I hate to." But he too comforted himself with a projection onto his opponents expressing a belief that you have to "just show them that you cannot win this next match, I'll stop you." Both male and female coresearchers shared positive responses to the question about a negative experience; however, the male coresearchers emphasized the positive responses, whereas the female coresearchers appeared to be able to reflect on the experience in a deeper, more reflective way.

Question: What does it feel like to win? Winning is important in US soccer. The US distinguishes itself from the rest of the world in that they have a "golden goal" period of extra time in its soccer matches so as to avoid a draw or tied score. Naturally perhaps, when coresearchers were asked about winning, they all reported positive statements about the experience. Beneath the surface, answers were predictable (i.e., "it feels good"), but there were more statements relating to elevation, and also a sense of being given something, a kind of freedom. Jane described her experience: "well it feels like a number of things, it's liberating," then repeated her earlier sentiments about a "sense of accomplishment after working so hard." Carly also referred to a "good reward for hard work," adding, "I did something good." Diane spoke about a feeling of "being in a good family," again echoing a sense of things coming together at these moments. She reaffirmed the idea of "that accomplishment together, of bringing football together and the individual."

Diane then spoke of something ecstatic; the experience for her "is just like a high, it's all unexplainable." Diane talked about feelings after the "sacrifice" they had made together and again referring to a numinous quality in terms of a "five-minute" feeling of elation. She regaled how "after the sacrifice," "that little five you get again and again," concluding with her sense that this is an "essential accomplishment." Diane mentioned sacrifices three times, once about her parents, and then again about the importance of her achievements. Gabrielle said less on the subject but did chime with the others when describing a time when "you get to celebrate with your family on the field, and you just raise up." Staying with the transcendent theme, she added, "It's work and yet it's just, just so happy."

Jamal was the only male coresearcher to speak about the impact of winning by directly referencing the team. As with the female coresearchers, he spoke of something being gained that is kept: "I feel like it gives the team confidence," immediately adding a sharper word not spoken by anyone else; "I feel like it gives you an edge." As if a realization has occurred, he reflected, "we know we can do it, and it gives to you" and then more of the same theme, in that winning also "gives me confidence." The other three male coresearchers expressed positive themes, but it appeared that they were different in that they spoke only of the impact on themselves, with no mention of the team. Andrew said, "it feels tremendous to win and I love winning, I have the mindset of a winner and I feel tremendous but I only feel tremendous if things I've been practicing were accomplished." Oscar reflected more soberly, "there's a great difference between getting a win against a good team and getting a win against a bad team," and that "getting a win against a big opponent, this is just more motivating." Like Jamal, Kevin spoke of this in terms of an insight in that there is a *knowing* something has been achieved. Using terms of conquest, he added, "Knowing that you beat your opponent on that day and you're triumphant over him." He speaks as if something has been put to the test: "It kind of makes you feel like in a way like you're better than the other person." He ended his answer by correcting himself with modesty: "but just on that day you're better than them."

Whereas the majority of the coresearchers related *up* and *down* experiences with regard to winning and losing, some themes were more nuanced, and the responses to losing were in some respects the most taxing to interpret. Giorgi spoke to the expectations of effective phenomenological research in that "the method demands that something be 'lived' rather than intellectualized" (2009, p. 182). This means in terms of interpreting the data that a kind of suspension must take place within the researcher in order to see the picture as a whole. After spending time trying to shed light on this answer set, it seemed to me that the male coresearchers in this section spoke quite differently than the female coresearchers, but also in a lexicon not used anywhere else. The meanings of the data were not obvious because the terms were often cloaked in positive statements or intentions, things you "shouldn't do." The data refrained from any real expressions relating to the inner experience of losing, instead focusing on solution-based statements, which might indicate they would not, or could not relate the inner experience.

Word cloud results

Below are the images produced after using the word cloud system to compute the data and produce an image where the word font sizes correlate to the frequency the word is used by the coresearcher. The most commonly-used words have been copied and identified for the reader below each image. Those sections have been gathered and will be explored in more detail later. The individual male coresearcher word clouds will be presented first, followed by the combined male coresearchers word cloud. Then the individual female coresearcher word clouds will be presented, followed by the combined female coresearchers word cloud. Finally, a combined coresearchers word cloud will be presented which aggregated all coresearcher responses.

Figure 4.1 Jamal: Like, kind, family, feel, just, bad good, confidence, know.

Figure 4.2 Andrew: Think, things, get, life, always, game, going, day.

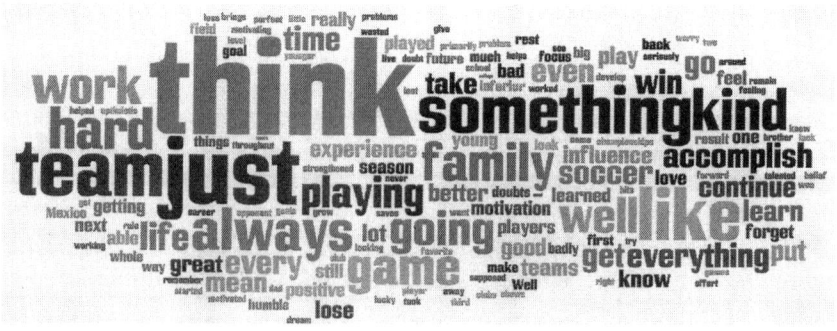

Figure 4.3 Oscar: Think, just, team, something, like, kind, always, game, going.

Figure 4.4 Kevin: Just, know, think, like, game, able, work, field, feel, need.

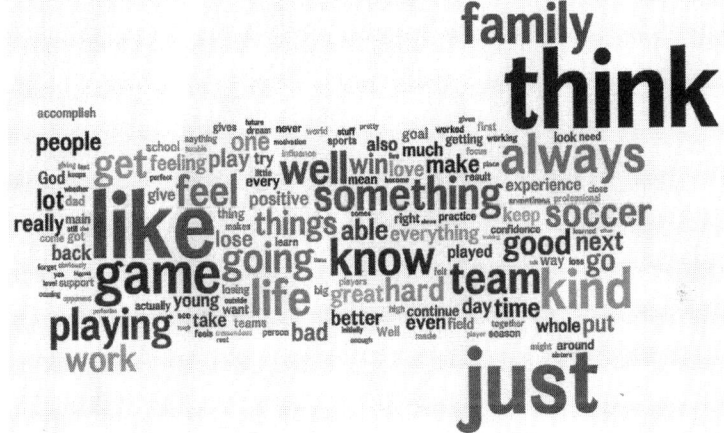

Figure 4.5 Combined male coresearchers word cloud: Think, like, just, family, game, playing, something, kind, going, life.

Figure 4.6 Jane: Just, like, know, good, feel, want, team, well, really, play.

Figure 4.7 Carly: Just, like, really, much, lot, pretty, soccer, everything, big.

Figure 4.8 Diane: Like, family, just, think, life, something, good, soccer, accomplishment, team, always.

Figure 4.9 Gabrielle: Just, family, feel, always, hard, lose, good, play, soccer, like, really, sisters.

Figure 4.10 Combined female coresearchers word cloud: Just, like, family, good, really, soccer, think, feel, get, life, always, hard, play.

Figure 4.11 Combined male and female coresearchers word cloud: Just, think, like, family, good, always, know, team, soccer, hard, get, game, work, play, playing.

Word cloud results—words only

Below are the significant words that the word cloud system produced, with the most frequent words to the right and less frequently used words to the left. Rather than comparing the pictures, this system provided an opportunity to compare the words without the images as well. At first glance, it is apparent that words such as *just* have limited potential to reveal any meaning. However, some words such as *family* appear as a theme, as well as a frequently used word. In order to accurately use word clouds, documents were created which only included the words used by the coresearchers, and not my questions or headings. Therefore, it was simple to use these texts to analyze the numerical frequency of the words used. Scores and data are included below.

Table 4.1 Numerical word cloud table

Words	Number of times used	
	Female coresearchers	Male coresearchers
Total words used	5524	4438
Sister or sisters	6	0
Brother or brothers	0	5
Feel	26	22
Family	22	18
Play	18	12
Playing	8	23
Think	26	58
Want	14	7
Good	32	18
Get	24	22
Always	21	28
Love	5	11

As described above, when observing complete answer sets, it became apparent that the word *just* is used in a variety of forms (not to be confused with a sense of being just as in justice). The word was interchangeably used as an adjective (i.e., "we hope to be just") and an adverb (i.e., "this is just like").

Male coresearchers: individual
- Jamal: Like, kind, family, feel, just, bad good, confidence, know.
- Andrew: Think, things, get, life, always, game, going, day.
- Oscar: Think, just, team, something, like, kind, always, game, going.
- Kevin: Just, know, think, like, game, able, work, field, feel, need.

Male coresearchers: combined
- Think, like, just, family, game, playing, something, kind, going, life.

Female coresearchers: individual
- Jane: Just, like, know, good, feel, want, team, well, really, play.
- Carly: Just, like, really, much, lot, pretty, soccer, everything, big.
- Diane: Like, family, just, think, life, something, good, soccer, accomplishment, team, always.
- Gabrielle: Just, family, feel, always, hard, lose, good, play, soccer, like, really, sisters.

Female coresearchers: combined
- Just, like, family, good, really, soccer, think, feel, get.

Male and female coresearchers: combined
- Just, think, like, family, good, always, know, team, soccer, hard, get, game, work, play, playing.

In the following Discussion chapter we can explore the possible significance of these answer sets in more detail. Particularly as female coresearchers used fewer words than the men, it was noteworthy that they achieved similar frequencies or even surpassed the men with certain words already significant to the study such as family and play.

Chapter 5

Depth discussion and analysis of the data

By this stage, the study had now collected a lot of material and data from the source of this investigation—those who play the game of soccer. Earlier Nesti (2010), Leonard (2001) and Cousineau (2003) described a lacuna in modern sport compared to the past, apparently successfully bridged by Phil Jackson and indeed, in my own experience. But this approach appears the exception to the wider world of sports, and the wider Western world according to Campbell (1972), Johnson (1987), Goodchild (2001), Wallace (2006) and Corbett (2007). Earlier the question was asked, where have the philosophers gone? Research has revealed some notable historical figures from politics, literature, and the church that have been deeply invested in soccer. Some of their impressions are useful to consider as the study now turns to interpret the data on another level—in the depth tradition, with a role for the unconscious aspect of this study in the Alchemical Reflections section later in this chapter.

At times, in the following analysis, the Greek gods will be explored, utilizing the London 2012 Olympic Games. Many of the observations and themes revealed by our coresearchers can be related to archetypal mythological gods from Greece on show in London, and on a synchronistically-timed showing of the US Youth Soccer Show. The study has now gone through two deliberate stages in order to reach this point. First, by creating questions that could most usefully reveal their inner world, while thoughtfully maintaining a distance from the subject with the process of *epoche*. And now, one advantage of phenomenological enquiry is that having become intimate with the material there is now an opportunity to take the data onto another level, by following Hillman's (1982) advice to return again to the subject with fresh eyes.

Great minds and soccer

Before writing about the themes in detail, now is perhaps an appropriate point to revisit the connection described earlier by Cousineau (2003) concerning Socrates, Plato, and the early schools or academies. These places were schools of theoretical dialogue; none of the above appeared to have any confusion about working alongside athletes. Albert Camus (1913-1960) was a French philosopher, poet, political activist, and author. In 1957, he won the Nobel Prize for Literature for his work on capital punishment called "Réflexions sur la guillotine" (Reflections on the Guillotine). With Jean Paul Sartre, Camus led the French Existential movement, inspired by the philosophy of Martin Heidegger. It is not widely-known that Camus was also a goalkeeper for the university soccer team called RUA, who became national champions. He was a highly regarded player, but his life took another course and his soccer career ended at 17 due to tuberculosis. However, he never forgot his experiences with soccer.

The online Albert Camus Society of the UK cited a response Camus gave about his relationship to soccer (he uses the term *football*) to a question posed by the university alumni magazine in the 1950s: "After many years during which I saw many things, what I know most surely about morality and the duty of man I owe to sport and learned it in the RUA" (2012). Camus was a modern philosopher who saw principles alive within soccer that he believed had become dissipated or forgotten in the wider world. The website went on to suggest that "Camus believed that the people of politics and religion try to confuse us with convoluted moral systems to make things appear more complicated than they really are, possibly to suit their own agendas" (Albert Camus Society UK, 2012).

Andrew Cooper (1998), in his book *Playing in the zone: Exploring the spiritual dimensions of sports,* believed that modern sport has undergone a kind of degradation, in Western society at least. Like Camus, Cooper also believed sport is understated in terms of significance to the psyche and society, suggesting that "we have relegated sports to the realm of entertainment" (p. 25). Camus suggested a deeper, more significant expression of humanity occurring in soccer, at least, that somehow remains out of sight or of a lesser significance to most of us. Echoing Andrew Samuels' ideas about outreach, Cooper believed that psychology has been limited by only focusing on pathology, and that "until recently, it has had next to nothing to say about states that are of higher order than normal waking consciousness" (p. 25). Sports psychologist Mark Nesti (2010) obviously agrees, complaining that "there has been a dearth of published papers" (p. 176) on the perspectives of the players that are hard to access. Thanks to the data volunteered by our coresearchers, this study can make an attempt at providing a Jungian depth exception to this rule.

It is conceivably not coincidental that Camus was also interested in the work of Plotinus, whose work was cited by Hillman (1976) earlier when describing the expression and the possible source of the soul. As described earlier, Plotinus was very much interested in human expression and unity in all its forms. He was not confident in Platonic "forms" being the whole truth and felt that some deeper expression was at play. Camus was also interested in the deeper expressions of the soul. His statement about learning "morality and the duty of man" from soccer appears to resonate with some of the expressions already recorded by our coresearchers in the study.

What does this tell us about the game of soccer, and why this "simple morality" has thrived and expanded in a world potentially more complicated in the West due to the rise of technology, celebrity culture, and material values? Fortuitously for this study, synchronistically at the time of writing the Olympic Games were being held in London. This provided a useful opportunity to view the phenomenon through a contemporary lens and see how it relates to the subject of sports and soccer. Interestingly, Cousineau also wrote *Soul moments* (1997), a book about synchronicity. Much of his work relates creativity to the soul and psyche, and his works have been immensely helpful to this enquiry.

London 2012 Olympic Games

At the time of writing this Discussion, the 30th London 2012 Olympics opened, on July 28. The BBC Opening Ceremony was reportedly watched by a local viewing audience of 26.9 million at its peak (British Broadcasting Company, 2012). This would represent nearly half of all the people in the United Kingdom. Various reporters estimated global viewing figures of one billion, although as explained earlier, these figures are difficult to verify with any certainty. However, the opening ceremony was a spectacle where many of the archetypes being discussed here appeared incarnate. The opening is traditionally an extravaganza, and in Britain it was no different. The exhibition sometimes took the guise of theatre, with actors portraying scenes in the stadium interspersed with movie excerpts on large screens in the stadium and at home. The 90-minute show was a narrative of British history and sport, designed by the Oscar-winning director Danny Boyle.

The ceremony began with rural and agricultural scenes, which then evolved into a retelling of British history through the industrial revolution, to the National Health Service, highlighting throughout current prominent people on the British cultural scene. Remarkably, at one point, the Queen appeared as an actress, portraying herself en-route to the stadium. The actor Daniel Craig, the current James Bond, in films such as *Casino Royale* and *Quantum of Solace*, was filmed arriving at Buckingham Palace as an escort for the Queen, to take her to the stadium. The film contrived to make the audience believe that it was the Queen jumping out of a helicopter above the stadium, accompanied by James Bond. From a traditional perspective, the Queen's appearance as an actress might have been as shocking as Nero's appearances as an actor was in Roman times. Although the Queen did not in fact parachute into the stadium, a stunt double in a similar dress emerged from the helicopter. Nevertheless, it was an extraordinary moment when the Queen became an "actress," joining the worlds of acting and sport together.

The arrival from the skies was in keeping with many of the archetypal images familiar to the Greeks. Although this remains an investigation of soccer, the extraordinary behavior of the Queen did testify to the significance and gravity of the event. The Olympic tradition, like soccer, seems to be growing, at least in part due to the media and the online revolution. The events at London 2012 demonstrate that archetypal identities, which would have been familiar to the Greeks, are still portrayed in the world of sport. As the ceremony drew to its finale, the audience awaited the delivery of the Olympic flame to the stadium after its journey from China to herald the official opening of the Games. Remembering David Rock's (2009) assertion that our emotional connections as viewers can have a link to the past without us being conscious of it. The torch or flame is a central symbol of the Games, bringing the light into the darkness.

Soccer player David Beckham was given the task and responsibility of safely delivering the flame, regarded as the symbol and key to opening the Games. Dressed like a kind of James Bond, Beckham drove a powerful speedboat with red, white and blue flashing lights. Global followers on television joined the waiting audience to witness his rapid progress up the Thames, accompanied by fireworks set off on the riverbanks as he passed. The ceremony and happenings within the Games provided this study a rich opportunity to explore the sometimes hidden, unrecognized archetypal forces from the past that appear a very part of us today.

Fox Soccer Channel: US Youth Soccer Show

During the time of writing the Discussion chapter, another television program was broadcast that could be a useful resource for the further discussion of these topics. The US Youth Soccer Show on the Fox Soccer Channel (USYSS, 2012) is a program aimed at a younger audience (ages 12-18), who have an interest in soccer, including magazine items relating to tournaments and developments for youth soccer across the country. A recent episode featured four current US international professional soccer players who were asked questions about their relationship to soccer, including questions on their interest in the game when they were younger, their achievements, and dreams. These professional players also discussed their feelings about the role that the sport has played in their lives. Coincidentally, one of the players interviewed for the program was mentioned earlier—Landon Donovan. Other interviewees were Tim Howard, Hercules Gomez, and Clint Dempsey, all of whom are at the height of their careers, playing in the best leagues in the world. Their answers had many similarities with the data given by our coresearchers, and selections from these interviews have been included to supplement the discussion of the themes below. Regrettably, there were no female professionals interviewed. Nevertheless, the inclusion of the professional perspective appeared to illuminate and corroborate the data offered by our coresearchers. After all, they may well represent the very people our coresearchers might aspire to become.

Discussion of each theme in depth

Theme 1: Family as the reason they play soccer

After initial consideration, it may not be surprising that the majority of our coresearchers described family to explain how and why they had become involved in soccer. Obviously, children normally originate from a family, so it cannot be too surprising that the coresearchers reference theirs. Many players talked about sacrifices made by their parents, and in order to pursue the game they needed this cooperation. What is surprising or revealing about this? With further thought, we realize that the family is not the only reality for a child. It is perhaps significant that the emphasis of the answers avoided a focus on friends, and didn't seem to indicate that peer pressure or "all my friends played so I did," which might have been an equally feasible response to offer. But when coresearchers were asked how they came to play soccer, they all referred to family as the source.

In the following discussion, this study will look at conventional stereotypes in terms of gender and sport and the possible origins of these expectations, distinguishing cultural values and those of the individual for women and sport. Then there will be a chance to explore in depth the finding that no particular gender was ascribed as their initial involvement in soccer, and what that reveals about the cultural expectations of gender and sport. The study can then go onto the role of children in the family and implications of that connection to sport, ending with excerpts from the interviews with the professional players.

In terms of a superficial look at the culture of soccer, it may be reasonable to assume that soccer is essentially a masculine tradition. The professional soccer leagues are male, and as described earlier, they attract vast followings and players are paid veritable fortunes. Women's leagues are comparatively tiny concerns, and very few women in the world are professional soccer players. In this case, one might expect a tendency for coresearchers to have male role models and inspirations for the sport. The only female coresearcher to name a hero outside of the family named a male professional soccer player. Nevertheless, the answers given by our coresearchers did not suggest that soccer is a man's game but rather a family game. However, culturally speaking, the evidence suggests that it is a man's game, especially at the professional level.

However, after exploring the first answers the coresearchers gave, it seems that this idea may be open to question. Perhaps most noteworthy was the fact that no common idea of a gender identification appeared to relate to the original playing of soccer. Carly mentioned her brother as an inspiration; Andrew mentioned his sisters. Gabrielle's whole family played, "especially my sisters," and Diane said that she valued making both her parents proud. From the researcher's perspective, this is an intriguing response, one that was to some extent surprising. However, there are clues that the game, in the United States at least, has broader gender identification for soccer. By observing the world of women in sport today, there is perhaps a suggestion that the traditional idea of women who are mothers not being suitable for sport may be changing, and women may naturally become heroes or be celebrated nationally as sportswomen rather than mothers. By exploring the relationship of women and sport, perhaps a better understanding can be achieved about women and their relationship to sport and soccer.

Women and the archetypes of sport and culture

On July 26 2012, the United States Women's Soccer team was pictured as the feature on the front pages of *The New York Times* and *The Wall Street Journal*. In 2012 United States Women were the world champions of soccer. As a tradition, it appears that women's soccer is a significant part of the US psyche, and organized women's leagues exist all over the nation. Evidence suggests that, globally, women's sport appears to be flourishing and is seen as a more acceptable option for females in the twenty-first century. In the London 2012 Olympics, for the first time the US women competitors outnumbered the male competitors and cultures such as Afghanistan and Saudi Arabia entered female competitors for the first time. In the Olympic women's soccer tournament, one preliminary round match on July 31 2012 between Great Britain and Brazil attracted the third-largest crowd (70,584) ever to watch a women's match. Audience figures testify that something in women's sport is shifting and expanding, and it is good to ask why. On August 10, the US women's team won the gold medal, beating Japan 2-1 in a final that was watched by the new record audience of 80,203. Evidence suggests that women's involvement in sport has been influenced in the past by cultural expectations and rules rather than by natural capabilities or inclinations to play. Perhaps this is one explanation of why our coresearchers identified their families as the original inspiration to play rather than gender.

The evidence presented by our coresearchers suggested that soccer was not so much related to gender identification, as to relationships and the importance of them. The idea that sport or soccer is an essentially masculine venture may be a result of culturally imposed ideas rather than a reflection of the deeper archetypes played out by women. That is, when they get the chance to play them. Ideas of family rather than gender seemed to be most apparent in the data, suggesting that sport is a natural expression for both male and female players. In *Sport, femininity and the promises of the theology of the Body,* Dr. Synthia Sydnor (2011) asserted that "qualities such as strength, aggression, boldness, and muscularity take feminine and masculine form" (p. 89). The coresearchers indicated that for them, family remained a significant issue throughout the study, with all coresearchers describing the team as a kind of family. Syndor also described:

> K. Cahn's highly regarded *Coming on Strong: Gender and sexuality in twentieth century women's sport* that emphasized the changing, nuanced definitions of

femininity, making a call for attributes long defined as masculine—skill, strength, speed, physical dominance, uninhibited use of space and motion—to become human qualities and not those of a particular gender.

(p. 86)

This is a reflection of a deeper archetype beneath the doing of soccer that this study revealed and aims to explore. Evidence suggested that the challenges and identifications for women appeared to be the same as the males. This was an expression of non-gender-specific ideas relating to the challenges that they faced being a soccer player. The English Football Association (FA) is the governing body for soccer in England, overseeing the rules of the game in the country. They have only allowed women to play the game since 1971, removing a ban previously set in 1921 on the grounds that it was inappropriate conduct for women. However, the first recorded game between women was in 1895, when the North of England played the South (The Football Association, 2012). It certainly appears that women desired to play the game from an early date, and not playing was more a result of cultural mores of the time and not the desire or capacity to play. In Andrew's case at least, it seemed perfectly natural to him that he was inspired to play by his sisters. It seems our coresearchers naturally accept that their impetus for the sport came from or was identified with either gender.

An argument can be made to suggest that different archetypes are indeed related to different team sports. American football, for example, is a game that is concerned with tackling and disabling an opposing player with or without the ball by butting them like rams to put them off their stride. Soccer, as a sport, is more about the relationships of the players to the ball and each other. The aim is not the physical disabling of an opponent, but is more related to skill and control of the ball. American football became organized in 1925, and as a sport has few if any women playing on record. Specific equipment is needed, such as helmets and padding, to protect players from the forces of collision required by the game. American football's original ancestor, rugby, is different in many ways, primarily in that the rules allow an opponent to be tackled only if they have the ball. There are significant women's leagues for rugby in the UK and other countries that play the game such as South Africa, Ireland, Australia, New Zealand, and Canada.

American football appears more of a warrior combative sport, whereas soccer has a different emphasis. Is this why women's soccer is culturally accepted compared to women playing American football? Even though in the US women are now allowed to become soldiers, it seems for some reason American football is still out of their reach. But as this study relates to soccer archetypes, can it be said that another, unisex, perhaps deeper archetype is being expressed? The evidence suggested that our coresearchers had a deep sense of gratitude and identification with their families of origin, and the idea of family in their current family of the soccer team. Evidence also suggested that soccer is a phenomenon that women can embody as naturally as men, and that both parents seem to provide the necessary inspirational qualities for young people to play the game.

Family, childhood and sports

Earlier in the study the seminal works of Huizinga (1955) and Schechner (2002) were described in regard to their ideas about the role of play. Huizinga suggested that deeper archetypes even beyond humankind were in motion during play, as animals played long before humans. Gardiner (2011) stated:

> As children, we run, and dance, and weave, and wrestle, and throw objects, and play tricks, and experiment with tunes, and mimic adults in role playing. Especially where our circumstances allow "free time" away from the necessities of subsistence and production, as adults and communities we create opportunities, facilities and competitions to recreate these early childhood experiences of play, and institutionalize them in sports.
>
> (p. 132)

Gardiner (2011) suggested that humans have since codified play and childlike activity into organized sport. So is this perhaps what the sport of soccer is all about? Gardiner's codified form of childhood? In a speech by President Nelson Mandela at the launch of the Nelson Mandela Children's Fund on May 8 1995, Mandela said "There can be no keener revelation of a society's soul than the way in which it treats its children." The sports world does indeed appear to reserve a place for children and for the purposes of the soul of this work there is a little room to provide a few illustrations. For example, at the beginning of each Premier League game in England, the players walk through the tunnel onto the pitch, each holding a child's hand; at the opening ceremony of the London 2012 Olympics, an entire section of the show was devoted to the care and protection of children. At one stage an army of "Mary Poppins" flew in from the sky and banished the bad ghosts that were hunting and haunting vulnerable babies. In fact, the very opening scene of the ceremony showed children dancing around a Maypole, an ancient pagan fertility ritual and part of the English mainstream cultural tradition. Moreover, the symbolic opening of the Olympics is not the Queen's announcement, but the lighting of the flame—a symbolic spark anointed to the eternal flame of life and light to the venture. For London 2012, the privilege was given to seven young teenagers who represented the next generation of athletes. This leads us to ask if sport really is a child's game? This study indicated another purpose and place in the psyche, at least in part contradicting the idea that sport is a recreation of child like moments.

Professional players echo experience of coresearchers

The soccer professionals on the Fox Soccer Channel US Youth Soccer Show (USYSS) 2012, were also asked about the origins of their first interest in soccer. These statements provided the study with some comparable data from those who have scaled the heights of success in the game. Tim Howard said:

> I first fell in love with the game of soccer when I was about six years old. My parents sent me out for a youth league and I just loved running around and scoring goals and doing all fun things sliding and kicking a ball. So that was the beginning of it and I try to cast my mind back to those days.
>
> (USYSS, 2012, Howard Interview)

Similarly, on the same show, Hercules Gomez, a professional who plays in the German League, when asked about how he became a soccer player, related:

> It was instilled in me by my father who loves the game it's his passion and I think through his passion that got passed down to me. So from the time I was walking I had a soccer ball at my foot everywhere I went when I was kicking around the house getting into trouble and since that day I haven't stopped.
>
> (USYSS, 2012, Gomez Interview)

Clint Dempsey, a professional player currently playing in the United States was playing for Tottenham Hotspur FC in England at the time he was interviewed. He said of his early involvement in soccer:

> I think I fell in love with the game of soccer when I was in fifth grade. I had to make a decision about which sport to put everything into because my family was going to make a drive backwards and forwards from Dallas.
>
> (USYSS, 2012, Dempsey Interview)

Landon Donovan was described earlier in relation to meditation, so it was synchronistic that the study could benefit from his reflections on these topics. Donovan is perhaps the highest ranked player in America alongside Clint Dempsey. He also spoke about his family experience:

> I fell in love with the game of soccer at a very early age. I had an older brother he was five years older, and from what I'm told, as soon as I could start walking I was playing so my brother was sort of waiting for me to take my first steps to play with me and I think because he played, I fell in love with the two and was about a year and a half or two years old.
>
> (USYSS, 2012, Donovan Interview)

Interestingly, three of the players used the term *love* and how they "fell in love" with the game. The only exception, Gomez, uses the word *passion* as he described the game being "instilled" into him, by his own father's love of the game. It appears that soccer is a game that allows for much love and passionate expression. Of our coresearchers Jane "learned to love" the game and Kevin, although he did not speak much about his inner world, did say that he got into soccer to help "burst out some" of his energy that ended in "growing into the passionate love I have for the game."

As with our coresearchers, the older professionals expressed a familial context for their interest in soccer, speaking about bonds of love for family and the game. The game of soccer appears to be much more related to the family archetype at play. Is a domestic family a kind of team? It would seem natural to assume that the ideal of a family unit involves teamwork, but this topic will be explored more usefully later in a section specifically dedicated to the nature of family in sports environments. The data suggested that they remain deeply connected to the ideas of loving, supportive, relationships that to some degree rely on trust. The Olympic opening ceremony did not solely represent competitive ideas, but celebrated family and the nurturing of children. Our coresearchers and professional players spoke of intimate ideals and relationships, perhaps representing a desire to recreate the earlier ties within the original family unit. In that sense there is a recreation of family emerging from the data, and also there are clues that this is not just a recreation for comfort, but perhaps there are reasons why these priorities are so often expressed within the culture of soccer.

Theme 2: God as a source of gifts

Coresearchers were asked, "Where do you think your gift for playing soccer comes from?" Five out of eight coresearchers described *God* in some way connected to their gift. From a superficial first reading, the suspicion is that this is a cultural reflection. What would a team from China or Tibet say? There is a limitation to the possibilities open to exploring what our coresearchers mean when they refer to *God*. However, as so many of them used the word, there must be significance in the theme somewhere. Each of the three players who did not use the term pointed to their family in some way as a source of their gifts. The following section will explore other older gods in world traditions which might amplify the data the coresearchers offered. These are the themes the coresearchers identified put alongside archetypal themes understood to be expressed by the gods. Also, the current relationship of the church and spirituality with sports and soccer can be usefully explored to see what are cultural conditions at the time, and what belongs to the realm of the transpersonal, timeless meaning.

On a national scale, Frank Newport from the Gallup organization reported that "more than 9 in ten Americans still say 'yes' when asked the basic question 'Do you believe in God?'; this is down only slightly from the 1940s, when

Gallup first asked this question" (Gallup 2011). However, for the purposes of this study it should be remembered that our coresearchers were not asked a question that used the word *God* or asked about attitudes regarding this subject. Consequently, there do not seem to be any significant implications in the divide between those who used the term and those who did not, because who can say if they believe in God anyway and didn't say it?

However, the use of the term indicated that somehow the connection between God and sport is significant, although there is little discussion regarding the subject. One author who does discuss this is Dr. Susan Sing, who holds a doctorate in sport history and philosophy from the University of Pennsylvania. As a former member of the US World rowing team, she has personal experience of elite sports in action and later wrote a book called *Spirituality of sport*. Sing (2004) described sport through the lens of her own religious beliefs and spoke about her relationship with God and sport:

> God can be experienced as the master artist who extends Herculean levels of spirit into vessels that come—either by force, as in injury or ordainment, or by birthright—as inheritors of the spirit of God, familiar enough and comfortable enough to play at the feet of their father Abba, as children and heirs.
>
> (p. 65)

Interestingly, Sing was comfortable relating to the Greeks as well as her traditional religious perspectives and this study shall do the same.

Synthia Sydnor (2011) referred to the work and thoughts of the recently deceased Catholic Pope John Paul II, who was a major force in the Catholic Church. Like Camus, he was serious about soccer and had also been a goalkeeper in his youth in Poland. He was naturally interested in the relationship of the church with sports, and possibilities for a general emancipation of the sexes through competitive recreation. Sydnor wrote about his relationship to sport in her essay "Sport, Femininity and the Promises of the Theology of the Body." She recounted a favorable view of the Pope's attempts to broaden the discourse between church and sport, which, since the rise of Christianity and the fall of the Romans had become distanced. Pope John Paul II tried to ameliorate this shortfall by founding commissions and church bodies that tried to bridge the gap. "In what he did say specifically about sport, Pope John Paul II comes to have a sophisticated understanding of sport as possessing cultural, transformational qualities" (p. 70). Like Camus, Pope John Paul II had experienced his soccer first-hand and held no attachments to culturally imposed ideas about gender and sports like soccer. He believed that sport embodied a value and essence universally appreciated for its own sake.

Sing (2004) suggested that beyond religious affiliation, sport has a dynamic that transcends exterior affiliations and speaks to the deeper senses and expressions of the soul.

Once you experience the soul within you and its spiritual orientation acting as guide for the body's course, you can't ignore it. You don't have to believe it, in the sense of having faith, because it does not require your faith in it to exist.

(p. 80)

Sing (2004) also suggested that something beyond our normal experience, a universal archetypal force is in motion. Pope John Paul II's interest perhaps represented the high water mark for the Catholic Church and its strained relationship with sport. Sydnor remarked that "John Paul's idea is not a falsity of personhood, but a gift of true self. No matter one's state of (dis)ability, fitness or intellect, the person's existence is 'legitimate and charged with meaning'" (p. 88). Thus far, the identifications that our coresearchers have given have indicated deeper forces at play that defy narrow interpretations or marginalization through gender identifications.

From the data gathered so far, it appears that play and prayer are related activities, in that they are ideally singular pursuits. The aim of any performer is to be focused on the activity at hand, a kind of devotion to duty. The Danish author Tor Norretranders (1991) in *The user illusion* remarked, "it is not only at work and at home that we can feel great pleasure being at one with what we do. Religious practitioners have always talked of such feelings" (p. 267). Psychologist Mihaly Csikszentmihalyi (1990) suggested that humans on a broader level are at their happiest when they are in a state of flow, or what he refers to as *focused attention*. Perhaps Csikszentmihalyi has been the most successful in articulating a lexicon for states that are beyond the quantifiable. Research suggests that there is a common language expressed in spirituality that may be more difficult to articulate in the masculine world of sports. However, these forces are at play whether recognized or not.

The sports psychologist Mark Nesti (2010) noted that cultures in English soccer clubs, at least, have a division of labor with regard to the mind and soul, but also hinted at their mutuality.

Sports psychologists share a personal identity with chaplains, again, irrespective of their own attitude towards religion and belief. Players in particular will tend to see similarities between chaplains and sports psychologists; one deal with the soul, one with the mind.

(p. 175)

Is this a symptom of the modern mind-body-spirit split that the aikido master and journalist George Leonard (2001) related? Leonard suggested that this split was a problem for modern athletes and wider society in general. Nesti (2010) recognized this problem of the split between soul and mind and suggested that sports psychologists can become separated from some important sources of education and influence. The idea implicit in this modern division of labor is that the soul is divorced from sport and that the two can live in separate domains, while psychology remains absent and seemingly unable or unwilling to engage the subject of soul. Nesti suggested, "One of the best ways to address this is for sports psychologists to engage in extensive reading on philosophy and ethics" (p. 152). But what exactly did he mean by ethics and philosophy? His call sounds more like a wish for a return to the wisdom of the elders. This would perhaps explain why Karen Armstrong (2005) noted that "the shaman after all, worked with the hunters." In light of this it is perhaps understandable why my clinical depth background has dovetailed so easily into professional soccer culture. Evidence suggests that there is a role for the science of clinical psychology in that further acknowledgement of the soul may help reach the sport and the individuals concerned.

Was working with a shaman a pragmatic, early method for hunters to keep in touch with their soul? Author and analyst Andrew Cooper pointed out that the shortfall of the split is that it is not a good idea for the player or the culture. "Ironically, focusing just on what a player does and neglecting his or her inner experience may hinder the attainment of the highest levels of performance" (p. 31). This could be said of the culture of coaching staff, but not in this instance of our coresearchers, who all spoke of interior feelings and numinous ideas that related to the soul. Should the coaches catch up by looking backwards at how our ancestors lived? Earlier, we looked at the work of the chief coach of the LA Lakers Phil Jackson (1995). Jackson had much success using totems and Native American symbols and ideologies. He seems to have realized the power of combining spirit and sports, but ultimately it has to be the players that embrace it.

As mentioned previously, Jung (1964) said of early peoples that they "assume that a man has a 'bush soul' as well as his own, and that this bush soul is incarnate in a wild animal" (p. 6). This study has explored the Greeks and their impressions on the soul, but can we go back further? Natural sciences such as astrophysics, geology, cosmology, archeology, and biology, to name a few, rely on rewinding the clock to see where humans come from and what conditions existed before now. Understanding the past has always held significance for the humanities as well as science and it is surely legitimate that this study can also look back in time, beyond the Greeks, to see what can be found to inform our study.

What is the oldest known lineage that can be found? Recent DNA evidence suggested that the peoples of the Kalahari are the oldest peoples on Earth and that all of humanity descended from them. In 2011, Brenna Henn and Professor Marcus Feldman from Stanford University conducted DNA sampling research from all over Africa, which indicated that southern Africa was the most likely origin of modern humans (Ravindran, 2012, online). Separate research by Professor Sarah Tishkoff, a geneticist at the University of Pennsylvania, also indicates the Kalahari regions and Namibia as the oldest peoples we can trace using current understandings on DNA. In 2009, Tishkoff won the 2009

National Institutes of Health's Pioneer Award for her work on the origins of our ancestors through DNA analysis. She trekked on foot through Namibia, much as van der Post did, sometimes relying only on batteries to power testing machinery. In the *New York Times*, Nicholas Wade (2009) wrote about Tishkoff's research:

> The origin of a species is generally taken to be the place where its individuals show the greatest genetic diversity. For humans, when the new African data is combined with DNA information from the rest of the world, this spot lies on the coast of southwest Africa near the Kalahari Desert.
>
> (para. 5)

Evidence is now mounting that the lineage of the Bushmen of the Kalahari goes as far back as any peoples we know about on Earth. Fortuitously, one of the best illustrations of the Kalahari soul and spiritual philosophy is at hand in a book mentioned earlier; van der Post's *The heart of the hunter,* published in 1961. This study suggests that Greek culture and its subtle influence is still very much with us today. But what can the Kalahari and van der Post tell us about the Greek gods which relate to present day gods. A depth reading of van der Post's book reveals mythological stories that have subsequently informed this study.

Laurens van der Post was a recognized authority on the peoples of the Kalahari, and was also mentor for a time in Africa to a young Prince Charles, the next King of England. Van der Post (1961) dedicated his book "to Carl Gustav Jung, for many reasons but in particular because of his great love of Africa and reverence for the life of its aboriginal children." Jung, like van der Post, was interested in the soul of man, which he discovered in the Kalahari. Van der Post recounted an ancient myth that he was told by the Kalahari Bushmen called "The Young Man and the Lion." Interestingly, we saw earlier that professional player Steve Claridge was described (Claridge & Ridley, 1997) as having "the heart of a lion." Kalahari mythology and folklore were centered around the "Mantis," a being notably absent from this particular myth of the Lion and the Hunter, "implying this is a part of creation that man must take upon himself alone" (p. 253). The absence of the Mantis signified to the Bushmen the universality and importance of the message behind the myth.

Van der Post (1961) said the lion was seen by the Bushmen as the king of the plains. All other animals have limitations, for example, an elephant has poor eyesight, but the Bushmen recognized that the lion had strengths in abundance and in all respects. A lion was therefore divine in stature, and was also crucially, by nature, an individual. Van der Post recounted how it was a given truth for the Bushmen that the lion is an unpredictable and very dangerous animal to even attempt to predict. The myth of the Lion and the Hunter tells how a young man "from the early race" (p. 253), fell asleep while out hunting, and a lion, on the way to drink at the river, discovered him. Kalahari folklore believed that hunters could be become hypnotized by animals, seducing them into a trance. The greater the trance, the greater the animal and the greater the danger. In this myth, the lion discovers the young sleeping man and drags him up into a tree so that he can drink at the river before eating the man later. Despite being in great pain, the hunter now feigns death, so the lion will not kill him. Awkwardly stuck in the tree, his back is in great pain, and he cries tears, which the lion notices and licks away, before it goes to drink at the river.

The sharing of tears was a crucial element for the Bushmen, which meant that the hunter and the lion were now forever united, for good or bad. The young hunter escapes and runs back to the village and begs villagers, who are relieved to see him but also now frightened, to wrap him in animal skins to hide his scent. The lion tracks down the hunter and denies the villagers' attempts to save the hunter. The lion tells them that nature must take its course and they eventually have to disown the boy, acknowledging that their own survival is dependent on a harmonious relationship with nature. They knew that to withhold the young man was wrong and that the laws of nature had to be obeyed or they would all be destroyed. The hunter is killed by the lion, and then the lion, in turn, offers itself to the villagers, and is killed by them.

The Bushmen believed that the myth symbolized the importance of an individual not hiding within the community, but meeting his (or her?) obligations to meet our animal selves.

> There are matters wherein you cannot hide forever behind the attitude of the community and yourself. Nature demands in its supreme expression that it should be lived individually. You must not, therefore, fall asleep on the way to the waters of life.
>
> (van der Post, 1961, p. 257)

"The Young Man and the Lion" is possibly as ancient a myth as we can find, although we cannot know for sure how old it is. Even the Bushmen describe it as from the "early peoples" who came before them. However, we can identify themes within this story and relate them to current issues and dilemmas for our young coresearchers. They, too, have to deal with the issues of individuation; they are part of a community but cannot hide within it. They, too, have to somehow connect to their more natural spirits as the Bushmen insisted must be the case, by obeying the lion and giving him the young man. The inner animal helper is not a new idea to religion or depth psychology. Marie von Franz (1974) wrote on the subject:

> the animal plays this way and that, from an ethical standpoint, but if you go against it you are lost. This would mean that obedience to one's most basic inner being, one's instinctual inner being, is one thing that is more essential than anything else. In all nations and in all fairy tales material I have never found a different statement.
>
> (p. 146)

Part of my work is running process groups at a clinic with some disturbed patients. We meet as a group three times per week for an hour and a half, and my role is to facilitate the process of this meeting as a clinical depth practitioner. Around the same time that I read about the myth of the Lion and the Hunter, one of my clients was having a hard time staying awake in any session he attended, and the myth was used as a fitting illustration of the danger he was in from a pathology that could dispense with his life as readily as the lion did in the myth. As with the lion, if treatment does not help to "wake up" patients, they may pay with their life; they cannot hide from themselves forever.

The coresearchers are public performers, who are expected to succeed and play well in order to survive in the team. As the Kalahari myth suggests, they have to somehow simultaneously come out of themselves to become individuals and be part of a team. Perhaps this can also be seen as an illustration of a universal archetype and function of religious practice in that the process of individuation is sought by the coresearchers and they naturally seek to attach ideas of God and the numinous to the playing of their sport.

Theme 3: Achievement and initiation

This theme emerged from a question relating to "an achievement that stood out in your life." Although there was no mention of soccer in the question, all coresearchers related a soccer achievement of their lives. Perhaps the most significant factor in this answer set was the sense of induction or a sense of initiation as five of our coresearchers described this kind of experience as an achievement—a first goal, a debut, or being the youngest player. From what they said, the achievement that stood out seemed to have a capacity to move them to another place, perhaps socially in some way or internally. In this context, it does appear that our coresearchers were relating to some kind of initiation in that significant change occurred for the individual that related to identity.

At present, the Western world is perhaps distinct in the fact that young people do not have any defined rituals of initiation. Other cultures have long-standing, formalized ceremonies for their young people, for example, the Jewish bar mitzvah. But this is curiously absent in the West, beyond passing a driving test, going to college, or being old enough to join the army, smoke, or drink alcohol. Initiation as a ritual may not be a universal expression today, but anthropological research suggests that initiation was an important cultural rite of passage for most, if not all, of our ancestors.

Earlier, Erich Neumann's (1954) work *The origins and history of consciousness* was discussed. Neumann believed that initiation relates to the earliest origins and a reverence for the founding spirits of life.

> The spiritual collective as we find it in all initiations and all secret societies, sects, mysteries, and religions is essentially masculine and, despite its

communal character, essentially individual in the sense that each man is initiated as an individual and undergoes a unique experience that stamps his individuality.

(p. 146)

Neumann spoke also of a *stamp*, which rings true with how male coresearchers referred to the meaning of their greatest achievement. Andrew said of his debut at the Galaxy academy, "one of the things that I could check it off, say that I did it."

The professional interviewees from the Youth Soccer Show were asked about a favorite memory from their earlier career: "I would think that my favorite youth soccer memory would probably be when my youth team won the state cup for the first time" (USYSS, 2012, Howard Interview). Hercules Gomez recalled how he played in senior teams when he was young:

> My favorite memory from youth soccer would be playing club soccer when I was growing up. ...My junior year I went to the Sun bowl and we ended up winning the tournament and I got MVP (Most Voted Player) for that tournament so that was probably one of the most special memories.
>
> (USYSS, 2012, Gomez Interview)

Gomez then spoke about another opportunity that he had, later in life: he played in the World Cup™. Like the Olympics, the World Cup™ is the premier soccer competition in the world, held every four years. A World Cup™ appearance was defined by all of the professional players interviewed on the Youth Soccer Show as their most significant achievement. Dempsey (USYSS, 2012, Dempsey Interview) said of his relationship to the event:

> My coolest experience in soccer on the field was being able to accomplish your dream. You know I was a young kid playing in the World Cup and being able to score a goal and being able to do that and accomplish your dream as a kid I think it brings to fulfillment and it brings you that little bit of peace. So that's probably the coolest thing.

Our young coresearchers have much progress to make if they are to achieve the same standard as the professionals interviewed on the show and they will have to make substantial progress to achieve the status of being a World Cup™ player. For soccer players, and indeed for many performers, each new level reached can be like a new kind of initiation. What about our coresearchers, did they regard a debut for a professional team an initiation? Andrew certainly did, calling his debut in the academy as a "benchmark" in his life. If things go well for our coresearchers, perhaps the same might happen with their first international soccer match or in an important final. This initiation experience is surely common, for example, when someone gets a new job, promotion, academic degree or qualification.

In *The history of myth*, Armstrong (2005) discussed the caves of Almeria, Spain, and Lascaux in France as possible sites where initiations were performed. She proposed that tunnels were adopted by early peoples for the purpose of initiation and the painted murals of animals were part of this purpose. Armstrong suggests that initiates were led into the caves, and then shown the paintings of animals and the ancestors. Should this idea be correct, it is natural to assume that for a young person the images revealed by torchlight must have been awe-inspiring. After seeing the murals and then performing some other kind of ritual, Armstrong suggests the initiate would be returned through the tunnel back to the outside, being re-born as adults or perhaps hunters. Even though in the West, formal initiation ceremonies might not exist, there is an argument to say that in the modern age, the experience has not gone away entirely. It is still common, although more subtle, for example, for men and women work in teams but candidates must go through a job interview to get approval and acceptance to become inducted into the organization. Closer to home, psychotherapists often have to go through many ordeals in order to initiate a practice, pass examinations, and become professionals. As with the initiates of Almeria and Lascaux, soccer players pass through a tunnel to reach the pitch, into applause and adoration of the fans.

Landon Donovan is an unusual player because he publicly endorses meditation, and we are fortunate to have his reflections on his experiences. Donovan described a time in his career that bears all the hallmarks of an initiation, even though it came after he was a well-established player:

> My favorite was probably my first World Cup game in South Korea, walking down the tunnel before we played Portugal, and just realizing at that moment, seeing my whole youth soccer days flash before my eyes, and realizing how much I put in to get there, and how lucky I was to be there. And to take it all in and enjoy it was awesome.
>
> (USYSS, 2012, Donovan Interview)

Consistently throughout the London 2012 Olympics, events replicated the images of birth, beginnings and initiations. One case in point was when international soccer player David Beckham—who was born in East London, near to the site of the Olympic stadium—was given the crucial task of delivering the Olympic flame to the stadium so that the Olympic flame, the sign and symbol of life for the Games could be lit. This is no small responsibility given that the flame had travelled around the world to reach its final destination. Travelling up the Thames by speedboat, Beckham finished the flame's journey by delicately navigating the craft up a small canal. The care of the flame could only be given to one of England's favorite sons who would deliver it into the stadium where it would ignite the circle—a central symbol of the Games.

When the Games ended, the flame was transferred to a torch, this circle of fire in London was allowed to die, and the flame began its next journey around the world to Brazil. Similarly, coresearchers emphasized the importance of initiation as if it were a kind of conversion or maturation into another identity or form. Their statements indicated that having reached this new stage, they regarded themselves in a new light. Neumann is cited above, defining initiation as needing to be part of a "unique experience," something accorded with a "stamp" or perhaps, in the case of the Olympics, further recognized with a medal and a place on the podium. For London 2012, a group of teenagers were finally handed the torch to ignite the eternal flame. They represented the next generation of initiates into the athletic tradition.

Immediately after the eternal flame is lit, every Olympic ceremony enters a new phase. The teams from all over the world process into the stadium and are introduced to the crowd and assembled dignitaries. Significantly, those who partake in the ceremony are always entitled to call themselves "Olympians," as a recognition of their new status. In London 2012, after the athletes were introduced, a dramatic show began and a drum roll heralded a more Dionysian flavor to the proceedings. The Queen's humorous entrance from the sky was an illustration of the importance of this Dionysian element of drama and spontaneity, all created within the framework of Apollonian timing and precision in order to make it all run well. Being Dionysian in a public setting requires a lot of precision—so why was it done here?

Kast (1991) suggested that Dionysian festivals were intimately connected to ideas of life and death: "Dionysus is the symbol of indestructible life" (p. 116). This does resonate with the feelings expressed by our coresearchers, who related playing well to feelings of omnipotence and unstoppable force. Kast distinguished Dionysus as a spirit central to the psyche. Kast also cites Plotinus who "spoke of ecstasy as the exit from individuality into an intoxicating fusion. Not only do individuals find accord with each other, but human beings find accord with nature as well" (p. 127). As described earlier, soccer is a sport where interconnectivity is a crucial factor in the ability to play. Finding accord with each other is a core skill in competitive soccer that every individual needs to accomplish in order to do well and our coresearchers didn't hold back on speaking about it. During Beckham's journey along the Thames, the flame was carried by a young "maiden" who stood at the bow of the speedboat, facing forward. In this moment Beckham was the Apollonian figure, a man known for his accuracy in scoring goals from the dead ball; the maiden's safety was entrusted to him. There was a sense of speed, élan, and urgency behind the situation. Would such trust have been given to a wilder, Dionysian figure? Guthrie (1955) wrote in *The Greeks and their gods*: "Dionysus, by the license of which his cult bestows on women is a subverter of the marriage-tie" (p. 159). Beckham was the safe choice for the task, and only when the life blood had been passed on via the divine spark could the fun of the ceremony begin, a more jovial moment.

Other options were available for delivering the flame—there is no reason that instead a candle could have gently delivered the flame to the stadium by horse and cart, steered by an old Dickensian figure, who perhaps stops off en route to have a cup of tea. Equally English but would it have had the same effect? The London 2012 ceremony was styled by a dramatist, Danny Boyle. Remembering that the Greeks used the same term for actors and athletes—*agonistes*—they would surely have understood why Boyle was chosen for the job. Connections to Greek gods were evident throughout the ceremony, and were played out by contemporary personalities who embodied the sense of the occasion. As Sing (2004) pointed out earlier, you do not have to believe in faith to experience it, and so perhaps, humans do not always have to be aware of deeper symbolic archetypal representations to be able to enjoy the feeling and join in the spirit of them.

Our coresearchers too must live a life of initiation: they are reborn in the stadium every game, and they must take the concomitant risks of winning and losing, which they compare to life and death. Our coresearchers have to seek life and some kind of spirit in order to live for another day, to get a chance to play in the big leagues. For their stadium matches, coresearchers wait on the sidelines for their names to be announced, with flourish, their previous clubs and experience described as they enter the field. At this level, our coresearchers are trying to get to the next level, the desire for an initiation into a bigger, better family is a crucial element of their experience. Coresearchers struggle with the reality that sooner or later they will have to find a new *supra family* if they are to succeed. The times when this happened were so deeply felt that they related initiation as critical factors related to who or what they are in the world, and what they have to offer.

When describing initiation, coresearchers expressed ideas related to a kind of conversion. This was the changing of form, morphing into a new being, an experience and longing which may be familiar to us all. In *Awakening the hero within*, Carol Pearson describes a more contemporary, broader sense of initiation: "In modern life we may experience initiation through love initially as sexual passion and later by experiencing a passionate connection (with our work, with God, with a cause or an idea), by experiencing divine redemptive love, or by experiencing a profound inner union in love which brings the dispersed parts of the psyche together" (1991, p. 4). Pearson implies that amidst the inner dialogue that can make up the psyche, there is a thirst for union with ourselves and a chance to be able to live again. None of the coresearchers attached ideas of exclusion or alienation to initiation, rather they attached ideas of conversion and a new, better union. The combination of the archetypal contradictory spirits of Dionysus and Apollo sparks new beginnings and new life: soccer players must train, both precision and spontaneity are required. This combination is the challenge they must overcome to be granted new initiations.

Theme 4: Dreams of growth and finishing

The data from this section asked a question about personal achievement, and then a supplementary question about the personal significance of the achievement. The second question relating to significance was designed to catch a more internally reflective perspective. This following section will explore the differences in the answer sets and some perspectives on why the data contained gender differences regarding achievements. The female coresearchers tended to relate achievement in terms of inner growth and development. Jane spoke of "things" and "the work I put in paid off in the end," Carly said she "realized a lot of things," and Diane spoke of "five or six years work" coming together in the end, and Gabrielle described a "sense of pride." The female coresearchers appeared to distinguish themselves by being more insightful than male coresearchers about their achievements and goals. The male coresearchers offered answer sets which had a different sense of discernment. It feels stereotypical to suggest that women are more in tune with their feelings, but if we look back through history, we see that even the Greeks might have had the same sense. Women held the important role of *pythia*, or oracle at Delphi, interpreting and intuiting messages from the gods. In the context of the study, the female coresearchers did appear more intuitive and self-searching when confronted with failure and challenge, which may illustrate one reason why the Greeks chose women to perform this task.

Jamal said immediately "before then I was always coming close," lamenting that "I just wasn't finishing." In *Sport and spirituality* Gardiner (2011) noted, "we humans, it seems, naturally 'benchmark' ourselves. We play a game against another person or team, not just as a barrier to overcome, but so as to know, by comparison, how clever, how excellent we really are" (Ed, Preece, & Hess, 2011, p. 133). As discussed in the previous section, male coresearchers in particular said that they had changed as a result; a new status had been achieved. The subject of *other* came into the frame in this section. Kevin said directly, "I was able to prove to them and myself that I was able to overcome many difficulties." The female coresearchers did not mention the *other* at all, as if the significance of the event was a personal one, whereas the male coresearchers inferred that the importance of the event was not only for them, but was significant in terms of their relationship, or status, in relation to other people. This does not necessarily imply that the relationship to others is not important for the female coresearchers, but it does indicate that male coresearchers were sensitive to this, and for them the implications are not just personal, but are emphasized in relation to others.

Earlier in the study, it was discussed how Neumann (1954) believed that initiation was a "masculine" (p. 146) tradition. Indeed, male coresearchers in the study did indicate that they felt a desire to prove themselves to others in some way, whereas female coresearchers tended to relate this in regard to each other. The evidence suggested that finishing, one of the aims of the sport, was more important to our male coresearchers than to female coresearchers. However, our male coresearchers did distinguish themselves in that they spoke of finishing and their relationship to the *other*. Neumann explained his masculine perspective:

> This is not to say that the matriarchate knows no law; but the law by which it is informed is the law of instinct, of unconscious, natural functioning, and this law subserves the propagation, preservation, and evolution of the species rather than the development of a single individual.
>
> (p. 147)

This may well be a fitting support for the explanation as to why the achievements were no less for the female coresearchers but the significance was of a different order to the male coresearchers. Males perhaps have different pressures to visibly distinguish themselves in some way, to each other, in wider spheres. Looking at this through an anthropological lens, it is plausible to suggest that males seeking status would once have had to demonstrate an ability to hunt and kill something, to see it through, in order to be regarded as a peer. To this day, the business term *to make a killing* is perhaps an echo of our ancestors' past priorities that are no longer a reality, namely the need to go out and hunt. Although needs have changed for our coresearchers in the twenty-first century, it is notable that in this study, success for the female coresearchers was about internal growth, but for the male coresearchers it was about finishing. These needs may have long histories and our young researchers may represent ancient archetypal realties, which have been issues for young men and women for millennia.

Theme 5: Parents as heroes

All coresearchers named a member of their immediate family as a hero. Was this something they thought they ought to say? The coresearchers certainly appeared to speak with sincerity when they spoke of their family members in these terms. Jane, Oscar, and Andrew all named professional soccer players as an initial response, but then went on to describe parents as their heroes. Andrew, for example, mentioned a soccer hero first, but then qualified it with "my biggest heroes are my parents." What is a hero? The following section will discuss the historical antecedents regarding heroes, including the anti-hero and the differences between the two. Current cultural ideas about what constitutes a hero will be explored, and if that has changed over time.

Historical antecedents

Today, we are perhaps very familiar with the idea of a hero: soccer players, historical figures, and film stars all fit the category. In the US, the term is also used to describe troops based in a foreign war. But for the Greeks, the idea of a hero was very different, according to Jungian author on sport Andrew Cooper. Certainly for the Greeks, the status of hero was reserved for the Pantheon. Remembering his interview with the Jungian analyst Tom Singer, Cooper wrote that in earliest Greece, a person "could not be considered a hero until after death, when that heroic energy went into the society's store of ancestral blessings. Heroic energy was an impersonal force, what we would call archetypal" (1998, p. 65). However, in discussing their heroes, our modern coresearchers related the theme of home and named their parents, all of whom were very much alive. Many coresearchers then spoke in grateful terms about the chance they have to play soccer, offering thanks and praise to their parents. Some then spoke of sacrifices their parents had made and the coresearchers' constant awareness of that fact.

Susan Sing (2004) also spoke of heroes and sacrifice:

> When we are sacrificing, offering ourselves for the greater good, the outcome, the finish line—we have broken the barrier of fear, gone through the limit of self and embody creaturehood, gratitude, and humility. This is when champions become heroes. We all have them; some may not look athletic at all as they age. But the heart within them is tangible and infectious. It makes us seek them out so we can be around it.
>
> (p. 88)

Heroes that are in some way life affirming are being alluded to here, and not in the sense of heroes portrayed by the media in the world of sport, celebrity culture, fantasy, and films. Our coresearchers identified heroes who need not be champions on the field, but who represent those qualities in the expression of their lives and what they had given to them.

Norretranders (1991) traced the earliest-known hero back to Greek mythology. Erich Neumann's (1954) interpretation of the *Odyssey* was that the myth represented a testament to the birth of consciousness for modern humans as we know it today. He related that Homer's creation of the *Odyssey* happened at a crucial turning point in the development of the human brain. Likewise, American historian Morris Berman wrote extensively on the significance of the *Odyssey* as a story that related heavily to the psyche of modern humans. Believing that the story related to the fate of Odysseus as a hero, in *Coming to our senses*, Berman (1989) suggested:

> Again and again, Odysseus experiences the enormous pull of the great unconscious, undifferentiated female power, the desire to melt or merge back into it, to go unconscious, as he once was a very young infant or fetus. But what makes him a hero is that he refuses that option.
>
> (p. 239)

Berman concluded that the killing of the Cyclops in the end was representative of the symbolic victory of intuitive understanding. He believed that the heroic journey is the battle between opposing forces of the soul, and that the power of differentiation is the saving factor, a theme that remains with modern humans today. In *The heart of a hunter,* van der Post described his friend Tom Hardbattle, who he regarded to be heroic. Along with many other soldiers of the Second World War, Hardbattle returned to the desert to live and be around the Bushmen of the Kalahari. Hardbattle formed relationships with tribal peoples in the Kalahari, and resided in many villages throughout the year, and van der Post (1961), said of him:

> There is deep in him a sense of heroic quest; and our modern way of life, with its emphasis on security, its distrust of the unknown and its elevation of collective values, has repressed the heroic impulse to such a degree that may produce the most dangerous consequences.
>
> (p. 81)

While the playing of sports may be a "heroic" struggle by athletes to transcend themselves above the forces of death and darkness, it is played out in a game. Individuals in the wider world, engaged in the same heroic battle for transcendence, may not be so lucky. The nature of the anti-hero and unconscious predator will be explored at the end of the chapter.

Our coresearchers constellated their answers about their heroes around the family. Coresearchers did not appear to select any particular gender for the honor of hero. At the same time, male soccer heroes were a predominant factor, in that only males were identified by coresearchers. If we think about status in the soccer world, the coresearchers' choices were male. Outside of the world of soccer, it may have been reasonable to assume that there would be a majority of male archetypes identified, or deeper identifications with the masculine. To follow more stereotypical cultural norms, most heroes in public culture appear to be male and a predominance may be expected. However, the data did not indicate this; coresearchers offered no gender or even age-specific qualities and all age groups were offered as heroes.

Three male coresearchers identified male professional soccer players, whereas only one female coresearcher did, and he was also male. Realistically speaking, soccer is a far more viable possibility for our male coresearchers, who can aspire to the organized professional league MLS, whereas the female coresearchers have less identifiable or widely publicized models. For this reason, it is difficult to speculate about the deeper meanings concerning selection of heroes outside of the family. However, the female coresearchers were no different from the males in that they named their parents and siblings as their selection as fitting for the title of hero. That family is the source of soccer for our players, and that it is a source of their heroes, too, appears to be significant.

The identification with parents and family seems to be a central part of the coresearchers' overall experience. Whatever the Greeks felt about the place for heroes, our coresearchers identify with positive figures at home. However, as van der Post (1961) pointed out previously, our modern twenty-first century mindsets, cut off from the heroic possibilities, cannot shield us from the realities of the psyche and the realities of becoming an individual. Perhaps technology might one day find a way to raise a child on the Internet, but it is likely that questions of self can only be resolved in the wider world by actual experience and the myths of Kalahari Bushmen would suggest that you cannot hide in the community forever. Being public performers, however, our coresearchers' quests, to some extent certainly, have to be based out of the home. It is on the field where they must face and overcome themselves as much as any opponent.

The anti-hero and hero

In order to catch a sense of the hero, it is perhaps required of the author to explore its *shadow* side, the anti-hero. In 2012, a neuroscience student James Holmes shot and killed 12 people, mostly the very young, at a cinema in Aurora, Colorado. It appears that the choice of the film for his crime was not coincidental. The murders were committed during a screening of the 2012 Batman film, *The Dark Knight Rises,* directed by Christopher Nolan. The film was a customary archetypal narrative about the dark *shadow* side of the soul and its battle against evil and darkness. Even though he was perhaps familiar with the structure of the brain, it seems Holmes' mind and soul collapsed into the mad realm of the possessed. In court, Holmes appearance—wild tousled red hair—made him look like a mad Dionysus, perhaps fitting for his wild rampage. As Kast warned us, we cannot identify with the gods: "Only as much of the Dionysian spirit should enter into consciousness as can be appropriated by the Apollonian power of clarification" (1991, p. 128). Robert Johnson, the Jungian author and analyst, spoke of the dangers of ignoring or colliding with the undifferentiated unconscious, "more people have sunk after collisions with the unconscious than Titanics' after collisions with Icebergs" (1986, p. 8).

This is the realm of the anti-hero, a *shadow* archetype perhaps enhanced by an age that concentrates on the mechanistic side of the human psyche and denies or mistrusts the deeper soul. Cooper (1998) remarked that "while we may ignore the gods, they do not ignore us. Forced from our world the numina have retreated underground to the unconscious" (p. 57). Perhaps the heroic quest in the ethic and codes expressed by our coresearchers is the same as related by Odysseus. They too must overcome their self-centered impulses and join with the team while remaining in touch with their soul and sense of self. Van der Post (1961), Kast (1991), and Johnson (1986) join with Cooper (1998) in warning about the potential for danger in those conditions where self-centeredness appears to collapse in on itself. Perhaps what most clearly distinguishes the hero is that he or she has to return, or give something back, whereas the anti-hero always appears only to take away.

Theme 6: The unstoppable body, elevation and descent

In response to being asked about the experience of playing well, seven out of eight coresearchers described feelings of elevation and freedom, whereas the experience of playing badly was described in terms of descending and thinking too much. Beyond their immediate identifications in the wider world, coresearchers were asked about their experiences when playing the game. Universal expressions were related in the transcripts which might be illuminating as to the nature of what archetypal forces are being experienced. So far ethics, the role of family, and the place of the hero have been highlighted as significant by our coresearchers, but what of their own inner sensations and experiences? As players, our coresearchers are placed in an ever-changing environment where they must somehow deal with the unpredictability of actions as they unfold. In this way we can see soccer as a kind of chaos. "Chaos, as undifferentiated, *massa confusa*, is usually that reality out of which a new form or organization is seen to arise, or more accurately, is crafted." (Goodchild, 2001, p. 204) Could it be that if they don't play the game the game will play them?

The highs

Earlier Andrew Cooper (1998) related an interview he had with comparative mythologist Joseph Campbell, who described to Cooper his past experience of running in races. Campbell described a moment when he was racing and losing, and then despite being behind, Campbell "describes an exhilarating moment in which he was seized by an irrational certainty that he simply could not be beaten. And sure enough he was right" (p. 30). Our coresearchers also described these kinds of feelings: Diane related that "at that time nothing could go wrong," and Jamal said, "I feel like I can do everything right, not just think about it." Is this just an inflated state of omnipotence? If it is, considering the favorable sporting results that tend to come from this state, perhaps it is a good fit? Evidence suggests that a deeper sense and expression are in motion. Sing (2004) related her own view:

> I see sport as a communion, a sacramentality in several layers. Certainly effort is a communion singularly or as a group to become something greater than what was. And in this quest for transformation we participate in the liturgy. We are the liturgy in that we seek to lift up and elevate our broken selves in order to become something greater, or at least be accepted in union with something greater.
>
> (p. 64)

Where is this something greater? Why is it always up? Will it always be elusive? Where does it live? What can modern science contribute to this idea of the deeper layers that Sing reported as critical to the experience of elite performance? The German phenomenological psychologist Ludwig Binswanger was a contemporary and colleague of Freud and Jung, and he was interested in all forms of mania and tried to interpret these forces. In 1960, he published *Melancholie und manie*, a study of heightened emotions and mania in the psyche. He was curious as to why there has to be an inevitable arrest of the senses at some point, and why what goes up must come down. He might have appreciated coresearcher Andrew's sense of caution, saying that he didn't want to go "too high." Binswanger (1960) suggested that human beings live on a vertical as well as a horizontal plane. There was a relationship with how high we could safely go and how far we have gone on the horizontal plane in life, which would relate to experience. Experience can also be gained through insight and reflection for human beings, which can help us satisfy our longings to be high and keep going.

However, like Icarus, we run the possibility of losing our judgment and flying too high, melting the glue that keeps our wings intact. Something becomes disconnected and disjointed in the psyche, and maintaining the appropriate relationship between the up and the down is a crucial skill and capability, that presumably needs to be learned. Daedelus made wings for Icarus, and Daedelus knew the strategy, suggested by Clint Dempsey and others in the study, not to "get too high." The suggestion is that individuals do not become too inflated or become lost in a state of mania. The advice is that they remain in touch with themselves and on the path of safety.

Psychologist Cardwell C. Nuckols (2010) has written extensively on the relationship between addictions and the workings of the soul. In his book *The ego-less self,* Nuckols stated:

> so as the self emerges, we see higher and higher levels of consciousness prevailing. Going back to the mountain metaphor, it makes sense that, as we climb higher and higher, everything becomes clearer. We can see farther, understand better, and are not limited to just a narrow view of what is happening around us. We can see the interrelatedness of things and how nothing really stands by itself.
>
> (p. 211)

Nuckols wasn't writing about soccer players, but our coresearchers might relate this to the experience of when they play well. The author and psychologist Sian Beilock wrote extensively about the experiences of playing poorly under pressure at the wrong moments and stated, "people choke under pressure because they worry" (p. 183). Yet again we are presented with "worry," where can it be found and can it be mastered?

I and Me

In *The user illusion,* Tor Norretranders (1991) referred to the work of Australian psychologists Taylor and McCloskey (1990), who published research on human reaction times entitled "Triggering of Preprogrammed Movements as Reactions to Masked Stimuli." Taylor and McCloskey were able to demonstrate the existence of a subconscious mechanism that enables subliminal perception. The results proved that we can react to a stimuli and not be conscious of it, or rather that a mechanism in the brain actually exists that is separate and autonomous. Norretranders (1991) amplified this research and suggested that evidence now defines the existence of an *I* and the distinct and deeper part of us *Me.* Norretranders tied together findings of modern science and related insights that seem to speak to Jung's (1964) "bush soul," Maier's (1931) experiment with swinging ropes, and Gladwell's (2005) "locked room."

According to Norretranders (1991), the *I* is concerned with traditional ideas of the *ego*, thoughts that are more self-conscious, echoing Beilock's (2010) idea about worry that she calls *choking*. Norretranders suggested these thoughts are often defined by ideas of ourselves in regard to others. The *Me,* however, is a deeper part of our psychic structure, and a system in itself. Put simply, the idea is that our more self-consciousness inner voice vies with a deeper sensing side of us; the *Me*. Norretranders suggests that for an individual to grow and develop, the *I* must learn to trust the *Me* (p. 253).

It is curious that many philosophical thinkers and religious figures express so much interest in soccer and sporting traditions. In 1992, Denmark won the European Championships in soccer, and Norretranders (1991) is no different than Camus or Pope John Paul II in expressing an interest and identification with soccer. Although Norretranders reveals that one of his country's great scientific figures, Niels Bohr (1885-1962), had a penchant for spaghetti westerns, Norretranders did not mention, when describing the *I* and the *Me,* that Bohr was also interested in soccer and at one time nearly played for Denmark as a goalkeeper.

Perhaps many would-be modern-day philosophers are goalkeepers. Norretranders (1991) uses soccer examples on the field to illustrate his points to do with the mind, suggesting in one instance that "soccer players are not conscious while they are playing. But nobody who plays the game would claim that a superb, original mental process does not take place." He then went on to say, "except that is, in unique situations where there is time to think things over. And where things go wrong as a result" (p. 253). Jane described the experience of playing badly as a state where you "talk to yourself a lot mentally." Jamal said, "it kind of puts me in a bad mood and it kind of makes me initially worse." Practitioners of meditation often report the Buddhist notion of the "monkey mind." This animal representation of a system of the mind seems to haunt many young people. For the Buddhists this mind state is characterized by internal chatter and an inability to be still.

We have already mentioned Malcolm Gladwell's (2005) "locked room," and Gladwell's recounting of the work of Norman Maier (1974) and his study with swinging ropes in 1931. This experiment also suggested that an active deeper thinking part of the mind was in action even without the person knowing it. This is the place beyond our conscious decision-making mind, which athletes need to access in order to play to their potential. Our coresearchers clearly indicated that they aspired to reach conditions and states within themselves that would produce good results. The author and editor of *Sport and spirituality*, Gordon Preece (2012) quoted a conversation with basketball player Melissa King, who said:

> I've played because, when the game is good, when everyone is doing, not thinking, it happens, little stillnesses in the moments when you see your open man and nothing else, or you feel your shot going in the hoop as it leaves your hands, or you share a laugh with someone you've never spoken to. Race, money, gender, age, they're still there. But the junk we're all saddled with is gone.

> (Preece & Hess, p. 35)

The "junk" she is referring to may be a reference to all those daily conscious concerns and insecurities in life, and her view of a space where we are beyond or above ourselves. Csikszentmihalyi's (1990) concept of *flow* also comes to mind here.

Investigation of the subject does reveal that the transcendent function is particularly relevant to sport and the expression of competitive excellence. This study will hold a space for the unconscious side of the work during the Alchemical Reflections section, a reflective diary of my own experience conducting the study, attempting our own fusion, inspired by the work of Robert Romanyshyn. In *The wounded researcher*, Romanyshyn (2007) suggested that Plotinus believed that Platonic forms need more explanation and that diversity can be explained by its unity. Romanyshyn described his views on Plotinus: "The principle states, 'all knowing comes by likeness' and the method is one of 'reversion,' which is 'the idea that all things desire to return to the archetypal origins of which they are copies and from which they proceed" (p. 47). This may also resonate with Edward Tylor, cited earlier, who asserted that we all carry forward and inherit certain earlier formed traits and instincts that he called "survivals."

But what of *reversion*? To what, or by what, are we being pulled, as Romanyshyn suggested above? In 1976, Julian Jaynes, a Princeton University professor, was interested in the early developments of the human mind. He wrote *The Origin of consciousness and the breakdown of the bicameral mind*. It was his belief that consciousness as we know it is only 3,000 years old. "If our research has been correct, it is perfectly possible that there could have existed a race of men who spoke, judged, reasoned, solved problems, indeed do most of the things we do, but were not conscious of it at all" (p. 17). The implicit idea is that the time of the writing of Homer's *Odyssey* was also a turning point for humanity and that humans began to have a new sense of self-consciousness, which in turn would influence the systems of society.

Norretranders (1991), when discussing the work of Jaynes, remarked that Christianity reflected this by being monotheistic: "For the really huge difference between polytheism and monotheism is not so much superstition, hallucinations, or rain dancing: The big difference is the perception of who the real executor of human action is" (p. 214). It seems fitting that the Greeks felt that our personal results come from a force acting through us, as Plotinus referred to earlier. Camus was also interested in the expression of the soul in all its forms, resisting outside influences and seeking a more complete, honest human expression. For Camus and the existentialists, we have all been corrupted by our governments and institutions to some degree and we have lost part of our soul. Plato also was perhaps referring to this in *Apology* with his admiration for the poet.

The Greeks appeared very conscious of the capacity of sport to access other states, a state where the gods could speak through selected humans. But who are these gods? What can knowing more about them speak to this state of ecstasy that our coresearchers described? Of all our coresearchers, Diane had the most to say on this theme, relating the experience of playing well as:

> almost like a kind of a high, like adrenaline junkies will search for that, it's a high once you have it, you crave it, you get motivated to practice every day to go out and do your best, because the feeling after a game is almost indescribable.

Certainly my clinical experiences can testify that that heroin junkies will indeed often go out at any hour of the day or night to find their next high. Hillman (1982) joined Novak (1993), Leonard (2001) and Cousineau (2003) in the idea that the modern age has split us away from earlier important archetypes embodied by the Greeks through mythology, religion, and sport. That our coresearchers seem to be suggesting senses and drives that relate to these gods indicates the power of the archetypes whether they are seen, called or not.

Norretranders (1991) remarked that practice and technical development is the route to getting the "*I* to trust the *Me*" (p. 254). He argued that the *Me* is the one that experiences the experience, and the *I* takes the credit, meaning that our self in relation the "the other." Norretranders' idea is that a kind of Freudian *Superego* appears to be at work, derailing the potential for the *Me* with what he calls the "conscious veto," the rejection or repression of the *Me*. Diane is not a heroin addict, but by default used an analogy to a significant modern issue and social problem for young people, the junkie. But how can this "high" feeling in sports be intoxication like that experience of a heroin junkie? Or is this the natural state of ecstasy that the Greeks well understood, and referred to when they spoke of ecstatic, exuberant gods like Dionysus and the dithyramb? Norretranders suggested that the *Me* has to be set free by the *I*, but this is a risk:

> When we go to our soccer club, or our on the field of play, our *I* has made the decision to put the person into the situation in which the *I* has no say at all. We long for this experience of the now. We spent much of our spare time pursuing it, in sports, dancing, playing games, intense conversation, sex, and intoxication.
>
> (p. 263)

But where is the *I* to be found? In 1935, Roger Wolcott Sperry graduated in English from Oberlin College in Ohio where he was the basketball captain and a passionate sportsman, also taking part in varsity football and track events. In 1981, he won the Nobel Prize for medicine for his work identifying the functions of the right and left brain. His work proved that both hemispheres work closely together, but are also to some extent separate entities each with their own systems of consciousness, echoing Norretranders and his *Me*. Put simply, the left brain system is related to language and more logical, mathematical kinds of problems and is unable to effectively manage the more spatial tasks the brain must carry out, such as playing in a soccer match. Coresearchers reported that an inner kind of talking occurred during times of bad play, and Sperry's work would indicate that for a soccer player, a capacity to stop or reduce the left brain's more self-conscious kinds of thinking patterns is important. The nature of the task of soccer is predominantly a right-brain activity, involving a need for agile perceptions in judging distances. Spatial skills are required to judge ellipses of the ball in motion, as well as the inter-relationship with other members of the team, as well as opponents. There is a demand literally to let go and play, and a performer seems to need the skill of utilizing the right brain while reducing the functioning and call of the left brain. It is not that these functions are not required, but perhaps more they are inflated or become disorganized.

Ascribing functional areas of the brain as locations where the processing of information can take place can be misleading. Evidence suggests that in children, if a hemisphere has to be removed in surgery, they will develop left and right brain functioning anyway. Jung also was interested in the way the brain has certain functions as a way of perceiving the world. On a superficial level, his four functions of sensing, thinking, feeling and intuition can be discerned in soccer. Anyone associated with the competitive game understands on a conscious or unconscious level that the "feelings" of an individual cannot take priority over decisions concerning the team. This means that decisions or selections will be made by a coach or manager irrespective of how someone "feels" about it. The priority for selection is performance, and a special condition for this *supra family*. Therefore those who get their feelings hurt, and become upset, often tend not to thrive in such environments if they cannot overcome these feelings somehow.

I have heard it said that life is not an intellectual exercise in that we cannot only "think" our way through life, but we also have to "feel" our way. Many clinical patients are tormented by their fate, they are very clever in an academic sense, but emotionally they are constricted, blocked and often suicidal. The dominant thinker type may not find much use for "thinking about things" in the playing of soccer, an environment where it would seem that actions speak louder than words or thoughts. As for Jung's sensing function, players do indeed require an enhanced sense of the ever-changing space around them. Likewise, the intuitive function plays a role in soccer although to my knowledge this topic has never been explored. Having an insight into what is about to happen may be a crucial skill that a player may master over years of experience. Intuition and sensing appear to be the most influential and relevant functions in soccer, compared to thinker or feeler types. Hall & Nordby (1973) describe how Jung labeled thinking and feeling as the *rational* functions, countering them with their opposite functions sensing and intuiting, describing them as *irrational* functions (p. 99). "Jung does not mean by irrational that which is contrary to reason. They are nonrational and nonjudgmental" (p. 99). This echoed Gadamers' (1980) earlier assertion that logic is a "detour."

Having the benefit of Roger Sperry's discoveries in 1981, we can now correlate them to Jung's ideas about rational and irrational functions and see they are to some extent sympathetic. As rationality has been linked to the left brain, alternatively, sensing and intuition can be appropriately regarded as a process involving right-brain activity. Jung also suggested that concerning the four types, individuals will have strengths and weaknesses, with one function being regarded as inferior. Certainly, if everyone has an inferior function, then for soccer players inferior sensing or intuitive functions may put them at some disadvantage. Conversely, there are other fields where the rational functions predominate and intuition or sensing is downplayed or disregarded. The accusation of people involved in psychology being "nerdy" may be unfair, but perhaps it is a reflection of reality and another reason why philosophy and sports have divided in the modern age in the way they have.

The research indicates that a capacity to leave internal chatter behind and enter into another state is a goal shared by many people, including soccer players and followers of religion. The coresearcher Diane said that during this time "you feel like on top of the world." The author Verena Kast (1991) spoke also of elevation and intoxication through ecstasy, where

> by overcoming gravity, we are lifted above the anxiety and pressure of daily life, to where we can gain an overall view of things, a higher insight. Apparently it is a human need to overcome gravity. This mild form of mania bordering on ecstasy—what I am calling joy—is sought by fasting, meditation, intoxication, drugs, and other ways.
>
> (p. 104)

From what our coresearchers suggested, senses of elevation and happiness seem to be states that go together. A function and purpose for attaining such states could be that the brain operates more effectively during certain tasks during these states. In *Your brain at work*, author David Rock (2009) remarked that "increasing happiness increases the likelihood of insight, while increasing anxiety decreases the likelihood of insight" (p. 81). Our coresearchers appear to be accessing, in the playing of soccer, a function of the brain that perhaps is not a modern incarnation, something familiar is happening, speaking as it does to so many people around the world.

Whatever is happening by achieving these higher states, it is becoming a bigger business by the day. Sing's (2004) suggestion that "when a human being is elevated for a moment to the heights of the gods, the audience wants to know" (p. 29) speaks to that intrinsic interest the public has in performers carrying out these plays before us in sport. Considering that the potential and actual audiences for soccer are growing exponentially, this appears to be an accurate idea (*Telegraph Sport*, 2012). Later in the Discussion section, the recent work of Andrew Samuels (2012) and the relationship of the audience to the player will be discussed. While the desire to "get high" is a boon in soccer, for the rest of the population it can be deadly. This is perhaps the *shadow* side of getting high. For example, the sad reality for many heroin addicts is that the temporary elevation and "fix" produces little joy over long-term use and is so very often fatal. Heroin has a close relative in the also abused and dangerous drug morphine. Both are named after the Greek gods representing the induced state of mind they embody. Morphine, stems from *mort*, the French word for death, is often used to relieve pain in people who have been grievously (and thus fatally) injured, but unfortunately many young people also die by abusing morphine as a prescription painkiller.

Greek gods and the embodiment of soccer

Morpheus was the Greek god of dreams and is traditionally represented with wings. Morpheus was primarily concerned with the human element in dreams. His brothers were Phobetor, who related to the animals within a dream and Phantasos, who was concerned with inanimate objects. The experience of heroin may well be like a dream, but for heroin addicts their dreams are mostly broken by the drug. The Kalahari Bushmen suggest that we keep in touch with the animal side within us and perhaps the same idea was true for the Greeks with Phobetor and the animal spirits. Conversely, in my practice, new clients who are in the grip of heroin addiction are rarely animated. Addiction to heroin or pain-killers are national issues, separate from the wider world of addiction to prescription drugs. Apart from the criminalization of many people, heroin use creates a morbid culture and death is often the fate for an addict. In my experience, many addicts live like soldiers, who lose friends all of the time. Fortunately our coresearchers remain able to access this high state by playing soccer on the field. Our coresearchers suggested that something is gained in this particular fix that they can keep in a positive way, and not become jeopardized or lost in the compulsive, moribund world of addiction. Our coresearchers described unstoppable, exuberant feelings, and a high that many people in wider society die trying to reach, reporting what seems to be a battle between the heights of emotion and the depths of despair. As described earlier, Dionysus was the god of fertility, ecstasy, wildness, and creativity. Dionysus has consistently appeared as a fitting archetypal force that our players attempt to embody, representing spontaneous creativity, power, and a chance to become high whilst remaining indestructible. But what does this say for our female coresearchers? Even with his undoubted feminine qualities, Dionysus is a male god, so how can he wholly be a representation for the expression of womanhood? Earlier in this chapter, it was noted that in this study soccer did not appear to have a direct gender identification. If the female coresearchers represented or embodied Dionysus, then as post feminists might correctly suggest, are female coresearchers just attempting to be male? But so far, there has been evidence that female coresearchers own this archetype in relation to themselves, not as a copy of the men—so what now? Our female coresearchers are embodying something in sport that appears to be naturally theirs as much as their male counterparts in the study. Sing (2004) and Sydnor (2011) both suggested that women can own their own sporting archetypes.

Even if Dionysian logic was right for our male coresearchers, is there anyone in the Pantheon for the women to embody? Apollo was also a god of archery, but why should archery be the domain of the male? Apollo's twin sister Artemis was also an archer—a goddess connected to hunting, often depicted with a bow and arrow. Perhaps American Annie Oakley was a good example of a modern incarnation of Artemis. An archer of a kind, she was regarded as one of the greatest sharpshooters. She is not unique, the archetype of the girl master is still with us today. In the London 2012 Olympics US team member Kim Rhode won gold in the shooting competition, but she won her first world championship at the age of 13 and by winning gold in London 2012 she became the first ever American to earn a gold medal in five consecutive Olympics. We also see the girl master archetype on screen—*Brave*, the 2012 Pixar film (Andrews, Chapman, & Purcell) centered around a young Scottish girl, Merida, who was an archer with long flowing red hair. But Artemis is also a measured archetype, offering precision to sport with consummate skill and dexterity. Recently, in a group therapy session I had cause to describe the archetype of Artemis when a client enthusiastically interjected with "that's the Hunger Games!" referring to another film that portrays a heroine who is a skilful archer. And we know that Annie Oakley's powers of precision were better than any man.

If Artemis and Apollo seem well matched, then who is Dionysus' female counterpart? The study needed to find a "wild" woman, and a good candidate would be Cybele, a goddess of the mountains, bears, and hawks. Cybele is an ancient deity, originally from Phrygia in the eighth century BC. Kast (1991) wrote of her, "Cybele was also depicted on a panther cart, and I believe that Dionysus' close relationship with her and with the feminine included his ability to behave like a wildcat" (p. 118). As the early Dionysian female followers demonstrated by worshipping a male god, the gods are for both sexes. It seems reasonable that if depth psychologists worked with female soccer players, we might choose to explore the female gods. As the evidence in the study suggested, the female coresearchers have their own distinct mindsets, delineated by their more intuitive approach to problems and ideas of working together.

The current mayor of London, Boris Johnson, a well-known public figure in Britain, sports tousled white hair, which is to some extent his hallmark. It is perhaps a traditional connection with Dionysus that hair is wild and Johnson is indeed a creative, spontaneous kind of man and politician. There is an unpredictable and often humorous quality to his actions, yet he remains a popular political figure in England. He is also a successful novelist and writer and recently wrote a book called *Johnson's life of London: The people who built the modern world* (2012). The book explored many of the luminaries who have inhabited London. He includes a section about Cybele, and the Magna Marta. Recently, right where David Beckham passed under London Bridge on his speedboat, archeologists discovered "a fearful set of serrated forceps" (p. 20) dedicated to Cybele by the current church of the Magna Marta. Earlier we explored the central women's-only festival of Dionysus. Perhaps, then, it is natural that followers of Cybele were male, and it appears that some at least castrated themselves, which would certainly have been of interest to Freudian scholars. In fact, Freud himself may have known about this kind of self-castration that appears to have reached London. Cybele is a powerful deity, embodying the spirit of animals and the wild.

Is the art of soccer as simple as forming a balance between the Apollonian and Artemesian traditions of measure and the wilder spirit of Dionysus or Cybele? Hillman (1983) took issue with this idea in that "Dionysus has been written off, or adulterated, for his hysteria. He has come to mean simply the opposite of Apollo" (p. 37). Hillman believed that to understand either archetype, it was better not to regard them as a simple polarity, but to consider the purpose and the logic of the state, in particular Dionysus, who represents life forces and creativity.

Neumann (1954) also wrote about Cybele, also known as the Alma Mater or Great Mother, in *Origins and history of the unconscious*, suggesting that the figure signifies an important function of the psyche. The purpose of consciousness, for Neumann, is to ward off the threat of an enveloping unconscious and to resist the primal destructive forces inherent in the psychic structure of the mind. He related that "the psychic structure of the mind builds an active element of defense against the unconscious and against the danger of being overpowered by it" (p. 327). Neumann attributed the text below in his book to Sabrina Spielrein's 1912 essay: "Destruktion als Ursuche des Werdens" or "Destruction as the Cause of Coming Into Being" (1912/1994). Spielrein, a contemporary and colleague of both Jung and Freud, was interested in the pull of the underworld in the "death complex" Thanatos. Although a century old, her ideas reflect and resonate with many of the life and death aspects apparent within soccer archetypal forces that our coresearchers face. Coresearcher Diane spoke of dying if she didn't rely on her teammates. Neumann (1954) remarked:

> The uroboric tendency of the unconscious to reabsorb all its products, by destroying them so as to give them back in new, changed form is repeated on the higher plane of the ego consciousness. Here too the analytical process precedes the synthesis, and differentiation is the prime requisite for a later integration.
>
> (p. 327)

The "later integration" referred to here is perhaps best interpreted as the need to carry on, and go out again, as all our earliest ancestors must have had to do. Soccer players in a club do have to do this. Our player coresearchers strove to achieve these higher planes of consciousness, but like Icarus, they had to return back to Earth, the pull is so great. Significantly, the Middle English word *desporten* comes from the Latin *des porto*, to carry away. These are indeed the sensations and experiences our coresearchers reported. They also related experiencing states of ecstasy, sensing unstoppable forces at work within them. Perhaps it is the strict set of rules in the game of soccer that provides the container within which these archetypes can safely play out. Yet this raises questions about Gardiner's (2011) ideas of adults representing and replaying childhood roles on the field. Could it be that soccer is a representation of an adult game of letting go, ascending and then coming back down to earth?

This sense of a world where we have to leave ourselves and return by entering into the spirit of sport is described by Cooper (1998) as something with a powerful, archetypal draw on the psyche. In conversation with the Jungian analyst Tom Singer he explained:

> The primal pull is great, but one can connect with the powerful energies sport unleashes without losing oneself in them. One can participate in the workings of potent symbols without literalizing them. In so doing, that border-line realm between jest and earnest—the home ground of both sport and myth—is maintained and nurtured.
>
> (p. 67)

Perhaps this mutuality and connection Singer described between sport and myth can help explain how the Queen was willing to become involved with the acting in the Olympics in London 2012. As described earlier the Greeks used the term *agonistes*, referring to the mutual name the performers held in both the fields of acting and sport. This is a borderline realm, according to Cooper (1998), and many of our coresearchers and other authors were unable to describe their experience in words. Jane didn't "know how to explain" and Diane revealed that "the feeling after a game is almost indescribable." Gabrielle described an immersion, saying she is "light" and "it's easier to breathe." The male coresearchers didn't speak of indescribable emotions as the female coresearchers did. However, there appeared no disparity in the direction: upwards.

Hillman (1983) felt that there is a distinct logic and purpose to the Dionysian archetype that our players report a desire to embody. He noted that:

> this means the dream is not a coded message at all, but a display, a *Schau*, in which the dreamer himself plays a part or is in the audience, and thus always involved. No wonder that Aristotle placed psychotherapy (catharsis) in the context of theatre. Our lives are the enactment of our dreams, our case histories are from the very beginning.
>
> (p. 38)

Our coresearchers spoke of beginnings freely and concerned themselves with an expression of an archetype that humans are drawn toward. "If the structure of Dionysian logic is drama, the particular embodiment of Dionysian logic is the actor" (Hillman, p. 38). For example, my background is in live professional acting, and here I am working in the sports world. There is a hinterland realm we can recognize where the actor or the athlete must become part of a show, and as a result, they constantly play out treading a fine line between success and disaster.

The findings described above suggested that the rise of Christianity and the modern creation of consciousness have to some extent, split the conscious aspect of the psyche away from the body. What about the desire our coresearchers express to heal the mind body-spirit-split that remains? Something has not changed, that is, the desire to reach a higher place of inner unity amongst our coresearchers. Irrespective of our modern culture, and the standard of our current conscious relationship to our *Me's*, our coresearchers expressed a desire to heal this split and play the game like the gods. Can we find ways, as depth psychologists, to help these players and others understand our splits, and develop a language that is mutual and can help them find a way to trust their *Me's*?

Theme 7: Dreams of giving back

Coresearchers were asked to speak about a dream they had for their lives. This was the section where female coresearchers used the word *success* in a generalized way, which will also be explored in the Alchemical Reflections section below. The male coresearchers identified a professional career in soccer as an option for them. As outlined earlier, the significance of this in terms of this study may be limited here in that the male coresearchers have much more chance of having a professional career than the female coresearchers. Therefore this will not reflect as much of what is happening on the inside, rather than what is happening in the outside world. However, the male coresearchers did speak about *giving back* while the female coresearchers did not use the term. Why is this happening? What implications does this infer for the psyches of our coresearchers and the game?

Andrew wanted to give back to the whole world, Oscar saw himself "hopefully giving back to my family," and Jamal saw himself "being able to give my family and the people who have supported and loved me something back what they deserve." Kevin, who spoke the least of anyone, said he had a "passion for athletes," and wanted to be involved in some kind of medical support for them. Diane also wanted to be in a medical field, and Gabrielle wanted to be an elementary school teacher, which also involves "giving back." The emphasis of *giving back* for the males was also reflected by Clint Dempsey who said he was conscious of the "three hour drive" his parents made for him, "so to be able to pay my family back, my parents for those drives back and forth to Dallas and stuff like that. You know it makes me feel good. Being able to give them a better lifestyle to what I had when I was growing up, and make sure that they can be comfortable, is what it's all about" (USYSS, 2012, Dempsey Interview).

The theme conjured up many more stereotypical ideas and expectations regarding gender and roles. For the male coresearchers, giving back seemed to suggest the ethos of needing to "bring home the bacon." This is a cultural expectation that is associated with men by societies' norms, in that males are the "breadwinners." In the same way that a soccer career is more accessible to the male coresearchers, it is also the chance to give something back. However, as we shall see later in the study "the other" is a significant factor that distinguished male coresearchers from their female counterparts. Therefore, this answer set could reflect the male coresearchers' priorities in terms of being seen to be a provider and a giver, rather than the more generic theme of *success*, which the female coresearchers indicated. Female coresearchers are of course also naturally givers and providers, but the male coresearchers' responses indicated they were more conscious of what this means to others. This could also equally relate to cultural values, norms and expectations.

The pull of the heroic impulse or at least identification with it seemed to be a commonly-reported idea that all of the coresearchers were able to identify and speak about. As indicated earlier Neumann (1954) appreciated the primal pull of the unconscious forces he called "The World Parents and the Hero Myth, the latter stage being formally contained in the former." (p. 315) It is curious that Neumann placed the Hero as central in the human drama, as our coresearchers did when they named their parents as natural heroes. The spirit of family and children is so often represented in soccer and sport, symbolizing that something here ultimately needs to be preserved and protected from darker forces, for example, illustrated by the presence of a protective flock of Mary Poppins in the opening ceremony of London 2012.

The heroic function and archetype may speak to this psychic need, priority, and central theme. Jung remarked:

> In the visions the saints behold the sun of this power, the plenitude of its light. According to the old view, the soul itself is this power; in the idea of the soul's immortality there is implicit its conservation, and in the Buddhist and primitive notion of metempsychosis – transmission of the souls – is implicit its unlimited changeability together with its constant preservation.
>
> (p. 70)

Coresearchers naturally constellated notions of heroes, family and giving back, all of them set in a world of unlimited changeability, which is the nature of the game. This ever-changing nature may require the presence and psychic need for a heroic archetype to withstand the risks and pain involved with psychic death and defeat. It is perhaps natural then, that our coresearchers looked to home for the source of their heroes on Earth, because, of course, their lives originated there and to them their parents represent the ultimate givers of life, and of sacrifice they reported.

Theme 8: Team as a supra family and assistors

All eight coresearchers reported that a soccer team is like a family, a relationship which earlier evidence suggested did not conflict with their own affiliations with family. As a result, this implies a kind of *supra family*. All eight coresearchers qualified this idea by referring to the team as a source of assistance, support, and learning. *Supra* is a prefix defined by *Webster's dictionary* as being "'over' 'above' or 'beyond' or 'above'" or "beyond the limits of, outside of" (Bridgeman, Cummings, & Goez 1975, p. 1171). This section will explore the connections between family, soccer and the purposes and functions of the family archetype in a competitive environment.

The term *supra family* is not a new one for clinical psychology. In their book *Marital family systems,* Glick, Berman, and Clarkin (2000) define a *supra family* where "a blended family is occurring and children have new aunts and uncles who also have input into the family" (p. 96). In the current research, the notion of *supra family* seems appropriate for the coresearchers' descriptions, especially considering the answers given by them relating to team as a family, while obviously maintaining their own family of origin as a central motif. Perhaps a coach is like a new uncle with an input into the family. Certainly for younger students of the game, the role of the coach as an intermediary between the family and their new "family" is a crucial relationship. Curiously, our coresearchers did not speak often of their coaches, but the relationship is significant and perhaps suitable for further research.

The Jungian analyst and author Lionel Corbett noted that modern society is virtually falling in on itself, spiritually speaking, "given our essential unity, our contemporary Western cultural attitudes must be seen as spiritually unhealthy to the extent that they value individual achievement at the expense of the collective" (2007, p. 105). Corbett suggested that modern culture is in danger of inverted priorities that threaten the whole. However, our coresearchers expressed an ethos that might contradict this observation, or what any outside observer might expect to find in a competitive culture like soccer. Ideas of togetherness and fidelity were very present for our coresearchers and the professionals interviewed, perhaps resonating with older cultural approaches that remain with us today.

In 2007, Matt Pain and Chris Harwood conducted a qualitative analysis of the England soccer youth team cultures across age ranges, interviewing coaches and staff also attached to the team. The analysis researched what players saw as positive and negative experiences in their experience as soccer players. They found that "Of the 155 factors listed as impacting performance, team cohesion clearly emerged as the most frequently cited positive factor. On the negative side psychologically, player anxiety was most frequently cited" (p. 1316). Unity, it seems, is not just a pragmatic idea that can help with a team's efficiency; as with the coresearchers in this study. Players report that cohesion in a group provides a source of practical relief from stress in and of itself. In 2009, Pain and Harwood conducted more research, initiating team meetings where open and supportive sharing could occur. It became an effective strategy, rated by the players as helpful for overall performance: "Players reported improvements in cohesion, trust and confidence in teammates, training quality, self understanding, player ownership and team performance" (p. 523).

Sports psychologists such as Pain and Harwood (2007; 2009) are beginning to demonstrate the value of interconnectedness and making connections with each other. The author Guy Claxton asserted that this is a representation of a past imperative, also a blueprint of the human psyche. In his book *The wayward mind: An intimate history of the unconscious*, Claxton (2005) discussed some of the recent findings in neuroscience and the implications they present for current understandings of the brain. "Both evolutionary psychology and neuroscience are revealing that earlier conceptions and metaphors for the brain have been widely oversimplified" (p. 252). As observed earlier with the results of children who have brain surgery, he went on to suggest that the brain defies being "dismantled" and regarding it as separate parts is erroneous. He remarked "the brain is not like a clock, or any other kind of mechanism. It is a system, that evolved, and now functions, second by second, all of a piece. It is like a football team. 'Manchester United' cannot be boiled down to eleven individuals" (p. 252). Indeed, according to the *Daily Telegraph* (2012) Manchester United is in fact 659 million individuals. Our coresearchers suggested that there is an imperative for the team system to function properly in an interdependent way, the *supra family*, much in the same way the brain works itself.

The male or female coresearchers did not appear to differ in their expressions of fidelity and what they receive or expect from membership on the team. Jamal said "yes, I think it is exactly like being in a family, sometimes more like my own family." Jane related "on the field you automatically become a family." Diane had the most to tell about this subject, "it's all about building each other up, keeping each other together because we're all in it together, it's a team thing that's more of a family than anything else I've experienced before outside of my own family." Oscar said "every time I see them, I feel as if they are all part of me and that they've left something in me that I continue to use on and off the field." Our coresearchers indicated that *supra family* relationships can be as intense, and even greater in some respects than in their original family. This may explain why coresearchers described the family as more like a family than their own family.

The evidence indicates an ancient constellation of values are being expressed in this setting that relate to an older purpose and need. When describing "teams" that arose in the tribal conditions of our ancestors Erich Neumann (1954) suggested that:

> the formation of a group is thus dependent on the existence of *participation mystique* between its members, upon unconscious processes whose emotional significance we have already discussed. Symptomatic of this situation is, for instance, the fact that the group members call themselves brothers and sisters, and so by analogy reproduce the original family group where these ties are taken for granted.
>
> (p. 421)

Coresearchers consistently referred to the team as brothers or sisters. Fundamental to this study was the theme that the family of players our coresearchers play with, are there to help, there to assist in times of trouble, reflecting the mystical participation Neumann described.

The family of origin might be conventionally understood as an environment of learning lessons that a child can successfully take into the outside world. On the US *Youth Soccer Show,* goalkeeper Tim Howard spoke about the broader life skills that he feels are crucial to the doing or playing of the sport, as well as a potential benefit gained from the playing of soccer:

> Soccer has helped me develop as a person because it's taught me a lot of life lessons. It's taught me how to be competitive, how to play fair, it's taught me a lot of discipline, and certainly as I have gotten older I've learned how to handle myself professionally on and off the field, and a lot of those lessons come from the game itself.
>
> (USYSS, 2012, Howard Interview)

Hercules Gomez echoed this in his interview.

> I think playing soccer is helped me a lot, you learn a lot from playing
> soccer you learn how to be competitive, you make a good leader you learn
> character you learn sacrifice you learn things in general wouldn't necessarily
> learn in other places, you wouldn't get the chance. And it doesn't matter
> from where you come from principles apply, and if you like to or not you
> learn them.
>
> (USYSS, 2012, Gomez Interview)

Gomez implied that by participating in soccer you have to learn lessons "if you
like to or not." It seems that the purpose of ethics may be deeper than just
being nice to each other. Gomez also implied that they are not negotiable. The
implication is that, by default, playing of soccer recreates or represents other
issues that are present in life outside of the game. Clint Dempsey is no different
than the others in his perspectives:

> I think sports, especially soccer prepares you for life really because you
> have the ups and downs and you have to be able to battle through the
> good and the bad times because when things are good you might get on
> too much of a high and you know when things are bad you get too low.
> So it keeps you grounded, focused and you know it's like a roller coaster
> that's going to have its ups and downs but you got to stay level-headed and
> keep working hard and things will work out.
>
> (USYSS, 2012, Dempsey Interview)

Dempsey mirrored Binswanger's (1960) and coresearcher Andrew's concerns
by relating the necessity of the "even keel" in not going too high or low.
Landon Donovan also suggested in the show that being on a soccer team is an
experience which has a value that is universally useful:

> While doing this competitively and for a living I think it helps us a lot, as
> people I think. A lot of people say that athletes in general make good very
> good people in the workplace once they're done with their careers.
> Because they're obviously very determined for the most part, very hard
> workers and we are very dedicated to what we do. We work well in team
> environment so we make other people better. And the lessons that you
> learn naturally, without thinking about it, by being part of a team and
> doing this for a living.
>
> (USYSS, 2012, Donovan Interview)

Donovan implied that good people help others improve. Certainly the
traditions of love, ethics, and sharing seem to be self-evident in soccer, and

identifications with family are codified throughout the game. So do our coresearchers confirm that this *supra family* is a mirror and reflection of a family?

An important truth about soccer and all competitive team sport might be overlooked by the assumptions implicit in the aforementioned questions. In the competitive world, the reality of a team is that it cannot be a family in a traditional sense. Our coresearchers cannot escape the fact that their membership and selection is based on performance. As soon as a player is not competent enough, the necessities of the team will outweigh any considerations for them and they will be replaced. It is not unreasonable to assume that our coresearchers live with this reality as much as the professionals of soccer do.

It is normally the case that within only a few years the personnel playing on the field in a club can radically change. Our coresearchers, as well as the academy players in London, only have three or four years to prove themselves. But even they will be asked to leave before then if they fall below certain standards. What kind of family is that? Families are usually "for life," so what can be happening here? Does a family abandon its child if it is not good enough? If we look back, the family was not guaranteed to survive for many of our ancestors. The reality may be that *supra families* are omnipresent in many other guises, most often represented by employment in companies, employment in a small business must feel very similar to being in a soccer team. Many people may have to continually face the trials of adoption and abandonment when seeking a job or being issued with a redundancy notice. Whatever the case elsewhere, the coresearchers express a desire to be a family and at the same time deal with the *shadow* side of that, abandonment, if you are not good enough.

The latest research studies of soccer players in England have produced some unexpected results. In their article "The rocky road to the top" Collins and MacNamara (2012) discovered that there are important links to past trauma and achievement. The big surprise for many was that those with past trauma in their lives were more likely to succeed in the sport. Reasons for this are not conclusive, but the study indicated that a difficult beginning in life might not push an individual off course, especially if they are able to integrate themselves into a *supra* soccer family. Perhaps the importance of family culture that our coresearchers reported may be very appealing to those who have experienced loss of family or trauma. But there is surely nothing new in that. As this study testifies, my past trauma of losing my parents may well have inspired in me a need and drive to be a significant member of a team. But not just any team, the kind of team that has to fight for its life against others, in a league. Our coresearchers overwhelmingly described family kinds of identifications in their team, which may have an impact on and be essential for those without much experience of family.

Recent research from the Trimbos Institute in the Netherlands suggested that being in a team is beneficial in itself for young people. The researchers conducted research in over 7,000 Dutch secondary schools that took part in the 'Health Behaviour in School-Aged Children Survey' known as the HBSC.

Karin Monshouwer reported that "youngsters who were physically inactive were found to be at greater risk of mental health problems such as depressive feelings and anxiety, but also aggressive behaviour" (2012, online). While the physiological effects of exercise are well know, the study implied that self image, friendships and mood were all improved by being in a team. It may be natural to assume that many of the most troubled in our society may have disrupted relationships and no experience of family at home or in the world at large. The horrendous slaughter of the children at Sandy Hook, Connecticut, in December 2012 was committed by a boy who came from a broken home and who had an isolated existence.

Theme 9: Winning and losing, inner doubt, solutions, and shadow language

This *supra family*, if it is a family, seems to be living with the reality of winning and losing as part and parcel of being on the team. Perhaps in the longer term that reality does represent some of the deeper truths behind family life and death. But what about the other reality for a player? The feelings of loss and grieving when things go wrong? Earlier, Cozolino's (2007) ideas about *social death* were discussed, which may explain the need for the protection of the family. This section will explore the attachments and identifications that our coresearchers expressed in regard to this important theme in soccer and in life. The study endeavors to be a witness to the psyche's relationship to darkness, light and the heroic journey. Then perhaps we can catch a glimpse of the historic forces that our coresearchers seek to connect with by wanting to achieve and excel in this sport.

In response to losing, three out of four male coresearchers expressed solutions but did not relate their inner experience. There was also change in the language used by the male coresearchers, which appeared a significant deviation from the rest of the data. America, it is said, "loves a winner." If the family is such a crucial element, presumably our coresearchers want to be loved? Diane spoke again of being "high," getting a "little five that you can feel again and again." Perhaps the feelings of ecstasy may have an element that can stay with a player, encoded in a memory and reusable feeling after the event that Diane called her "little five." Jane said that winning is a "liberation," and Carly remarked it "feels fortunate." Echoing the themes of levity described when playing well, Gabrielle said of winning "you get to celebrate with your family on the field and you just rise up." Likewise, the male coresearchers spoke brightly about the experience, but this time the men spoke of "the other" again. Of the female coresearchers, only Diane and Gabrielle spoke of anyone else in this answer set and they both mentioned "family." Oscar spoke about the different feelings for beating a good team, and Kevin spoke about showing your opponent that "on that day" he can claim to be the better man and be "triumphant."

It does appear from this data that male coresearchers are more conscious of the relationship to the "other." Defeats, dreams, and triumphs impinge on others in a way that did not seem to be true for the female coresearchers. For the female coresearchers, the impact of winning seemed to be more significant in terms of their relationship to each other. While relationships with each other were important for the males, it also seemed that for them, their relationship to *the other* and whatever that may be for them is also a factor. Jamal said that he gets confidence from winning and also gets "an edge." For such an important subject as winning, the data in general did not reveal as much as the data on losing. As could be expected, our coresearchers spoke favorably about the experience of winning, and there were parallels with answers about playing well. The object of the game is to win, and losing can be a dire experience for our coresearchers and everyone who supports a soccer team.

Perhaps Cooper's (1998) earlier criticism of psychology only ever concentrating on pathology may be unsympathetic, in the sense that in this study the most revealing answers came from the experience of defeat and losing. As psychotherapists and depth workers, we perhaps need to understand a patient's painful experience in order to better understand a person. Earlier, we spoke about Homer's *Odyssey*, the importance of the myth and its relationship to the soul and consciousness of modern man. At one point in the myth, the disguised Odysseus is discovered by his scar. Homer implied that we can only know ourselves, or be seen, through our scars. As practitioners of healing, we surely have to be present and be part of the process where patients come to better know themselves. I have noticed that the professional players I work with in England often say to me that they changed most as people during tougher times and not during successful times. Our female coresearchers seemed to take the burden of loss on themselves, whereas the male coresearchers were more likely to make a positive exhortation rather than consider it further. All of the male coresearchers answered the question about losing by eventually offering a positive suggestion or sentiment. Why should they do this? Our female coresearchers seemed more comfortable relating the experience as it was, without a need to change the reality or reinvent the world with another positive exhortation.

There is room here to suggest that the male coresearchers were merely offering sentiments about something I would like to hear. However, it cannot be said that male coresearchers hung back from experiencing and expressing their feelings. Oscar spoke most of all about his experience, beginning with "losing, there are always two sides to it." Oscar further explained: "it just kills me inside," followed by "wasted time" and then "it just feels depressing in a way," all interspersed with sentiments that "you can learn something," and "you've got to focus," as he tried to convey the confusing feelings he experienced. He ended his answer with what seemed like a reflexive attempt to correct himself: "you have to look towards the result in the future and ask what I can do to make that victory in the next game, so it's optimism." It is perhaps easy to minimize the positive exhortations and solutions offered by the males, but at least it seems that alchemically speaking, they are trying to change the chemistry they are presented with, perhaps a kind of soccer philosopher's stone?

When playing badly, only Kevin said he was able to divorce himself from the outcomes and feel fine "as long as I am giving 100 per cent." He said nothing of the inner experience except that he "hate[s] losing, you know I hate to," resorting to the offensive, a wish to play again and "just show them that you can't win this next match, I'll stop you." It felt as if the words that the males used were unique in this section, an expression of the depth of their feelings. Jamal was the only male who did not use acerbic terms, and he described a feeling of "humility" in the face of defeat. In terms of the resultant projective language, the male coresearchers indicated that the experience was difficult to digest. Many of them appeared to latch onto positive sentiments, rather than fully express the feelings. Words that male coresearchers used indicated a wish to expel the experience, sometimes directing their attention immediately to "the other."

Failure is no doubt a bad feeling for a group of soccer players and perhaps for any team that does not achieve its target. Considering the Greek role of the *hermeneuin*, the women who interpreted and mediated the meaning at the oracle of Delphi, discussed previously in the theme dedicated to growth and finishing, it is perhaps not surprising that women appear better able to integrate the experience and speak of self-responsibility first. Although losing was difficult for both genders, female coresearchers appeared to handle it better. Or is this an assumption? Clinical psychology would suggest that integrated emotional states are better, but is this true for the soccer player? Their job is to play soccer. Our male coresearchers always wished to place an emphasis on the positive, mixed with a series of words indicating depression, hatred, and death, such as "it kills me inside." Diane said earlier, "the coach can't be the only person to motivate you or you will die." As described earlier, the battle seems to be with the darker forces of death and aspiring toward the ever present spirit of rebirth, incarnated through their parents and in their sense of family and carrying on together.

The family appears to be the unit that fends off the darker risks of the challenge and shields the coresearchers, as described earlier by Neumann (1954). From what they expressed, the coresearchers appeared to be aware of an inner voice that they could not escape. The men were distinct with their positive exhortations so inextricably woven into their sense of pain. Jung (1934/1991) in *The development of personality* spoke about this issue, and as with the Kalahari peoples, was aware that "to develop personality is a gamble, and the tragedy is the daemon of the inner voice is at once our greatest danger and an indispensible help. It is tragic, but logical, for it is the nature of things to be so" (p. 186).

In the *Wounded researcher,* Romanyshyn (2007) discussed Andrew Samuels' work on the space that is the relationship between therapist and patient, what he refers to as the *mundus imaginalis*. Samuels described the world of the imagination, represented by the analyst themselves and held by the analyst, so that it can be linked up with the analyst and ideally integrated by them. Romanyshyn described how Samuels drew upon the work of Henri Corbin (p. 147) and his work *Mundus imaginalis* published in 1964, in which Corbin explored the transcendental world and its relationship to the psyche. Andrew Samuels is also a passionate soccer supporter and follower. At the Freud Museum analytical conference called *Sport and psychoanalysis* held in London in June 2012, Samuels discussed his sense of the relationship of the audience (known in England as the "crowd") at a soccer game in England. He sees the alchemical process and function of the crowd as a kind of therapist, healing the wounds of the players.

Samuels' current investigations and writings on the subject moves this part of the discussion to a close and to some extent a full circle. However, the final circle shall be reserved for the Conclusion section of this book. Samuels is interested in another intimate aspect of this subject, the supporters of soccer clubs. It is the supporters of a club who fervently chant and sing in support of their heroes, willing them on to victory. Samuels is interested in the chemistry of the interaction and the undoubted effect encouragement can have upon an individual and team. "Specifically, I am saying that crowds manage the physical and above all the psychological process of injury for the players" (A. Samuels, personal communication, September 29 2012).

Romanyshyn (2007) explained that the role of the unconscious and its relationship to the *mundus imaginalis* is a significant space that we can perhaps integrate into this study. He stated:

> In this work, I am extending the range of the transference field as an intermediate landscape to the research process. For the researcher who would keep soul in mind, the work is an in-between. It is a real text within the broader sense of this term within a tradition that stirs the researchers' emotional complexes, and a text with a history carried by "the other" in the work as its unfinished business.
>
> (p. 147)

Romanyshyn (2007) then noted, "these psychological dialogues de-center the researcher's position and invite him or her to listen to the stranger's point of view on the work" (p. 147). Curiously, I had written about a "stranger" in the following section, and then only afterwards discovered this quote by Romanyshyn. In the spirit of this method of working with the unconscious within the subject and study, the discussion will now move into another realm, which will pay attention to the soul of the work, the alchemical relationship and *mundus imaginalis* of the world of soccer, set within the wider world of the inner psyche.

Alchemical reflections

This section aims to contribute to the study with a different approach to the Discussion section of the material, by allowing and regarding the role of my unconscious in the execution of this project. By doing so I shall express myself in a different manner, in that there will be no reliance on empirically qualified or supported statements; instead I will record the highs, lows, and experiences that often accompany any meaningful endeavor. It is the Apollonian traditions that inspire science and wisdom, allowing one to step back and observe the data, rather than getting lost within it. Thus a phenomenological study is by necessity Apollonian, in that we have to step back from the material with *epoche* and simultaneously look at it from a distance and "go inside" of the material. This section will perhaps be more related to the Dionysian approach, which will pay less attention to boundaries and qualification. Here I can at least record some of my feelings and stream of consciousness, with less emphasis on the empirical and more on the sensations and experiences of working with this material. The reason for doing this is that in the midst of so much data, perhaps something new can be found that can help illuminate the research further.

This approach is in keeping with the alchemical hermeneutics work of Robert Romanyshyn, as previously discussed, and his belief that to ignore this aspect would be a detriment to the wholeness of the work. Remembering that in the wider world the ignorance of the unconscious produces "epidemiological violence," for example, in prisons where the very experience of being an inmate in prison makes it much more likely for them to reoffend and be sent back again. I will refrain from alchemical dialogues, but will at least refer to the unconscious through dreams and my experience.

The journey of beginning to explore this topic as a dissertation began four years ago. I could say now that it began 40 years ago probably when I first experienced the game of soccer. It has been a long passage to make some sense of the material and the world our coresearchers inhabit. The relationship to the work has been a journey of commitment that has defied any of my attempts to place a timeline on its completion. If I thought a portion of it would be done in a month, in my experience, it was more likely to be three months. I have been conscious, at times, that what I think of the project is not as important as what the project is telling me. As this section unfolds, I will be referring to the first person, so that the *Me* of this project can be expressed. To maintain any kind of rigorous scientific approach, the phenomenological counsel has been to create a space for *epoche*, in forming a distance between myself and the material. Themes emerged that demanded attention, and some initially defied understanding and comprehension but became clearer after time. The discipline of writing a dissertation worthy of the name is a difficult task, and part of me wanted to speak in different, less precise language. The Apollonian traditions of precision can be side-stepped in this section, and a different response to the material can be expressed.

As I mentioned, this project took time to complete. As it went on, I confess that I suspected that all I was doing was mirroring what I had written in the Introduction. I didn't want this study to be only about hunting and hunters, as I even mentioned in the procedures section, I dismissed any questions in the *epoche* that related to that. I mistrusted my ideas, and had no intention of writing a dissertation that merely confirmed what I thought. Perhaps it is honest to say as well that my relationship to the "other" forbade it. Perhaps it was also that I didn't want it to look like that.

I have worked in soccer cultures for a long time and I am aware that presumption can be a dangerous thing. But in the end, the study seemed to confirm some of my intuition about what was happening with our young coresearchers. My working life seems to center on real life and death in the clinical world and imagined life and death in the world of competitive soccer. My background was in acting, and I knew there was a connection there, although discovering that the Greeks called actors and sports people *agonistes* made me think there was more to the connection than met my eye. People often ask me about the connection between theatre and sports, and I felt I was beginning to have an answer. The legendary actor Richard Burton said that he would have exchanged his career to score a winning try (rugby goal) for Wales.

The first day I began to transcribe the interviews was the day I began the process of teasing out the material, dividing it, and eventually refining it into the meaning units. Initially, I was disappointed. There was no mention of exciting things like devils, spirit guides, ancestor-based ideas, supernatural experiences, alchemical interactions, or even hunting! Even though I had listened to what the coresearchers said in the interviews. I remember reflecting that I felt I wasn't able to listen deeply to them, as I would if they were a clinical patient. Perhaps it was because I was using a recording, I knew the deep listening would take a while to come. My first response to the emerging data was ambivalent. I had no idea that the coresearchers had really said anything at all that could be considered illuminating. I passed through a phase of wondering if I should start all over again, but it was too late.

The references about family did not inspire me. I thought I had collected a set of statements that would leave us all none the wiser. I feared I would be compromised; I would have to somehow weave a blanket out of the material by stretching out connections and meanings out of whole cloth, as it were. I remember sitting in my garden, wondering what had I gotten myself into and how awful it was, and what a mistake that I had chosen the phenomenological path. Frequently at times when I would try to rest a negative fantasy visited me that would make me jump as my nerves recoiled with a kind of terror—I felt there was nothing in this project and I had wasted my time.

Nor did the writing of the transcripts from the audio to the page initially reveal anything to me. I saw no correlations and I discerned nothing that stood out as a theme that offered any mileage to explore. More days of defeat followed, as I worked through the transcripts, seeing it all (on a bad day) as a kind of trial of Sisyphus. The writing of the transcripts felt monotonous and the process seemed endless. I went through each candidate and didn't see anything interesting beyond nice sentiments of togetherness. After advice from my internal reader Karey Pohn, I created a spreadsheet to be able to set the meaning units side by side and get a picture of the whole. "Great, more work to do," I thought. But as I was finishing the transcripts and began creating the spreadsheet, things began to shift. It was at this point that the whole paradigm started to change. Again, particularly at times of rest, phrases or sentiments I had heard and read began to return to me, sometimes small links and connections would become apparent to me that I had previously not seen. Even during my work as a psychotherapist, things clients would say would remind me of a transcript or expression.

The whole process felt like laying out some huge jigsaw puzzle. It had taken many hours, but the contents of the data were finally beginning to sink into my unconscious process. I began to make connections between the material and some deeper expressions. The material was disparate and all over the place, and somehow I had to make some meaning from it all, drawing things together or seeing the distance between the pieces.

But it was still a tiresome task; sometimes I consoled myself by reading rather than converting more data. Curiously, the books that I read also informed my work and eventually became elemental in the Discussion section. On reflection, reading those books was a good idea because the information I often stumbled upon became very useful. It is my best compliment to Hillman that I would read his work in order to rest. I was fortunate that sometimes I just opened a book at the right page and it told me what to say. Hillman's *Healing fictions* (1983) was a good example of this. I didn't expect to find anything for the dissertation in this work, but I find Hillman entertaining and always illuminating. I once had the good fortune to write a play in the same room where he apparently wrote *Re-visioning psychology* at the Eranos Center in Switzerland. Hillman's work on Plotinus began the chain, and I then began to see Plotinus everywhere—in other writings from Kast, Romanyshyn, and Camus! I cannot say I knew anything about Plotinus before the study called him forward. There is the truth of the experience: the gods had to come to me, not I to them. Perhaps the courage to wait is the process of *epoche*.

I remember, one day, staring at a passage spoken by a soccer player when I became conscious of a pause within me. An impression overtook me that I really had heard this before, said by someone else, better still, I had heard this many times. I would return to the spreadsheet and discover more connected statements. Like a stranger, the theme introduced itself to me. For example, the insight that the males were speaking about imitation, the way the women reflected differently about loss, and the *shadow* language of the males. I took the process of *epoche* very seriously, perhaps too seriously, and in relational terms I had separated myself from the project. But I had begun to make some connections in my mind and from that, larger pictures were forming. Forgive the analogy, but I had spent time in the garden digging and in mud but now I was surprised to see green shoots and small flowers emerging. But then the task was not done yet, they still had to be understood and appreciated, so as I could try to discern what they were telling me. Ideas and insights relating to the study were forming and appearing in this manner.

This phase was like a coming together and a happy reunion and I wanted this to be a serious investigation, and I wanted to separate myself as much as I could. I was perhaps overly self-conscious of my experience in the sport—repressing it in this way into the *shadow,* it was denied. Perhaps I even resorted to the *epoche* as the safest place to be, somehow separated from the material but at a cost. Perhaps like the players themselves, I was talking to myself too much, and not really in touch with the life of the project. But this was now a rising phase for me, where I began to see connections in many places. I had intended to cut the two worst answer sets, but in the end after seeking advice from my internal reader, I kept them all. Now, in what seemed like no time at all, there was too much material! I worked on things religiously every day to complete each stage: the transcribed interviews, meaning units, the Individual and the General Situated Structures. Now I was in a kind of obligation, with a kind of optimistic love that I had knocked on the door and someone was answering.

It is now my impression that on reflection, I was simply trying to complete the significant task of organizing so much material and avoiding any interpretation. I had hoped that interpretations would and should come later, but not as they did. I separated the material, attempting a goal for one segment a day. At this time, I learned about the recent DNA evidence linking us all with the Kalahari tribesmen. It was striking to me that of course van der Post or Jung had no idea of this kind of evidence, and I imagine that they would have both been fascinated. This information gave the book *The heart of the hunter* new impetus, so I revisited it and discovered the myth of "The Lion and the Young Man." Van der Post describes the myth beautifully; somehow I had missed it in my first reading, and the timing of my rediscovery of it could not have been better.

The first theme to emerge was like chemistry in motion. I realized that there was no particular gender association with references to family and original interest or inspiration to play soccer. Initially, the coresearchers' talk of family did not inspired me, but now there was something unexpected that I was not able to explain. My cynical side had even concluded that expressions about family were a diversion adopted by interviewees. Family—"the last refuge of the sentimental"—but I was wrong.

I had at one time stared at answer sets and groups of meaning units together not knowing what the coresearchers were telling me. What they did say began to get more and more significant as the study progressed and as I worked through the data. I got the sense of what could be possible as I went through the highs and the lows of the experience. It was only at this stage that I was able to see some lights come on, that stayed on. My dreams began to change, although strange to me, I would often only have statements not recollections of narrative dreams or stories. One morning I wrote "the feminine wants to be united." I went to bed cogitating about what was different about the men and why the material was of a different texture in terms of their dreams for their lives.

Another word, *redaction*, started to haunt me, although I had no idea what it meant. Of course is sounds like reduction, but I thought redaction was a word I had made up. I discovered redaction meant exactly the process that I was working on. It is the idea that by editing and reducing we can approach the purer meanings of things; perhaps Plotinus would have agreed. However, it is a good example of the kinds of processes that were then transpiring inside of me. It seemed that my continual laboring over the editing and refining of the material was producing smaller, more meaningful chunks. I believe, as Romanyshyn suggested, that this project began to own me, and a distinctly unconscious process was in motion. The Excel spreadsheet was a very useful idea, although it involved more labor and learning how to work with the Microsoft software. However, the process of extracting meaning units and placing them side by side further deepened my affinity with the data.

Individual styles of the coresearchers became apparent. I was now so familiar with the content that themes started to emerge on their own. The earlier transcripts in isolation did not really mean much to me, but together they all formed a kind of mosaic, which appeared over the period of the months it took to transcribe and further work on the data. The states of elevation described by the coresearchers were illuminating for me, as I came to understand that the states of ecstasy and joy being described were covered by Verena Kast (1991) so beautifully. Even though I have observed players all my life and now work with them, I had never thought to ask the question what is happening when players play well.

I remember the first time I heard Dr. Romanyshyn speaking about one's own unconscious being in touch with the unconscious of the material. I did not believe that it was really true, or at least thought that "clever idea, but I will never get a sense of it in my own experience." I am a product of the twenty-first century; I know that the unconscious isn't something you will ever get to know. But this is exactly what occurred, and I am very grateful to have had this experience of consciously connecting to the level of *Me* that moves unseen. Perhaps this is what "getting to know yourself better" means.

My dreams began to come to me like lectures. I would wake and write only a statement. I wrote: "women want to work in unison," "you hold the book of power," "Machismo is a masquerade," "love is our eternal protection," and "common sense is an uncommon sense." Occasionally, I would dream and be so confident that I could remember the dream that I did not write anything. Many times I had an expression in my head to write down as I awoke, but I would say to myself that it was so obvious I would remember it, but, of course, I never could. During the writing of the Discussion chapter in particular, some dreams did stay with me in my consciousness and were very vivid. I will include an example of one here that ended up being useful to the process.

In the dream I was on a big ship at sea and there were naval officers everywhere, but it wasn't a military ship. All the naval staff were disparate types, all with different characters and ages. They wore smart uniforms with white piping, almost military. None were young like the coresearchers though, they were older more middle aged, and some were very old. I remember being conscious that there were children on board, but they were below and out of sight. It was a large ship and I remember that there was a bright sun a little over the horizon. It was bright and there were blue skies and calm seas. I stood on the deck by an officer with jet black, spiky hair and we watched the iridescent vista before us. He pointed to the sea as he noticed there was a storm on the horizon, like a typhoon. We could see that it was reaching down to the ocean, touching the surface. It had a beauty, gray and distinct, and part of me was awestruck. I also knew it would be coming this way. The officer with smart hair startled me and began shouting, not panicking, but he was very cross, and he was hitting himself. He ran away and went down into the ship for some reason and I didn't follow.

I had a sense that it was up to me to tend to the children. They were oblivious as to what was happening. I went below into a large room where children were playing. The lights flickered, and I became conscious that outside the door, in the hallways, men began swearing. I remember shouting to them to stop swearing, but they wouldn't stop. The boat began to rock, one big sway sent me through a door and I was at the bridge. An officer looked at me and called me the captain and I didn't find that strange. I was the captain now, and I felt calm, even as we were in the middle of this storm. There were great wiper blades and all spray quickly vanished. I wasn't worried at this point, nor were the other captains. I remember the bow smashing into a wave, but the ship cut through it and we all expressed awe.

I woke up and was able to write the dream down just in time. (Again, I thought I would be able to remember it, but thankfully I wrote it down.) During the preparation of the questions phase at the outset of the work, I changed the question "tell me about a dream you often have," and changed it to "tell me about a dream for your life." I was concerned that the data might become a minefield of speculative assumptions that would not be as useful as I might receive by asking the latter question on a "dream for your life." This dream occurred as I was preparing the spreadsheet and transferring the meaning units into it. Perhaps as the study did not get answers about dreams, I can include my own interpretation here.

Using the Romanyshyn model, it is conceivable that I was dreaming a soccer dream, something that the unconscious of the material had conveyed to me. The study had moved into a new phase for me personally. All of the material I had been working on was becoming one through redaction, and my subconscious was definitely responding. I was becoming emotionally upset if I didn't visit the material each day, but my dreams would still be expressing images and words. I was impressed by this particular dream, in that it was vivid, and I think I may even have remembered it without writing it down. During the next day I wrote the significant elements onto a page and revisited the images that were still in my mind. Impressions came to me, which may be worth relating.

I felt as if the ship was part of being around the team. Our coresearchers are all to some extent passengers, but also staff, in that they wear uniforms and often have smart haircuts. The man who saw the storm was, to me, a *shadow* figure. His hair was black and even spiky. He alerted me to the storm and then began a series of expletives and hitting himself. It was only the next day that I became aware of the language that the male coresearchers had used in the last question about losing. The language had a significance that I had unconsciously struggled to acknowledge. Also there are men in the soccer culture who I have witnessed often acting and behaving in this way, using expletives and often blaming themselves. The children perhaps represented for me the responsibility of my role to younger minds. As the research has suggested, the team embodies something of childhood, holds and protects it, as we have seen represented in the wider world of sport. I felt as if the approaching storm was inevitable. The children did not know what was really happening, and I tried to protect them, but also to acknowledge the curses of the people outside the door. I was the calm captain, the one who could see the ship through this storm. I remember feeling no anxiety when I was the captain and why that was I am not sure, but in that world I was confident as a result of my past experience, as I am in this world.

The strangest thing about the dream was that it appeared to be telling me something about the data relating to loss. I was reluctant to entertain any idea that losing was worse for men than it was for women. I still can't accept the idea. The depth of the expressions in the men indicated something else, and I realized that the words were coated in positive exhortations and solution-based thinking. In that way one could suggest the character next to me who pointed out the storm was indeed a *shadow* archetype. It is also fitting that the *shadow* figure in this sense provided the clue to opening up and acknowledging an aspect of the data that was difficult for me to recognize. There were no women in this dream, something that only occurred to me later, signifying for me that this was perhaps a dream about the data our male coresearchers offered.

I was haunted by Camus' title "Réflexions sur la Guillotine." Both Camus and the title kept coming back to me. I imagined him watching an execution, and how it is linked with him somehow loving soccer, which is about life and death and we don't need to know that to experience it. The dissertation often was an experience of the unexpected becoming significant, and my expectations of what was significant became less useful. Likewise, the word cloud data seemed to have possibilities I was initially optimistic about. I had expected only to be able to see and use pictures, but a by-product of the work was the ability to produce statistical facts about the frequency of words used. I could feel my Apollonian gods relaxing. I can only venture suggestions and not explanations as to why some of the data below might have been as it was. Nevertheless, after so much contact with the data, there is a little room to venture thoughts about the significance of what transpired, and how this was reflected in the word cloud data.

- Women used the word *feel* 26 times; men used the word 22 times.
  Even after revisiting the material and exploring in detail the context each time the word was used, it would be in keeping with the broader results that the female coresearchers were indeed more connected to their feelings. Female coresearchers indicated that they were indeed better able to digest difficult feelings and to express them meaningfully in terms of self and others.
- Women used the word *family* 22 times; men used the term 18 times.
  There was not any discernible difference in the emphasis that either gender applied to the question asking "Is the team like a family?" in that all coresearchers related affirmatively to the idea. But even though women spoke less than the men in total, they used this term more than the men.
- Women used the word *think* 26 times; men used the word 58 times.
  Male researchers here have used the word with twice the frequency of the female coresearchers. Reviewing the material, it appeared that for 75 per cent of the time, people used the word with *I* before it, as in "I think that."
- Women used the word *love* 5 times; men used the word 11 times.
  Reviewing the data showed that Jane used the term three times when describing her love for the game, whereas use of the word by the male coresearchers appeared more evenly spread throughout the data with all participants using the word once. Earlier in the Discussion section, Neumann (1954) described how a *participation mystique* emerges between co-operating adults that encourages the retention of family terms such as *brother* and *sister*.

Below are some word statistics from the data that appear too intangible for me to usefully explore for possible explanations, but which have been included, as they do demonstrate differences and comparisons between the genders. As soon as I began to write about possible significances for the disparity and frequency of word use, the speculative nature of the summaries that transpired did not feel safe as a way to interpret because of the many variables. There is no context here and it feels that phenomenology or alchemical enquiry might produce no data to help the study move ahead.

- Women used the word *play* 18 times; men used the term 12 times.
- Women used the word *want* 14 times; men used the word 7 times.
- Women used the term *playing* 9 times; men used the term 23 times.
- Women spoke of a *sister* or *sisters* 6 times in comparison to the men who mentioned *brothers* or *brother* 5 times.
- Women used the word *good* 32 times; men used the word 18 times.

- Women used the term *get* 24 times, men used the word 22 times.
- Women used the word *always* 21 times; men used the term 28 times.

During the writing of the study, as I began to encounter the concepts that the data presented, my relationship to the project changed. The work had been very laborious, as I had been warned by taking on a phenomenological approach. There was much time spent revisiting and scouring the material, checking and rechecking that the similarities or differences were accurate, and not just part of my imagination, or a desire to see what I might want to see.

In order to present the material in a cogent way, I had to do a lot of editing and then re-editing of the material as well as the *bracketing* process. I knew the paper pages in front of me very well. I remember becoming aware of the texture and touch of the papers as my palm passed over them; it occurred to me I was "feeling" the material as well as digesting it. It is said that "familiarity breeds contempt," but on this occasion it bred an affinity to the material that I had at first dismissed but came to respect.

As the project is near completion, it continues to defy me. I project times when the work will be done, but it resists and will not be finished. Some days I was very conscious of a different mood within me on days when I had accomplished some work, and when I had not. My computer was on its last legs (I write about it in the Conclusion) and should my battery have failed, I would be lost (thankfully I have a backup). To put my modern-day strife into perspective, our ancestors needed each other for their backup plan and life must have been very dangerous for them. The battle is without and within, and there's no escaping it. Improvements to the text or work still call out to me as I rest in the evening, reminding me that the work is not done and I must do more tomorrow. The ending of a project appears to need poise, in that I cannot rush the last stage. Having come so far I want to go home so to speak, but I have to carry on until I know it is finished. Perhaps a part of me knows that I would struggle to forgive myself or rather the project would struggle to forgive me.

Recommendations for future research

As Mark Nesti (2010) suggested, it is true that team environments are difficult to access. As the game expands so too will the public interest and players at the top level are likely to become even further removed than they are now from most people. There is not any real reason why clubs cannot work with the less definable issues such as emotional maturity and work ethic, particularly with the young. The coresearchers on this team embarked on this project readily, and were enthusiastic about expressing ideas on the subjects that were inquired. A strange result of this study is the correlation between goalkeepers and philosophers. Many great philosophers were mentioned in this work, and they all were goalkeepers, apart from Roger Sperry who played America Football. Why?

Some areas for future research would involve taking gender differences into account: In terms of current coaching styles in the game, is women's soccer copying methods used by men? Is this the most effective approach for women? If women do not think or play the same way as men, then there are implications for soccer training and psychology. Women might respond well to learning about archetypal forces of their own gender.

The study demonstrated many traits that reflected the serious nature of the competitive edge required to perform at this level. What of noncompetitive soccer? Conceivably, do more people play soccer in a noncompetitive fashion than play competitively? As stated earlier, the coresearchers relayed ideas about what a soccer team "should be." This work hopes to convey to prospective managers and coaches potential ideas as to what ways to work with the team as if they were a single individual. Further research could explore this idea and perhaps focus more on what happens if you work with the soul of the players using the lens of clinical psychology. What would a similar study of the coaches reveal?

Coaches were not mentioned much in this study by coresearchers or by me. However, the relationship of the parental figure of manager or coach to the team is an important one. The selection of players is a matter for a coach or manager, and there useful research could be undertaken on the transference relationships that do occur. Managers in soccer teams are much like father figures, and the coaches under him perhaps more like elder brothers and sisters. Is a female manager a father or a mother figure? Pain and Harwood (2007; 2009) identified coaches as a potential source of stress, a subject that invites research and further understanding if only for the coaches themselves.

If early hunting traditions can be discerned for soccer, then the implications of this could be usefully explored by those who play the game. Methods of training can perhaps reflect or incorporate some of these findings in the way they approach support and training for performers in this field. The results of this study indicated that teams and groups of "hunter families" may be a common reality for many people today. Perhaps further research could be conducted on the wider implications here.

Clinically speaking, in the course of this project parallels were observed illustrating how psychotherapy clients could benefit from being a part of a team or alternative family system as a route back from a sense of disconnection and feelings of unrelatedness. From the evidence provided by the coresearchers about their team experiences, their data related much satisfaction from being included. All of the interviewees and coresearchers in this study reported that being in a soccer team helped their lives, and that valuable life skills are learned as a result. This may have been part of the significance for the great philosophers and figures named above who were attracted to soccer and sport. Can this topic be explored further? Could soccer be used in schools as a way to build relatedness? Further research could explore this idea and perhaps focus more on what happens if you work with the soul of the players using the lens of clinical psychology. What would a similar study of the coaches reveal?

Mentioned earlier, the author David Rock (2009) has written extensively about research from neuroscience that has indicated specific conditions that will encourage neuronal wiring and significant learning to take place, a system he calls SCARF. Culture is important, and to forget the lessons of Dweck (2006) might be a mistake, as her evidence was proof that certain cultural ideas help learning. Much work complements Rock's research on the conditions needed for skills enhancement in the brain (2009, p. 82). More research on the relationships of neuroscience, culture, and relationships might be able to inform the practitioner or coach in new ways, with a certainty that was not possible before the latest understandings in neuroscience.

In keeping with depth traditions, the Greek gods have been explored. In particular, the figures of Apollo and Dionysus have been contrasted with each other, along with their female counterparts Artemis and Cybele. These archetypal representations might be easily recognizable archetypes on the field of play and in the wider community. Perhaps this also could be a topic of further writing and research. Do creative teams need a balance of these forces? Is there a place on a team for a blend of members with the more careful approach of the Apollonian spirit working alongside those with a more radical Dionysian spirit, the force that makes things happen, resulting in a combination that is creative as well as destructive. Research has shown that sports psychology is already leaning towards more qualitative kinds of research into soccer, and this study has indicated that sports psychologists in future should also consider the wealth of material available when we ask the players to speak for themselves.

Similar results from Tottenham Hotspur FC in London

Differences do exist between educational settings and the professional culture of English soccer. University environments are legally obliged to adopt community-based standards that incorporate more inclusive cultural protections for all, whereas the professional performance environment is comparatively unregulated. However, in my experience, at the academy level there are arguably more standards of child protection and safety than there are in many universities. It seems that, paradoxically, young people may be better protected in professional learning centers such as Tottenham FC than in the more conventional world of education. As part of their learning, soccer scholars in England are given regular weekly sessions relating to health and safety, driving, cooking (making their own food), first aid, awareness of racism and addictions, nutrition, exercise, financial planning, media training, and as in my case, psychology. As well as this, they are frequently visited by mentors who have made significant contributions to the game.

Part of my work at Tottenham FC involves getting to know players on a deeper level, hoping to learn more about what motivates them as individuals.

To help achieve this, I often survey soccer scholars in terms of their attitudes, beliefs and attachments. Coincidentally, in such a survey I undertook in 2013 I had asked a question which had appeared in the study: "who are your heroes?." By understanding the figures that scholars identify with, the hope is to have a deeper insight into their motivations and inspirations. The question was asked to 12 individuals, aged between 16-17 which makes them younger than any of the scholars in America.

Two factors emerged: one that distinguished this group of scholars, and one which correlated with the coresearchers in America. For whatever reason, the Tottenham FC scholars named many more cultural icons than their American counterparts. A coach at the club offered a plausible explanation that there is more pressure on the Tottenham scholars to identify heroes than young people out of the professional performance environment. Three scholars named God as the hero, four mentioned a sprinter, Usain Bolt, four named an actor (Will Smith, Jim Carey, Justin Timberlake, Tom Hanks), four mentioned Muhammad Ali, two mentioned a musician (Bob Marley and Jay Z), one nominated Martin Luther King and one scholar mentioned Barack Obama.

In addition, and of most interest to me, was that ten out of the 12 scholars polled named a member of their family as a hero. This result correlated with their American counterparts and suggests that the issue of family and soccer is a constellated factor on both sides of the Atlantic, indicating that the results in America have a more robust validity. As with the American coresearchers, scholars in England named both genders as heroes with similar sentiments about the roles their parents have played in their lives. Due to the magnified issues of confidentiality that exist at Tottenham FC, actual statements cannot be reproduced, however, they were similar to those expressed in America.

Conclusion

The Holy Trinity of Soccer

If phenomenology is ultimately a process of redaction and not discussion, then now is the time to seize the opportunity to reflect on what remains. If done effectively, this form of research takes no prisoners and here at the end, when only a few themes remain, it is time for the execution! So far in this book, there have been many connections made to the Greek gods and their creative energy. Certainly the original intention for the Olympics, as a medium to avoid warfare, has the same potential for good today. Sport is demonstrating an accelerated pulling power of a medium with the possibilities to help unite a world now connected by the internet super highways. Thanks to technology, we live in ways that, to the Greeks, would make us appear more like gods. Historically, even before the Greeks, the Kalahari myths such as the Lion and the Hunter resonate with universal issues relating to individuality and in the West they remain with us today.

Even though our coresearchers described the team as a family, we can be certain that in one real sense it is not. In fact, this is a *supra family* state made of the same archetypal forces that mingle with different realities. Soccer players face a different reality in that his or her place on the team—and his or her part in the family—is not a given. Young performers on the public stage make themselves vulnerable in enhanced conditions where they publicly live with the risk of loss, failure, exclusion from the team, and we can now assume, perhaps a sense of letting their families down. Coresearcher Diane said, "that's one of our biggest strengths, is acting like a family, the more you are like family the better you do as a team." The predominant work ethic expressed by coresearchers related to mutual assistance and encouragement. This ethic was about what *had* to happen. Mutuality and co-operation were the lifeblood and experience of this team at least, despite the reality of their respective competitive relationships to each other for places. However, this may be the exception and not the rule, the tragedy at Columbine proved how ugly sports cultures can become.

It has always seemed curious to me that Carol Dweck's (2006) apparently groundbreaking work on mindset did not have the impact on education that it deserved. Many learning organizations have not changed at all as a result of her work. However, on a brighter note, my employment alone suggests the world of soccer appears to be taking Dweck's ideas seriously, and there must be others. Dweck found that a regressive ethos regarding a child's "talent" may be something that resonates with Norretranders' (1991) "*I*" factor. His research suggests that there is a definable identity distinguishing the *I*, which he asserted is much less helpful in this environment than the *Me*. Roger Sperry's (1981) Nobel Prize work on the left and right brain posited language as a predominantly left-brain function. The spatial nature of football would certainly place this experience as a predominantly right-brain activity. Coresearchers certainly identified "talking too much" as a sign of playing poorly. This shows clearly that Landon Donovan's attachment to meditation is not so strange, and in the future, players may wish to learn more about controlling left-brain impulses when required. Sport psychology may be able to create a language of its own for this dynamic, being able to help players have a better command and influence over their right and left brain processes.

Cousineau (2003) described how the marriage of Ares (god of war) and Aphrodite (goddess of beauty and fertility) produce their love child, Harmony. Therefore, in soccer, if a player can produce the right amount of harmony at the right time for the soccer team, personal idiosyncrasies and foibles can be forgiven. The same is true of actors in film and television, who when prominent, possess their own power in relation to the wider team, sometimes dictating their own terms. The distinction here is to find a way to balance the repression of individuality and militaristic culture that demands obedience in a team (from Ares), and Aphrodite, evident in the fact that coresearchers made many loving expressions towards each other. They reported loving relationships with a purpose, so perhaps harmony is indeed what arrives when the middle ground is found.

Camus' work "Réflexions sur la Guillotine," which shows his passion for soccer, is a title that is fitting for the game. Expressions of life and death appear everywhere in soccer. In contrast to the life-giving energy of initiation, there are many "small deaths" to contend with—times when opportunities in games are squandered, mistakes and errors in play made, matches lost, injuries sustained, being "let go" from a team or club or being relegated from a league. Experience suggests that these painful experiences are also opportunities for emotional growth, if the culture is willing or able to help. All soccer players need to have the capacity to "comeback" and at least develop essential qualities of good character, a perspective endorsed by the senior players we heard from. For the coresearchers, the soccer *supra family* bears all of the hallmarks of a unit that offers many qualities of protection and healing. It is a defensive archetypal structure, there to help shield them from the precarious realities of this occupation, and ultimately life in general.

Soccer players need to be able to "go again" and again—as if they possess nine lives, like the cat-like James Bond figure. It is a matter of public record that Sean Connery was advised that he should audition for the role of Bond by embodying the spirit of a cat. And we see that for the Kalahari Bushmen, the lion was master of all things, including his inner kingdom—a way of life that soccer players must imitate. For the males in the study, to play good soccer appeared to involve the passion of Dionysus offset by the cultivation of more Apollonian qualities such as restraint and the capacity to remain grounded. Archetypal research suggested that the forces of Artemis and Cybele might also be embodied by the females in our study, and showed us that these archetypes are still very much with us today. Also, it seems that the trials of Odysseus are not completely offset by our concrete and technological realities today. For some, it appears progress in the West is at the cost of separating us from nature and even our own inner natures. But long before the Greeks, the Kalahari Bushmen spoke of the same concerns, predating the bicameral mind change that Julian Jaynes described in 1976. The young man in their myth was reluctant to leave the community and become an individual, to individuate, and face his destiny with the lion for good or bad. The word *individual* implies indivisible, and the expressions of unity about the team could as much represent their own struggle with themselves.

Today, our coresearchers have to try and find a life and future for themselves somehow, in or out of the world of soccer. The challenge is no less urgent for psychotherapy clients who also face this dilemma, and are very often in a low place when I meet them. In my experience, those who do not or cannot transcend their pathologies will often pay with their lives. The ethics for staying alive are similar in clinical settings and soccer settings, and the issues they face do seem to resonate with each other. The re-creation of family in a clinical group setting appears to be a crucial element for many people who come from damaged and broken homes. They too battle forces of isolation and loss, they are alone, unable to master the forces they battle inside of themselves to achieve a life worth living.

The coresearchers didn't relate the idea of broken homes, but they face a common enemy perhaps. Part of my work in Los Angeles is teaching life skills and meditation to a group of young men living together in a sober living house. Many might consider meditation to be a bourgeois, effete preoccupation with no real value. But I can testify that for those living with sobriety it can be a matter of life or death. All those who battle addiction are, in a sense, "fighting for their lives," fighting against forces of chaos and destitution. It seems that young people especially—those not experienced at getting through emotional stress or "carrying on" with their sobriety—will often engage in reckless and dangerous situations if a relapse occurs. My sessions there are almost universally attended, young people in my experience in soccer or sobriety are keen to learn ideas related to calming the mind and personal growth. Everyone who battles addiction is, in a sense, fighting for his or her life. This can help explain why my work in England with young soccer players is not so different to my clinical work in America. And it seems the same issues are faced by actors, soccer players, public speakers, soldiers, the unemployed, gang members, professional gamblers, the sick, young mothers, pregnant young women, politicians, sex workers, the evicted, the mentally ill and those struggling to live with an addiction—and of course many more. Many of us have to fight the forces of the Underworld, or the world that will send us under if we do not take care. Caring and the need to be cared for were amongst the more buoyant expressions our coresearchers made. Many people in my care express the belief that they are not worth caring about. They tell me that you don't have to lose your parents to feel like an unvalued orphan in the world.

An unanticipated theme for this study was the absence of the expression of gender identification by our coresearchers in regard to soccer. Hopefully access to sport for women and the appreciation of women in sport will continue to flourish in the future. History suggests that culturally-bound imperatives constrained women from playing sport, rather than any relationship to their ability or desire to participate. Would biological evolution have been so lazy as to create 50 per cent of the population incapable of hunting? What if times were tough? Women today are demonstrating they are capable of great feats of endurance and skill, and it was apparent to the author that the women *owned* this subject as much as the men. Artemis and the feminine image of the female archer is an archetypal presence that is still with us, yet few of us would know it is an ancient symbol and goddess. In a "Wild West" culture steeped in the gun, Annie Oakley reminded the world that the Artemesian spirit can also enable women to do some things better than men. An argument can easily be made that female archery at least would have had a distinct role in tribal societies of the past. Has time and the cultural stereotype of women airbrushed them out of the history of hunting?

Female coresearchers demonstrated different capacities for digesting emotions, and with an inclination for integrating their negative experiences, in contrast to the male coresearchers, who often expelled their negative experience onto "the other." The values women embodied could have been useful to the Australian male rowing team at the London 2012 Olympics. The rower Joshua Booth was unable to contain his more Dionysian (or rather Bacchanalian) impulses and was arrested after a drinking rampage in London that evening. He was forced to pay £1500 damages. The next day, as if pleading for his life, Booth begged for forgiveness before a worldwide television audience, calling for athletes to take "better emotional care of themselves" after losing. Josh Booth might well rescue his professional career, but anyone could see the extent of his humiliation, as he exposed his shame on a world-wide scale. However, notably, his teammates stood by him, and many men described a feeling of "rather him than me." Since the time he was flown home, I could not find any record of Josh Booth regaining his place on the team, although he is training to be a medical doctor. His request that players take more "emotional care" of themselves was a constructive comment to a culture that may be slow to see the need. Modern athletes have to sometimes deal with great pressures and projections cast by supporters. Particularly for the young, this may be a burden that the sports world might wish to consider on a deeper level, finding ways to help athletes take better care of themselves emotionally.

The path to emotional maturity is not straightforward. The coresearchers had to show devotion, discipline and self-restraint in order to be competitive at their level, which must have involved many long hours of physical training and technical practice. They also appeared bound to learn skills that are necessary for life, which must also include the capacity to let go, and let the *I* trust the *Me*. It may be fair to assume that our ancestors, who were dependent on hunters, lived a life of danger and uncertainty. Considering the dangers of nature, they must have faced the fear of not coming home that day, back to safety and the comforts to which they were accustomed. Only a cold science would see this as simply conjecture by assuming our earliest ancestors did not know affection, care, or attach value to things like home and important relationships. Hunting does require fitness and presumably hunters in the past were often young men, mixed with the more experienced and seasoned hunters. Perhaps like our coresearchers they were very conscious of their position and the pressures to do well. It may be natural to assume these individuals will have had status and it is logical to assume that the performance of a hunter was relevant to everyone in a community whatever its size.

Early peoples would have been dependent on what they could bring home, and gifted helpers for that cause would have been appreciated and presumably valued. In an evolutionary sense, they would be good mating material, male and female. Initiation into a hunting "team" for our distant young ancestors may have been meaningful for them for this reason alone. Hunters may also have been useful to trade between communities. Nowadays, the soccer leagues frequently send a player "on loan" meaning he will do a job for an opposition team while they are still theoretically in competition with each other. Reciprocity may be an ancient way of safeguarding a future if times got bad for a family, tribe or even a single individual. Hunters would have naturally been travelers, and might have carried representations of their tribe on them somehow, with accompanying symbols or objects to indicate their status within that group.

This study has so far relied on van der Post for his impressions of the Kalahari mindset. Marvin Konner (1982) also wrote about the character and traditions of the Kalahari, and the impact on human biology resulting from the necessities of dealing with the wild in order to survive. He describes the Kalahari "Sun" tribe having a collective ethic and mindset where "equality is strongly valued. Few social or economic distinctions are known, nor could they be maintained, since the powerful ethic of sharing separates a person from any accumulated wealth as soon as it becomes visible. Stinginess is the chief sin, punished by social ostracism; and where mutual aid is key, no one can tolerate ostracism for long" (p. 6). For the Kalahari, the values of collective resourcefulness, resilience, communication, and fidelity would all have been necessary functions in the dangerous world of hunting in teams. Considering the emphasis coresearchers ascribed to these values it suggests a connection between these two groups yet they are separated by the ages. It is hard to imagine two different cultures; in the twenty-first century young Americans in the internet age and the prehistoric Kalahari hunters. Yet one thing is the same, mutual relationships are a necessity rather than a nicety and ethics are for a reason. Although the word cloud may have its limitations in this study, interestingly the men's and women's combined cloud appeared to say "think just like good family life."

As I write these final chapters, my computer is not working properly. The power cable at the back needs much adjustment before the battery will charge from it. The final day before submission, I am desperately attending the task of trying to get the decreasingly effective power cable to charge. Something is fitting here, in that the whole project has had a life and death element to it. The task has to some extent owned me, from the initial stages of doubt and virtual despair through to the alchemical nature of the insights that emerged. As humans, we have always had to contend with nature and transcend difficulties to keep the dream of life and a future alive. The problems I faced in the creation of this document were helped by a capacity to remain conscious, keep cool and keep moving on. But I have been lucky, I have been schooled in the inner world learning of psychology. I have had mentors and aids, and like the soccer players, my issues just feel like life and death. Our ancestors didn't have to deal with computer cables, instead there burdens were more dangerous—insect or animal bites, kicks, punches, grazes, nicks, sprains, falls, breaks, gouges, bruises and cuts, all of which would have had the potential to end a brief life in some agony. With something to lose, they had to be brave.

Before I submitted the final manuscript of this book, I had a dream where I was on a roof of an old, tiled building looking through opaque, dirty skylights. It was at night and cold, below I could see some shapes and things happening, discernible voices and some moving bodies. After the dream, it occurred to me that perhaps this is the best this study can attempt to do, observing the movements and discernible voices in a simple *shadow* drama. Thanks to the work of Amedeo Giorgi and phenomenologists such as Husserl who went before him, there is a structure and format available to me with which I could open the window and hear some voices inside. Throughout this journey, the themes represented the dimly-lit, barely discernible bodies that spoke of hunting, initiation, and the need for family. Soccer is a kind of blueprint for us all, continually represented, repeated and replayed constantly in every country in the world. Thanks to the media, now ever growing numbers of people can play out this central archetypal drama and join with the actors in a recreation of the issues this study suggests that stretch back to prehistoric beginnings.

Champions in soccer get to lift a cup and goal scorers reach for the skies. Perhaps it is not difficult to imagine a group of hunters returning to the tribe, holding the catch proudly aloft for the recipients to see. After a goal in a soccer game, play stops, the score is recorded and the ball goes back to the half way line before play resumes. The "dead zone", the time when nothing is formally in motion, gives players an opportunity to embrace each other in mutual congratulation, often affectionately expressed. Many reach for the skies as if to give thanks to a god. Perhaps this is a part of the ritual that helps the scorer to return to ground themselves once more after the thrill of scoring a goal. As with players, after all of the action, the hunters have returned to triumphant homecoming, with all of the accompanying emotions. One can imagine singing, dancing and happy connection after a successful venture, celebrating the fact that the struggle against darkness and uncertainty was over, for the time being. But what happened after a bad hunting trip? It is not difficult to compare this to the experience of a soccer team that loses. There are no celebrations, only one choice, to mend themselves and go out again. It is said that "hope" was the last thing left in Pandora's Box before the door snapped shut, and perhaps the soccer teams close bonds and attachments are the symbol of the hope they carry, that which must be held for the life of a soccer team to continue.

This work has hopefully contributed an example of what can be discerned using a qualitative approach to research such as phenomenology. Sport remains a natural science, in that men and women must go out in all weathers onto the field alone, with no computers or machines. Seeking to vanquish a foe, they must face the opposition and possibility of loss. And crucially they have to be able to go back out again and again. Hillman said earlier "If the style is repetitious it is because of the way of the soul, according to Plotinus it is the way of the circle" (p. 213). It is only when writing these final pages that I have arrived at a new understanding of this perspective. It is certainly the final insight I have had on this journey, as I step away from the work.

The coresearchers related a digestive process in which there was a need to be able to move on to the next challenge. There is a beginning, a middle and end for soccer players, perhaps representing a kind of ancient trinity. First is the preparation, then the action of the game, and then having to deal with the result and come back to Earth. Preparation is perhaps represented by the necessary stage of entering appropriate heightened states of mental focus required for action. Then our players must cope with the ever-changing nature of the game, relying on their skills and connections to maximize the team's efficiency and help their own chances. Then they must deal with another unpredictable issue, the outcome. Every player must be able to deal with both winning and losing.

From the coresearchers interviews, we can also can see how a type of soccer Holy Trinity is played out repeatedly when they participate in the archetypal story of the father, the son and the Holy Ghost. The coresearchers are bound to tradition, the father, and what has gone before them. Data demonstrated clearly they identify themselves as the product of their own family, feelings conferred now onto their new, *supra family*. To which coresearchers paid their respects like the son or the daughter, brother or sister. This is not a soccer canon that necessarily speaks to gender or religion as shown by our female coresearchers who may equally be bound to the Mother, the daughter and their Holy Ghost. Importantly, the study showed that female coresearchers had their own archetypal identity—they do not require masculine images and they can also choose between Dionysus or Ronaldinhio. This trinity is explored in depth by the American analyst and author Edward Edinger. His book *The new God image* (1996) amplified the themes of rebirth and repair that we must all experience in order to develop emotional maturity, perhaps best described as the capacity to heal. He discusses Jung's beliefs on the subject, which could in itself be an account of a soccer match:

> The age of the Father corresponds to a state of original oneness before consciousness, before the God-image has undergone a state of reflection; the age of the Son corresponds to the great split we have just been talking about, in which the opposites come into view. The age of the Son is a period of doubt and doubleness. The age of the Holy Spirit represents, psychologically, a restitution of the state of original oneness on a conscious level.
>
> (p. 59)

Players always ask me about ways to prepare for a game. Preparation for a contest involves a need for a behavior that is distinct from more day-to-day states of being. Our coresearchers did relate a need to settle and get themselves into the mindset and altered state they reported necessary for good play. The capacity to calm down and settle appears relevant in clinical and soccer settings and is part of the preparation process that players report. Some clinical models are now incorporating subjects such as mindfulness and meditation that do appear to be successful. The coresearchers knew, as many young people know, as my clinical clients came to realize, that they had to prepare to take to the field one day and to go out like the Kalahari. The challenge for the coresearchers and patients is that their opposites must also come into view, forces that will defy their intentions to succeed. Earlier, von Franz stated that she knew of no mythological figure in the world that succeeded without an animal helper, which may in part explain the sports attachment to animals. Grof suggested also that hunting tribes did better if they embraced the spirits of the animals they were hunting, and perhaps this embodiment helps coresearchers to perform better. And after the sport, another critical factor comes into play for soccer players and clients alike: the need for restitution and repair. This must be when the family orientations, so much a feature expressed by the coresearchers, will come into their own.

With what can appear like a left brain dominated educational syllabus on offer, the wider bodies representing education and policy might be concerned with how to help our young people learn to prepare, play and repair. This is not to devalue the empirical sciences which have helped this very study come into being. The intuitive side of this study needs structure and form for the data to be meaningful. It could be more a question of balance; the brothers Apollo and Dionysus perhaps worked better together rather than divided. The thoughtful Trimbos study from Holland (2013) identified healthy emotional and social benefits for young people in teams, something mirrored by our coresearchers and supported by neuroscience. But if this study was to authentically speak to the *erlebis* of the aspiring player, then what of their immediate issues and concerns right now? How can they be better players, how can they "make it" in this world?

Another recent Dutch study by Toering (2011) looked at the different capacities required for success as a young player. Toering discovered that reflection, and the capacity to see the bigger picture, helped them distinguish themselves, a word used by Jung as quoted above. Remembering the Egyptians affinity to the bird was because it could see the bigger picture from above, it is interesting to discover that in the English Premier League 2015 season, there are more birds represented on club crests than lions or any other animal. The Toering study reinforces Dweck, in that those scholars who could use more intuitive, flexible functions distinguished those who made it to the first team and those who didn't. These skills are also useful for any clinician to cultivate; many of my best insights regarding clients occur many hours after our interactions. Perhaps it is the emotional, mending side of life that so many young people seem to have trouble with. Clients report that drugs and alcohol, including prescription drugs, offer a brief glimpse of what feels like repair, but it is often at a price and always transitory. The preparative potential and usefulness of educational models in many places may be falling short, due to an over emphasis on principles of measurable learning. Anxiety and worry are issues for many young people in my experience and I am often left wondering, how are we helping young people with this at school? Hopefully education and psychology can join together and offer new messages of support and information so young people can learn to cope on their own and also find a natural family feeling somewhere. There are optimistic changes occurring in Britain at a national level. The 2014 Mind-Ed conference in London, launched a new program aimed at taking children "out of the shadows" with regard to mental health and access to services and learning.

It is perhaps the duty of policy makers to create a syllabus that reflects the primary goal for education, to help create individuals capable of being in the world. Jung believed that Individuation was a primary goal that we all strive for whether conscious of it or not. He died before Roger Sperry's Nobel Prize work identified that the right brain has a separate, distinct consciousness. It is a fascinating scientific model that no doubt would have intrigued him, but like the Dweck study, the implications of this insight appear to have been lost or not understood. This part and function of the brain is perhaps the "bush soul" that fascinated Jung and van der Post, and the element that Norretranders (1991), Tylor and McCloskey (1990), Gladwell (2006), Goodchild (2001), Corbett (2007) have all discerned. For some, it may be an uncomfortable idea. Religious affiliation of any kind may be a way to speak to and get in touch with this element, and another way to do this appears to be through playing soccer. In the West there are many messages from many places suggesting that the way to repair emotional disorder or pain is found in the consumer world. In my experience, therapeutic engagement and psychiatric medications can be very helpful , especially when compared to medication alone. Furthermore, playing competitive soccer defies materialism, in that, ultimately, our soccer players have to rely on their own inner metal; they may be surrounded by a team but in another sense they are on their own.

In June 2014 the soccer FIFA World Cup™ in Brazil will no doubt inspire and captivate new record-breaking viewing audiences, but we will never know the exact number that join in. The Olympic movement was a factor in this study, and it is not a coincidence that Brazil are scheduled to host the Olympic Games in 2016. At many times during these events much of the planet will be engaged in the same alchemical experience. Although this will be very difficult to quantify or measure, it will all be very real. Many towns and city streets will be transformed, bearing a faint resemblance perhaps to earlier celebrations of Dionysus. It is a flourishing time, business booms, people are inspired, but sooner or later all champions emerge and athletes and nations are defeated. Then the supporters must mend themselves and return back to daily life. Our coresearchers may be the fortunate ones, not just by the fact that they are part of an inclusive cohesive team. The phenomenological method employed here was able to connect to their dreams and visions and to show their passions and love for play, to reveal how they have a chance to embody the gods and experience natural highs and lows. Then they return to Earth and repair within the safer world of their *supra family*, where everyone wins in the end, sooner or later.

References

Aanstoos, C. (1985). The structure of thinking in chess. In A. Giorgi (Ed.), *Phenomenology and psychological research* (pp. 86–117). Pittsburgh, PA: Duquesne University Press.

Adams, L., & Russakoff, D. (1999, June 12). Dissecting Columbine's cult of the athlete. *The Washington Post*. Retrieved January 29, 2010 from www.washingtonpost.com.wpsrv/national/daily/june99/columbine12.htm/

Albert Camus Society, UK. (2012). Retrieved November 14, 2011 from www.camus-society.com/camus-football.html

Andrews, M., Chapman, B., & Purcell, S. (Directors). (2012). *Brave* [Feature Film]. United States: Disney/Pixar.

Armstrong, K. (2005). *A short history of myth* [CD]. Edinburgh, UK: Canongate Books.

Ayto, J. (2008). *Dictionary of word origins*. New York, NY: Arcade.

Beck, A. (1976). *Cognitive therapy and the emotional disorder*. New York, NY: Meridian Books.

Beilock, S. (2010). *Choke: What the secrets of the brain reveal about getting it right when you have to*. New York, NY: Free Press.

Berman, M. (1989). *Coming to our senses: Body and spirit in the hidden history of the West*. New York, NY: Simon & Schuster.

Binswanger, L. (1960). *Melancholia and mania: Phenomenological studies*. Pfullingen, DE: Neske.

Bloom, H. (1997). *The Lucifer principle: A scientific expedition into the forces of history*. New York, NY: Atlantic Monthly Press.

Bondy, S. (2010). 'Landon Donovon sees opportunity not burden.' *The record*. Retrieved June 10, 2010 from www.northjersey.com

Bridgeman, C., Cummings, P., & Goez, P. (Eds.). (1975). *Merriam Webster's dictionary*. Springfield, MA: G. & C. Merriam.

British Broadcasting Company. (2012, July 28). Olympics ceremony: 27m UK viewers watched opening. Retrieved August 21, 2012 from www.bbc.co.uk/news/uk-19026694

Brooke, R. (1991). *Jung and Phenomenology*. Pittsburgh, PA: Trivium Publications.

Caillois, R. (2001). *Man, play and games (Les jeux et les hommes)* (M. Barash, Trans.). Chicago, IL: University of Illinois Press. (Original work published 1958).

Cale, A. (2004). *The official guide to psychology for football* (Football Association). London, UK: Hodder & Stoughton.

Campbell, J. (1972). *Myths to live by*. New York, NY: Penguin Books.

Claridge, S., & Ridley, I. (1997). *Tales from the bootcamps*. London, UK: Orion Books.

Claxton, G. (2005). *The wayward mind: An intimate history of the unconscious.* London, UK: Abacus Books.

Close, M., & Korr, C. (2009). *More than just a game.* New York, NY: St Martin's Press.

Collins, D., & MacNamara, A. (2012). The rocky road to the top. Why talent needs trauma. *Sports Medicine, 42*(11), 907–914. doi: 10.2165/11635140-000000000-00000.

Cooper, A. (1998). *Playing in the zone: Exploring the spiritual dimensions of sports.* Boston, MA: Shambhala.

Corbett, L. (2007). *Psyche and the sacred: Spirituality beyond religion.* New Orleans, LA: Spring Journal Books.

Cousineau, P. (1997). *Soul moments: Marvelous stories of synchronicity—meaningful coincidences from a seemingly random world.* Berkeley, CA: Conari Press.

Cousineau, P. (2003*). The Olympic odyssey: Rekindling the true spirit of the great games.* Wheaton, IL: Quest Books.

Cozolino, L. (2007). *The neuroscience of psychotherapy.* New York, NY: Norton Books.

Creswell, J. (1998). *Qualitative inquiry and research design: Choosing among the five traditions.* Thousand Oaks, CA: Sage.

Creswell, J. (2003). *Research design: Qualitative, quantitative and mixed method approaches.* Thousand Oaks, CA: Sage.

Csikszentmihalyi, M. (1990). *Flow: The psychology of optimal experience.* New York, NY: Harper & Row.

Dennett, D. (2003). *Freedom evolves.* New York, NY: Viking Penguin.

Diamond, S. (1999). *Anger, madness, and the daimonic: The psychological genesis of violence, evil and creativity.* Albany, NY: State University of New York Press.

Dweck, C. (2006). *Mindset: The new psychology of success.* New York, NY: Ballantine Books.

Dwyer, K. K., & Davidson, M. (2012). Dwyer, Davidson disprove public speaking fear as 'worse than death' [Press release]. Retrieved April, 24, 2014 from www.unomaha.edu/news/releases/2012/07/17_speaking.php

Edinger, E. (1996). *The new God image: A study of Jung's key letters concerning the evolution of the Western God image.* Asheville, NC: Chiron Publications.

Erikson, E. (1950). *Childhood and society.* New York, NY: Norton.

Eriksson, S.-G., & Railo, W. (2000). *Sven-Goran Eriksson on soccer.* Spring City, PA: Reedswain.

FIFA. (2010). Almost half the world tuned in at home to watch 2010 FIFA World Cup South Africa™ [Media release]. Retrieved 6, May, 2014 from www.fifa.com/newscentre/news/newsid=1473143/index.html

Gadamer, H. (1980). *Dialogue and dialectic: Eight hermeneutical studies on Plato* (P.C. Smith, Trans.). New Haven, CT: Yale University Press.

Gallup. (2011, June 3). More than 9 in 10 Americans continue to believe in God. Retrieved April, 24, 2014 from www.gallup.com/poll/147887/americans-continue-believe-god.aspx

Gardiner, C. (2011). The call of the game. In. G. Preece & R. Hess (Eds.), *An exercise in everyday theology* (pp. 131–146). Adelaide, Australia: ATF Press.

Giorgi, A. (1985). *Phenomenology and psychological research.* Pittsburgh, PA: Duquesne University Press.

Giorgi, A. (2009). *The descriptive phenomenological method in psychology: A modified Husserlian approach.* Pittsburgh, PA: Duquesne University Press.

Giorgi, A., Knowles, R., & Smith, D. L. (Eds.). (1979). *Duquesne studies in phenomenological psychology* (Vol. 3). Pittsburgh, PA: Duquesne University Press.

Gladwell, M. (2005). Blink. The power of thinking without thinking. New York, NY: Little Brown.

Glick, I. D., Berman, E. M., & Clarkin, J. F. (2000). Marital and family therapy (4th ed.). Arlington, VA: American Psychiatric.

Goldblatt, D. (2008). The ball is round: A global history of soccer. New York, NY: Riverhead Books.

Goodchild, V. (2001). Eros and Chaos. From Brooke, R. (Ed.). (2010). Pathways into the Jungian World. New York, NY: Routledge.

Grof, S. (1988). The adventure of self- discovery. Albany, NY: State University of New York Press.

Guthrie, W. K. C. (1955). The Greeks and their gods. Boston, MA: Beacon Press.

Hall, C. & Nordby, V. (Eds.). (1973). A primer of Jungian psychology. New York, NY: Meridian Books.

Hanson, R., & Mendius, M. (2009). Buddha's brain: The practical neuroscience of the happiness, love and wisdom. Oakland, CA: New Harbinger.

Heidegger, M. (2008). Being and time. New York, NY: Harper Perennial.

Hillman, J. (1976). Re-visioning psychology. New York, NY: Harper & Row.

Hillman, J. (1982). The thought of the heart and the soul of the world. Woodstock, CT: Spring.

Hillman, J. (1983). Healing fiction. Woodstock, CT: Spring.

Hoffman, P, S. (2014). On Acting: An 'Exhausting' And 'Satisfying' Art. Retrieved February 8, 2014 from www.npr.org/2014/02/03/270954011/philip-seymour-hoffman-on-acting-an-exhausting-and-satisfying-art

Homer. (n.d.). The odyssey (S. Butler, Trans.). Internet classics archive. Retrieved April, 24, 2014 from http://classics.mit.edu/Homer/odyssey.html

Homewood, B. (2010). Soccer-world-more than 700 million expected to watch Cup final. Retrieved April, 24, 2014 from www.reuters.com/article/2010/07/11/soccer-world-television-idUSLDE66A06620100711

Huizinga, J. (1955). Homo ludens: A study of the play elements in culture. Boston, MA: Beacon Press.

Husserl, E. (1970). The crisis of European sciences and transcendental phenomenology: An introduction to phenomenological philosophy (D. Carr, Trans.). Evanston, IL: Northwestern University Press. (Original work published 1954).

Jackson, P. (1995). Sacred hoops: Spiritual lessons of a hardwood warrior. New York, NY: Hyperion Books.

Jaynes, J. (1976). The origin of consciousness and the breakdown of the bicameral mind. New York, NY: Houghton-Mifflin.

Johnson, B. (2012). Johnson's life in London: The people who built the modern world. London, UK: HarperCollins.

Johnson, J. (2001). Is soccer the new religion? Retrieved October 15, 2008 from www.hackwriters.com/footyjj.htm

Johnson, R. A. (1986). Inner work: Using dreams and active imagination for personal growth. San Francisco, CA: Harper San Francisco.

Johnson, R. A. (1987). Ecstasy: Understanding the psychology of joy. San Francisco, CA: Harper San Francisco.

Johnson, R. A. (2008). Inner gold: Understanding psychological projection. Kihei, HI: Koa Books.

Jones, G., Hanton, S., & Connaughton, D. (2002). What is this thing called mental toughness? An investigation into elite sports performers. Journal of Applied Sports Psychology, 14, 205–218.

Josselson, R., & Leiblich, A. (1995). *Interpreting experience: The narrative study of lives* (The narrative study of lives series). Thousand Oaks, CA: Sage.

Jung, C. G. (1961). (R, & C, Winston. Trans.). *Memories, dreams, reflections.* New York, NY: Random House.

Jung, C. G. (1964). Approaching the unconscious. In C. G. Jung & M.-L. von Franz (Eds.), *Man and his symbols* (pp. 1–94). New York, NY: Dell.

Jung, C. G. (1990). Concerning rebirth (R. F. C. Hull, Trans.). In H. Read et al. (Series Eds.), *The collected works of C. G. Jung* (Vol. 9, Part 1, pp. 111–147). Princeton, NJ: Princeton University Press. (Original work published 1950).

Jung, C. G. (1990). The psychology of the child archetype (R. F. C. Hull, Trans.). In H. Read et al. (Series Eds.), *The collected works of C. G. Jung* (Vol. 9, Part 1, pp. 151–181). Princeton, NJ: Princeton University Press. (Original work published 1951).

Jung, C. G. (1991). The development of personality (R. F. C. Hull, Trans.). In H. Read et al. (Series Eds.), *The collected works of C. G. Jung* (Vol. 17, pp. 167–186). Princeton, NJ: Princeton University Press. (Original work published 1934).

Kast, V. (1991). *Joy, inspiration, and hope* (D. Whitcher, Trans). College Station, TX: Texas A&M University Press.

Keen, E. (1975). *A primer on phenomenological psychology.* New York, NY: Holt, Reinhart, & Wilson.

Konner, M. (1982). *The tangled wing: biological constraints on the human spirit.* New York, NY: Holt. Rinehart and Winston.

Krajewski, Bruce. (1992). *Traveling with Hermes: Hermeneutics and rhetoric.* Amherst, MA: University of Massachusetts Press.

Krakovsky, M. (2007, March-April,). The effort effect. *Stanford Magazine.* Retrieved October 12, 2011 from http://alumni.stanford.edu/get/page/magazine/article/?article_id=32124

Laing, R. D. (1960). *The divided self.* New York, NY: Penguin Books.

Leonard, G. (2001). *The ultimate athlete.* Berkeley, CA: North Atlantic Books.

Levenson, E. (1985). The interpersonal (Sullivanian) model. In A. Rothstein (Ed.), *Models of the mind: Their relationship to clinical work* (pp. 49–67). Madison, WI: International Universities Press.

Levy, G. (2011). Super Bowl sets record figures of 111 million. Retrieved January 7, 2012 from http://newsfeed.time.com/2011/02/08/super-bowl-sets-record-viewing-figures-of-111m/

Maier, N. R. F. (1931, August). Reasoning in Humans. II. The solution of the problem and its appearance in consciousness. *Journal of Comparative Psychology, 12,* 181–194. doi: 10.1037/h0071361

Marshall, C., & Rossman, G. (1999). *Designing qualitative research.* Thousand Oaks, CA: Sage.

Monshouwer, K. (2013). Participation in sport good for youth mental health. Retrieved January 16, 2013 from www.trimbos.org/news/trimbos-news/participation-in-sport-good-for-youth-mental-health

Moustakas, C. L. (1990). *Heuristic research: Design, methodology and applications.* Thousand Oaks, CA: Sage.

Moustakas, C. L. (1994). *Phenomenological research methods.* Thousand Oaks, CA: Sage.

Nesti, M. (2010). *Psychology in football: Working with elite and professional players.* New York, NY: Routledge.

Neumann, E. (1954). *The origins and history of consciousness*. Princeton, NJ: Princeton University Press.

Nolan, C. (Director). (2012). *The Dark Knight Rises* [Feature film]. United States: Warner Brothers.

Norretranders, T. (1991). *The user illusion: Cutting consciousness down to size*. New York, NY: Penguin Books.

Novak, M. (1993). *The joy of sports: Endzones, bases, baskets, balls, and the consecration of the American spirit* (Rev. Ed.). Lanham, MD: Madison Books.

Nuckols, C. (2010). *The ego-less self: Achieving peace and tranquility beyond all understanding*. Deerfield Beach, FL: Health Communications.

Odajnyk, V. (1976). *Jung and politics: The political and social ideas of C. G. Jung*. Lincoln, NE: Authors Choice Press.

Owen, J. (2004). Egyptian animals were mummified the same way as humans. Retrieved January 4, 2013 from http//news.nationalgeographic.com/news/2004/09/0915_040 915_petmummies_2.html

Pacifica Graduate Institute (2012). Mission statement. Retrieved April, 24, 2014 from www.pacifica.edu/missionstatement.aspx

Pain, M., & Harwood, C. (2007). The performance environment of the England youth soccer teams. *Journal of Sports Sciences, 25*, 1307–1324.

Pain, M., & Harwood, C. (2009). Team building through mutual sharing and open discussion of team functioning. *The Sport Psychologist, 23*, 523–542.

Palmer, R. (1969). *Hermeneutics: Interpretation theory in Schleiermacher, Dilthey, Heidegger, and Gadamer*. Evanston, IL: Northwestern University Press.

Patton, M. Q. (2002). *Qualitative research and evaluation methods* (3rd ed.). Thousand Oaks, CA: Sage.

Pearson, C. S. (1991). *Awakening the hero within: Twelve archetypes to help us find ourselves and transform our world*. New York, NY: HarperCollins.

Peters, S. (2011). *The chimp paradox: The mind management programme to help you achieve success, confidence and happiness*. London. Vermillion.

Polkinghorne, D. (1983). *Methodology for the human sciences* Albany, NY: State University of New York Press.

Preece, G., & Hess, R. (Eds.). (2012). *Sport and spirituality*. Adelaide: ATF Press.

Rauhala, L. (1984). The basic views of C.G. Jung in the light of hermeneutic metascience. From Papadopoulos R. & Saayman, G. (Eds.): *Jung in Modern Perspective,* pp. 229–44. Craighall: A.D. Donker.

Ravindran, S. (2012, March 7). Stanford researchers find that modern humans originated in southern Africa. *Stanford Online*. Retrieved September 24, 2012 from http://news. stanford.edu/news/2011/march/feldman-africa-genetics-030411.html

Reason, P., & Rowan, J. (Eds.). (1981). *Human inquiry: A sourcebook of new paradigm research*. New York, NY: John Wiley & Sons.

Richards, M. P. & Trinkaus, E. (2009). Isotopic evidence for the diets of European Neanderthals and early modern humans. *Proceedings of the National Academy of Sciences of the United States of America* 106, 16034–16039.

Riemersma, M. (2010, July-August). The typical California MFT 2010 CAMFT member practice and demographic survey. *The Therapist Magazine,* pp. 28–36.

Rock, D. (2009). *Your brain at work*. New York, NY: Harper Collins.

Romanyshyn, R. D. (2007). *The wounded researcher: Research with soul in mind*. New York, NY: Spring Journal Books.

Rooney, A. (2012). *The history of physics*. New York, NY: Rosen.

Sagar, S., Busch, B., & Jowett, S. (2010). Success and failure, fear of failure, and coping responses of adolescent academy football players. *Journal of Applied Psychology, 22*(2), 213–230.

Samuels, A. (1986a). *A critical dictionary of Jungian analysis*. London, UK: Routledge.

Samuels, A. (1986b). *Jung and the post Jungians*. London, UK: Routledge.

Samuels, A. (2012, June 30) *The crowd as therapist*. Sport and Psychoanalysis Conference. Freud Museum, London. UK.

Schechner, R. (1988). *Performance theory*. New York, NY: Routledge.

Schechner, R. (1993). *The future of ritual: Writings on culture and performance*. New York, NY: Routledge.

Schechner, R. (2002). *Performance studies: An introduction*. New York, NY: Routledge.

Schenk, R. (2010). From Brooke, R. (Ed.) *Pathways into the Jungian World; Phenomenology and Analytical Psychology*. New York, NY: Routledge.

Shamdasani, S. (2003). *Jung and the making of modern psychology: The dream of a science*. New York, NY: Cambridge University Press.

Sing, S. S. (2004). *Spirituality of sport: Balancing body and soul*. Cincinnati, OH: St. Anthony Messenger Press.

Spielrein, S. (1994). Destruction as the cause of coming into being. *Journal of Analytical Psychology, 39*, 155–186. Doi: 10.1111/j.1465-5922.1994.00155.x (Original work published 1912)

Storr, A. (1983). *The essential Jung*. Princeton, NJ: Princeton University Press.

Sullivan, H. S. (1953). *The interpersonal theory of psychiatry*. New York, NY: Norton.

Sutton-Smith, B. (1997). *The ambiguity of play*. Cambridge, MA: Harvard University Press.

Sydnor, S. (2011). Sport, femininity and the promises of the theology of the body. In. G. Preece & R. Hess (Eds.), *An exercise in everyday* theology (pp. 65–99). Adelaide, Australia: ATF Press.

Symington, N. (2002). *A pattern of madness*. London, UK: Karnack Books.

Taylor, J. L., & McCloskey, D. I. (1990). Triggering of preprogrammed movements as reactions to masked stimuli. *Journal of Neurophysiology. 63*, 439–446.

Telegraph Sport. (2012, May 29). Manchester United survey reveals they have doubled their global fan base to 659 million over five years. Retrieved April 24, 2014 from www.telegraph.co.uk/sport/football/teams/manchester-united/9298384/Manchester-United-survey-reveals-they-have-doubled-their-global-fan-base-to-659-million-over-five-years.html

Tharoor, K. (2008, February 25). Globalization of soccer kicks local fans. Worldwide popularity pushes the game from a club culture to a corporate one. *Yale Global*. Retrieved November 1, 2009 from http://yaleglobal.yale.edu/content/globalization-soccer-kicks-local-fans

The Football Association (FA). (2012). About the FA women's cup. *The FA cup and competitions*. Retrieved April 24, 2014 from www.thefa.com/Competitions/FACompetitions/TheFAWomensCup/History

Thelwell, R., & Weston, N. (2005). Defining and understanding mental toughness within soccer. *Journal of Applied Sports Psychology, 17*, 326–332.

Toering, T. (2011). Self-regulation of learning and the performance level of youth soccer players. University of Groningen. Retrieved on February 20, 2014 from www.academia.edu/2588854/SelfRegulation_of_Learning_and_Relative_Age_in_Elite_Youth_Soccer_International_versus_National_Level_Players

Treschel, J. (2002). *A morning cup of yoga*. Birmingham, AL: Crane Hill Publishers.

van der Post, L. (1961). *The heart of the hunter: Customs and myths of the African Bushman*. New York, NY: Morrow.

van Manen, M. (1990). *Researching lived experience: Human science for an action sensitive pedagogy*. Albany, NY: State University of New York Press.

von Franz, M.-L. (1964). The process of individuation. In C. G. Jung & M.-L. von Franz (Eds.), *Man and his symbols* (pp. 157–254). New York, NY: Dell.

von Franz, M.-L. (1974). *Shadow and evil in fairy tales*. Boston, MA: Shambhala Press.

von Franz, M.-L. (1975). *C. G. Jung: His myth in our time* (W. Kennedy, Trans.). Boston: Little, Brown.

Wade, N. (2009, May 1). Eden? Maybe. But where's the apple tree? *New York Times*. Retrieved December 28, 2012 from www.nytimes.com/2009/05/01/science/01eden.html?_r=0

Wallace, A. (2006). *The attention revolution*. Boston, MA: Wisdom.

Wyatt, B. (2010). Could the 2010 World Cup final be the most watched event ever? Retrieved January 3, 2011 from www.cnn.com/2010/SPORT/football/07/11/world.cup.final.television/index.html

Youth Soccer Show. (2012, July 7). Interviews with Hercules Gomez, Tim Howard, Clint Dempsey and Landon Donovan. On *US Youth Soccer Show*. [Television broadcast, Fox Sports Soccer Channel #394]. Retrieved April 24, 2014 from www.youtube.com/watch?v=gSd2msrDBBg&list=PL9996311E0D785048

Appendix

Informed Consent Form

Thanks very much for agreeing to participate in the study. Before you formally agree to continue there are certain issues and matters it would be good for you to be apprised of. Before you sign, make sure that you fully understand this part of the process, what has been shown to you, and that you are happy to continue.

This study is aimed at better understanding the life of an aspiring soccer player like you, trying to discover themes, which may tell us a little more about the game and individuals who aspire to play soccer at the highest level possible. This may tell us more about the wider community as well. The interview will be recorded and will become part of the research findings and therefore will be part of the finished document. This document will be available for public viewing after it has been accepted.

I will be asking you a series of questions. Every participant will be asked the same questions as you are. At the end of the questions, you will be given an opportunity to add anything else you would like to say. The questions are not designed to confuse or stress you in any way; we are just trying to find out more about how your life is. As a result of the findings we hope that perhaps some ways of working better with soccer players in the future can be achieved. The question sessions will probably last 45 minutes. You may withdraw your participation from the study at any time should you so wish.

Are there any questions you would like to ask before we begin?

Index